The Changing Ways of
SOUTHWESTERN INDIANS

PISCHEL YEARBOOKS
A DIVISION OF HERFF JONES
P.O. BOX 36, MARCELINE, MISSOURI 64658 816—376-3523

The Changing Ways of

SOUTHWESTERN INDIANS

A Historic Perspective

Edited by
ALBERT H. SCHROEDER, M.A.

El Corral de Santa Fe
Westerners Brand Book 1973

The Rio Grande Press, Inc.

GLORIETA, NEW MEXICO · 87535

Library of Congress Cataloging in Publication Data
Main entry under title:

The changing ways of southwestern Indians.

(El Corral de Santa Fe Westerners brand book, 1973)
(A Rio Grande classic)
Includes bibliographies.
1. Indians of North America--Southwest, New--
Addresses, essays, lectures. 2. Acculturation--
Addresses, essays, lectures. I. Schroeder, Albert H.,
ed. II. The Westerners. El Corral de Santa Fe.
III. Title. IV. Series: The Westerners. El Corral
de Santa Fe. Westerners brand book, 1973.
E78.S7C45   970.4'9   73-21765
ISBN 0-87380-106-7

A RIO GRANDE CLASSIC
First published in 1973
(not a reprint)

First Printing 1973

The Rio Grande Press, Inc.
GLORIETA, NEW MEXICO · 87535

Publisher's Preface

First off, we should observe that a Westerners Brand Book is not a book of western cattle brands; it is, in essence, an anthology of short papers, each about some particular aspect of Western American history. When history was being made in the trans-Mississippi West, between, say, A.D. 1540 and 1912, the rush of events in so many places over so vast a territory made it quite impossible for any one scribe to write about it all in a comprehensive way. So it was that many men (and women, of course) wrote briefly or at length about their own particular experiences, and these various accounts can, we believe, be properly termed as "fragments" of the overall history. Many of these "fragments" are important enough in the context of the time, but they are "fragments" now, largely because they are available mostly without context (what occurred before? what happened after?). Then the student or the scholar is left to puzzle for himself where this or that "fragment" fits into the ever-growing and ever-expanding reconstruction of the history of America's "Manifest Destiny".

A Westerners' Brand Book is thus, in effect, a collection of precious historical "fragments", most of which are not—of themselves—items about which an entire book can be written, or needs to be. These "fragments" fill in gaps here and there, like a jigsaw puzzle, perhaps, for researchers, historians, scholars and students, and hence, are important for the ongoing development of America's historical continuity.

There are many Brand Books published by various Westerner Corrals; since there has been no central "clearing house" (to our knowledge) to keep such information on hand, we know of no way to record just how many Corrals have published one or more Brand Books. This one is the first for El Corral de Santa Fe, but the Denver Corral has published many—and so has the Chicago, Los Angeles, and San Diego Corrals (we understand). We really do not know how many have been published, or by which Corrals, but we do know that every Brand Book that has been published has been exceedingly popular and much sought after by collectors and librarians.

But now the reader may say: ". . .so, I understand about Brand Books, but what is all of this about "Westerners", "Corrals", and the like?" Although both of us at The Rio Grande Press are Westerners (and have been for years), we went to the Fountainhead for the answer to that obvious question. The

Fountainhead, in this instance, is Leland D. Case, the Grand Old Man of the Westerners—one of the founders, the one we know best and cherish most. He sent us this squib, which seems self-explanatory:

". . .Up Santa Fe's then-dusty and rutty Camino del Monte Sol, an idea got started back in 1939 that ended up as The Westerners. I can report this because I was there—and discussed it with another musketeer, name of Clinton P. Anderson, who drove over from Albuquerque. Our old Upper Missouri Valley was groggy back in those dirty thirties with dust storms grasshoppers, and overdue mortgages. We felt up there that people could get sustenance for the spirit, as had been done in Sweden, by re-discovering their own history and developing an indigenous culture.

"That idea became the theme of Friends of the Middle Border, whose museum and art gallery are still an attraction at Mitchell in South Dakota. But it was Chicago's group of Friends of the Middle Border that spun off the first Corral of The Westerners. It was a snowy, wintry night in Chicago—February 25, 1944, to be exact—when a bunch of us history buffs got together and made a little history ourselves.

"From there on, it was—so to speak—all downhill; now we openly boast of 50-odd units in the U.S., one in Mexico and several in Europe. The "home ranch" of the gang is Westerners International; we hold forth on the mezzanine floor of the Campbell Street Branch of the Southern Arizona Bank in Tucson. Here compadres lick stamps, file papers, and put out the quarterly *Buckskin Bulletin.*

"Westerner fellowship is unique, we believe. We like to chomp together, chat the lore of cuspidor and corral, then haze or praise a speaker. At any Corral roundup you can find the professional and the buff, giving and taking information and fellowship.

"Do you have any other campus discipline like Western History," we once asked University of Arizona's Vice President "Swede" Johnson, "with an organization where expert and amateur get together this way?"

"Eldorado, no!" he roared, "not even the bird watchers do that!"

"Then, why do the Westerners?"

"Every member has his own answer. Mine is simple. It seems to me that this group provides a sort of solvent for the artificial social barriers which often divide 'town and gown', in a deep-down affection for our country's great and marvelous West—what English historian Lord Bryce once called ". . .the most American part of America".

So, now you know. There are "Corrals" of The Westerners in nearly every large American city, and in some foreign cities as well. In Tucson, Leland Case, Bob Johnson, John Marohn and Ray Mattison keep the whole enterprise moving under the general aegis of Westerners International, a foundation which has this creed on its letterhead:

"Incorporated to stimulate authentic interest and publishing related to America's frontier West. A particular project is to serve The Westerners, started by Leland D. Case and Elmo Scott Watson in Chicago, February 25, 1944, now a unique fellowship with organized units around the world."

Now that we think we have explained The Westerners Brand Books and The Westerners organization in general, we can turn our attention to El Corral de Santa Fe, where betimes we hold forth at La Posada Inn. Following these pages, the reader will find a mass portrait of the members present on a wintry March meeting night in 1973. Such a distinguished group has rarely been gathered under one roof, but it happens once a month (excepting June, July and August) in Santa Fe, and most of us have grown callous to the grandeur of it all. We think those who join together each meeting thoroughly enjoy the fellowship (if not the dinner), and each time the meeting ends we leave a little richer in comradeship and knowledge. We only wish some of the younger generation would join the group. . .they could learn a lot from us. The excellent photograph, incidentally, is the work of Corral member Ol' Len Bouché, who could not take the picture and be in it, too. Ol' Len is to a camera what Toscanini was to an orchestra.

Now about here we suppose we should comment briefly on "how come" The Rio Grande Press—known world-wide as a reprint publishing house—is publishing this new material. Well, it isn't a very long story, but we can pad a little. Most Westerners have a particular interest, and those who have a specialty become, in effect, a very real expert in that specialty—that "fragment" we spoke of earlier. Thus, with a considerable pool of talent to scoop from, why not gamble the cost of publishing a new Brand Book? Why not, indeed! One meeting night, carried away by it all, we volunteered to publish an El Corral de Santa Fe Brand Book if someone else would do the drudgery. We're not opposed to doing drudgery, per se, but we already have our share and then some. The drudgery that goes into any publishing operation is relentless, and not only that, unremitting. Somehow, Ol' Al Schroeder got the job as editor of this (we feel obliged to say it unblushingly) handsome effort, and he did what we opine was a superb job.

And what does Ol' Al Schroeder get for all his efforts? Ol' Al, friend, compadre, scholar and gentleman gets a pat on the back and a free copy of the book. That's what Ol' Al gets. But surely he must have, somewhere around, the immense personal satisfaction that comes from doing a tough job well. To some of us old timers, that sense of personal satisfaction is often more satisfying than a steak dinner at La Posada Inn.

This publishing project got under way in October 1971, nudged gently along by that indefatigable researcher and inimitable scholar Ol' Crawford Buell, then the Sheriff of El Corral de Santa Fe. He named an editorial committee, headed by the aforesaid Ol' Al Schroeder, who took a few weeks to line up papers, and a few months to get them all in hand. The editorial committee (Ol' Crawford Buell, Ol' George Fitzpatrick, Ol' Bob McCoy, Ol' Jack Wilson and of course, Ol' Al) had a number of meetings to swig coffee (freeze dried, of course) and make plans. As the completed papers arrived, Ol' Al went to work with the professional skill of a professional, and by March 1973, he handed the edited manuscript to us.

In a sense, The Rio Grande Press is "married" to a printer doing business in the late Walt Disney's home town, Marceline, Missouri. That printer specializes in institutional yearbooks. From about February until mid-August of every year, that printer publishes nothing but yearbooks. So, it was not until late August that he could start on our Brand Book. But surely there is not a man alive who doesn't know what a busy president these United States have had in 1973. Among other things, he instituted "price controls" on those things he and his friends could think of, and the results affected those things and everything else—one item being paper products. As surely as the rising sun is followed a few hours later by the setting sun, price controls bring on shortages, and among the shortages we can attribute to price controls was book paper.

Well, to make a short story long, we and the printer and Ol' Al Schroeder finally got the project completed, and you hold in your eager, trembling hands the end result of a gillion hours of effort by many interested intelligent and gifted Westerners. We hope you appreciate it. If you don't, kindly get lost. Go take a job in the Justice (ha! ha! ha!) Department.

We invite your wispy attention to Ol' Al Schroeder's Introduction, which follows the mob scene mentioned earlier. He goes real formal here, perhaps to put on the dawg (sic) just a little, but we are not impressed. Formal is as formal does. Take a look at how formally he dresses for our meetings—he's the good-looking guy in the right front seat, so informal he's about to collapse onto the floor. Anyway, he presents in his excellent (though formal) Introduction a little background germane to this project and El Corral de Santa Fe. It's worth reading, and we think you should take the time.

Again, we invite your attention (this time) to the fine art on the endpapers. This is a reproduction of a beautiful painting by R.C. Gorman, a Navajo Indian artist of Taos, N.M. The title is *"Return from Bosque Redondo"*; if you know the story of the Navajo's "Long March", then the art will have for you an added dimension of beauty. The work is owned now by one of Santa Fe's best-known citizens–Mr. Shelly Grossman, an artist in his own right. The painting hangs in Mr. Grossman's living room; he himself took the photo transparency from which our reproduction was made. We are most grateful for Mr. Grossman's cooperation, and for letting us use his painting as we have.

Most of us old codgers are in the Twilight Zone, so to speak, with more days behind us than ahead of us. The Great Rollcall is inexorably catching up to us; one by one, our name is called and we must go. We are saddened, always, when one of us leaves for The Last Roundup. Thus, while awaiting our turn, we report that on December 10, 1972, Ol' Frank McNitt was called while he peacefully slept. We like to think that maybe by this time he has joined El Corral del Cielo, and that when the roll is called up yonder for the rest of us, we'll all be there, too. In this volume, Frank wrote *The Long March,* a compassionate account of a sorrowful incident in American history. Jack Wilson wrote a few graceful words about compadre McNitt, and these appear–appropriately enough–at the end of *The Long March.*

Last, but certainly not least, we want to personally and publicly thank our friends and colleagues who took the time to send along from their expertise the "fragments" of history we have published here. We do not know first hand all of our authors, but we wish we did. Whimsy aside, we like to think that all of this knowledge rubs off a little as it passes through our hands; whether it does or not, it is a real pleasure to be exposed to it.

So, for now, compadres. . .hasta luego!

Robert B. McCoy

La Casa Escuela,
Glorieta, N.M. 87535
November 1973

A Gathering of Some of the Corral

X

Seated, left to right:
    Harris Warren, Registrador
    Stan Agnew, Alguacil
    William D. Powell, Deputado
    Albert H. Schroeder, Editor
Standing, left to right:
    Luther L. Lyon
    Robert Boshen
    Thomas Durston
    Merritt Barton
    Kenneth M. Grubb
    Clayton B. Schrock
    Will Eskite
    Homer Hastings
    Robert B. McCoy
    Charlie R. Steen
    Phillip St. G. Cooke III
    Paul Franke, Jr.
    Crawford Buell
    Thomas B. Catron III
    Stewart L. Peckham
    Saul Cohen
    Edward H. Tatum, Jr.
    Joseph J. Burns
    John P. Wilson
    John T. Strachan
    Neil C. Stillinger

1973-74 Membership
El Corral de Santa Fe Westerners
as of November, 1973

1. Agnew, Col. S. C.
2. Alexander, C. I.
3. Arrowsmith, Rex
4. Barton, Merritt
5. Boshen, Robert
6. Bouche, Len
7. Boyce, George A.
8. Boyer, Jack
9. Buell, Crawford R. (REP)
10. Bullock, Dale
11. Burns, James J.
12. Catron, T. B. III
13. Clary, David A.
14. Cleaveland, Norman
15. Cohen, Saul
16. Cooke, Phil St. George
17. Durston, Thomas
    (REGISTRADOR)
18. Edwards, Albert C., M. D.
19. Eskite, Will
20. Fenn, Forrest
21. Fitzpatrick, George
22. Franke, Paul Jr.
23. Frazer, Dr. Robert
24. Grubb, Kenneth M.
25. Hastings, Homer
26. Hester, Jack
27. Keller, W. J.
28. Kingsolver, Joe
29. Lash, Col. Eugene
30. Latimer, Roman
31. Lyon, Luther L.
32. McCoy, Robert B.
33. Meem, John Gaw (Honorary)
34. Miller, R. H. (CAPORAL)
35. Newby, Neal D. (LADRON)
36. Noss, Gary
37. Ogden, Bro. Raymond
38. Olson, Herbert A.
39. Peckham, Stewart L.
40. Platt, Robert
41. Powell, W. Carlos
42. Powell, William D.
    (ALGUACIL)
43. Schrock, Clayton B.
44. Schroeder, Al (EDITOR)
45. Solomon, Charles S.
46. Spence, R. W.
47. Steen, Charles
48. Stillinger, Neil C.
49. Strachan, John T.
50. Talbot, Orin H.
51. Talbot, Tom
52. Tatum, Edward H. Jr.
53. VanSoelen, D. D.
54. Warren, Harris G.
    (DIPUTADO ALGUACIL)
55. Wilson, John P.

Notes of Future Members

Introduction

On November 20, 1962, under the organizational bent of James T. Forrest, then Director of the Museum of New Mexico, and with the historical push of Robert M. Utley, then Southwest Regional Historian of the National Park Service, 14 potential *vaqueros* met at an informal dry camp provided by the Museum to consider the need for a Corral in Santa Fe.

The second organizational meeting, on December 13 at La Posada, indicated the need for a permanent Corral to contain the mounts of the increasing number of wranglers signing on. *The Reglas de Gobierno* (by-laws) were adopted and, with the aid of some Taos Lightning, various jobs were set up: *El Alguacil* (Sheriff), *El Diputado Alguacil* (Deputy Sheriff), *El Registrador de Marcas y Tizones* (Secretary), *El Ladrón Oficial* (Treasurer), *El Caporal* (Sergeant at Arms), *El Comisario General* (Arrangements), *El Hablador* (program chairman), and *El Publicador* (publications).

The first formal meeting took place at the Palace Restaurant on January 17, 1963, following which others were held at various eateries with appropriate refreshments until October, at which time La Posada became our headquarters. Members, local authorities, and visiting dignitaries served as speakers on a variety of western topics, and beginning in 1964, the last spring meeting was set aside as movie night for Philip Cooke's early "flicks", William S. Hart in "The Return of Draw Egan" being the first showing.

Jack Rittenhouse, our first *Alguacil*, turned to his trusty Stagecoach Press to produce the Corral's first document, a form calling for the payment of 1963 dues. Any unused slip of paper that happened to be handy served as a receipt for *El Ladron*. The February 1963 meeting was announced by a printed notice, another work of art from The Stagecoach Press, a practice followed until April 1968 when Jack moved to Albuquerque. Dale Bullock and his Rydal Press continued with these notices until they were replaced in December by a newsletter type of announcement inaugurated by *El Alguacil*, Albert H. Schroeder, telling of *La Junta Pasada* (The Past Meeting) and *La Junta que Viene* (The Coming Meeting). This was expanded in September 1971 by *El Alguacil* John P. Wilson to include newsworthy items of the early days.

October 1963, The Stagecoach Press gave birth to *La Gaceta,* a four to eight page publication issued five times a year for regular and corresponding members. Editor William E. Brown continued in this capacity through February 1966. Phil Cooke took over for the next two issues of that year. The last issue with this format, to meet obligations in this land of *mañana* to corresponding members waiting for the final 1966 number (Vol. IV, No. 5), came out in April 1969 with Al Schroeder as editor. A complete set of these early *La Gacetas* now is a rare item, each number having been produced in quantities of 100 to 150.

With some trepidation, the Corral set up an editorial committee, Crawford Buell, Dale Bullock, Phil Cooke, and George Fitzpatrick with Al Schroeder as Editor, to revive *La Gaceta* in a 32 page format beginning with Volume V. The first number appeared in September 1970, printed by Rydal Press. Three numbers each year were produced in sufficient quantity (minimum of 350) to offer for sale on newstands and in book stores. The Corral felt honored when J.K. Shishkin received the Jedediah Smith prize at the Westerners Breakfast, held during the 1971 Western History Association Meeting, for her article "The Wonderful Year of 1880 in Santa Fe" which appeared in Vol. 5, No. 3. Unfortunately, publication of the next volume will be delayed until the coffers are replenished, and corresponding members were so notified.

All was not as bad as it seemed to be. Señores Robert McCoy and John Strachan, President and Vice President (respectively) of the Rio Grande Press, Inc., members of the Corral, offered to publish a Brand Book if the Corral would handle the editing chores. Another editorial committee, meetings, discussions, and conferences resulted in an author's "fact sheet" for the Brand Book produced in time for distribution at the October 14-16, 1971 Western History Association Meeting in Santa Fe.

In preparing for this, its first Brand Book, the Corral conceived the idea of gathering material that would illustrate interchange or interaction between Indian and non-Indian groups of the Southwest, or within either group, and at the same time would portray a more or less significant aspect of the history of the groups or individuals involved. We felt that this approach not only would provide an interesting theme for the Brand Book, but also would serve as a timely topic to point to some of the processes that bring about culture change, particularly in the tri-cultural Southwest. This is the essence of history and anthropology.

The contributors to this volume selected subject matter of their own choice to demonstrate change or stress in material culture, economics, social organization, territorial claims, and/or in social or religious attitudes. Since all ethnic groups, be they a minority or a majority, have to adapt or adjust in some way to new situations, contacts, and ideas in order to survive within the sphere of their particular physical and human environments, the Southwest is a fertile field from which examples can be drawn. In the course of about 400 years, some ethnic groups retained their cultural identity with some alterations; others made economic adjustments through substitution or large scale changes; and some were completely assimilated by large population influxes or moves of their own that tended to break down resistance to cultural fragmentation. The articles herein, arranged more or less in chronological order, reflect either a category of change over a period of time or a specific cultural alteration of short duration, both of which had long term effects on the people involved.

Albert H. Schroeder
Editor

Santa Fe, N.M. 87501
November 1973

Contents

XXVIII

Illustrations

This book is dedicated to

all those who cherish and respect

the traditions and the cultures

of the many Southwestern ethnic societies.

THE SUMA INDIANS OF
NORTHERN CHIHUAHUA
AND WESTERN TEXAS

Rex E. Gerald

The Suma Indians were one of the more numerous native hunting and gathering groups to occupy the areas that are now parts of northern Chihuahua and western Texas during early historic time. Their ethnic identity has been debated at length but no consensus has been reached (for summaries of these discussions see Newcomb 1961:225-228; Kelley 1955:982; Forbes 1959; Naylor 1970; Schroeder 1962:17-20). Regardless of their ultimate affinities, however, it seems probable that during the late 17th century the group known as Sumas, in northern Chihuahua, northeastern Sonora, and along the Rio Grande from Paso del Norte (the El Paso-Ciudad Juarez area today) downriver for about 130 miles to El Cajon, were linguistically and culturally similar to a group known as Jumanos who occupied the region between the Rio Grande below El Paso and the upper Nueces River in the vicinity of the present city of San Angelo, Texas. Sauer (1934:65), Scholes (Scholes and Mera 1940: 287-289), Spicer (1962:235), Schroeder (1969:18-20), and Newcomb (1961:233,235) are in general agreement with this congruency.

Part of the difficulty in identifying the peoples of these two general areas east and west of the Rio Grande arises from the Spanish practice, born of necessity, of identifying individual bands in this extensive group by the names of their leaders, by geographical localities, or by native names used by the bands themselves or by other Indian groups. One example of the latter practice is the Arcos Tuertos band encountered in 1683 by Juan Dominguez de Mendoza in west Texas some 20 leagues east of the Pecos River and of whom it was said, "...their wearing apparel and all the rest is after the fashion of the Suma nation" (Bolton 1908:333). The name of this band was apparently furnished by the Jumano chief, Juan Sabeata, who guided the Spanish force, a party that had recently passed through a number of villages identified as Suma and located on both sides of the Rio Grande below Paso del Norte. The identification of Sumas in this area east of the Rio Grande is

1

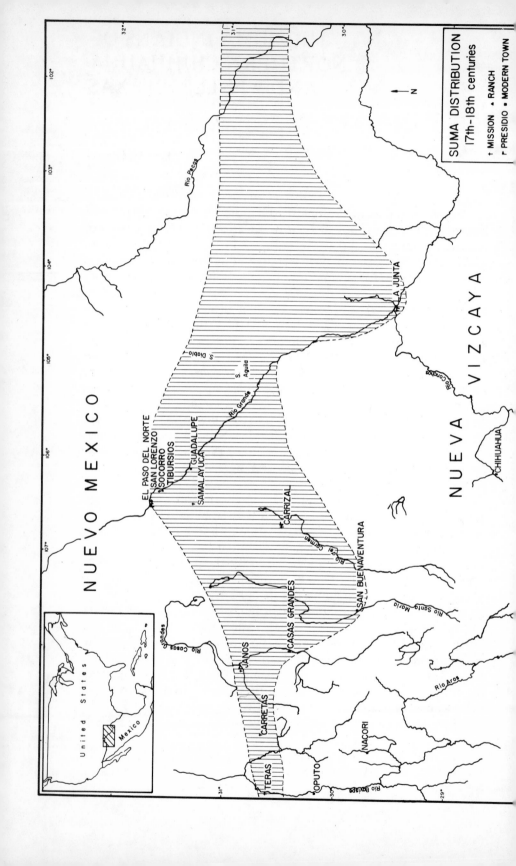

SUMA DISTRIBUTION
17th-18th centuries

† MISSION ▲ RANCH
ⵔ PRESIDIO ■ MODERN TOWN

NUEVO MEXICO

NUEVA VIZCAYA

United States

Mexico

LA JUNTA

EL PASO DEL NORTE
SAN LORENZO
SOCORRO
TIBURSIOS
GUADALUPE
SAMALAYUCA
CARRIZAL
SAN BUENAVENTURA
CASAS GRANDES
JANOS
CARRETAS
TERAS
OPUTO
NACORI
CHIHUAHUA

Rio Pecos
S. Diablo
S. Aquila
Rio Grande
Rio del Carmen
Rio Casas Grandes
Rio Santa Maria
Rio Conchos
Rio Aros
Rio Batepito

supported by a report in 1764, almost a century later, of a chief from a band occupying the Sierras Diablo and Cola de la Aguila, the Diablo and Eagle Mountains respectively, who was called to a meeting with governor Tomás Vélez Cachupín of New Mexico at Socorro in the Paso del Notre district *(Expediente)*.

A second difficulty confronting the student of these ethnic groups mentioned in early records is the absence of a standard orthography and poor calligraphy. Among the various terms identified as Suma and Jumano are the following: Suma, Zuma, Yuma, Zumana, Xumana, Humano, Jumano, Jumana (Sauer 1934:68), Umana, Xoman, Sumana (Newcomb 1961:226), and Shuman (Swanton 1952:324-325). A number of non-cognate forms are also identified with this group by various authors (cf. Newcomb 1961:227,233,235; Kelley 1955:982).

The Sumas occupied the northern and eastern frontier of the Spanish colonial domain, therefore, it is to be expected that most of the documentary references to them are to be found on the southern and western periphery of the territory frequented by them.

Along the Rio Grande itself, Sumas occupied both sides of the valley up to the vicinity of Paso del Norte where a mission was established for them and the Mansos in 1659 (Hughes 1914:305 ff.; Bolton 1908:321-323; Kelley 1955:982; McLaughlin 1962) and where a second was in operation in 1667 (Scholes 1929:56-57). West of the river, missions were established for them before 1684 at Torreon, near San Buenaventura, Chihuahua (Bancroft 1884: 365; Hughes 1914:363), Casas Grandes (Sauer 1934:71-75; Bandelier 1890:91, fn. 2), Janos (Hughes 1914:389-390), Carretas (Sauer 1934:70-71; Bandelier 1890:532,535), and Teras, Sonora (*Rudo Ensayo* 1951:114-115).

The southern portion of the salt lakes and sand dune area of Suma territory in north-central Chihuahua was inhabited by the Chinarras who were presumably close relatives of the Conchos living farther south. In the west, beyond Carretas, the area was occupied primarily by the sedentary Opatas (Sauer 1934:48,62), although Sumas frequently raided the area and some of them had been reduced to an Opata mission at Teras, located below the junction of the San Bernardino and Bavispe Rivers in northern Sonora. The Sumas often traveled outside their territory on raiding expeditions among the sedentary peoples to the west and southwest; many specific references exist concerning Suma raids in

3

the Fronteras area of northeastern Sonora (Bancroft 1884:253, fn. 27; *Rudo Ensayo* 1951:114-115), and as far south as Nacozari (Sauer 1934:75).

The Suma language became extinct before qualified linguists were able to reach them, but several students have attempted to relate their dialects to one or another of the language stocks known from the surrounding area. Sauer (1934:80) and Kroeber (1934:15) have tentatively placed the Sumas in the Uto-Aztecan language family on the basis of a short vocabulary. Forbes (1959) has marshalled a mass of circumstantial evidence that he interprets in favor of an Athabascan affinity. Orozco y Berra (1864:25) was inclined to the latter relationship also, although he did not state the basis of his opinion. Other authors have declined to express themselves in the absence of more concrete evidence (Naylor 1969: 8; Kelley 1955:982; Schroeder 1969:18-20), a practice that will be followed here.

The physical characteristics of the Sumas seem to have been no different from other tribes in the region. The group living in the La Junta area and to the east may have painted, tattooed, or scarified their faces with stripes, according to the etymology of the word "Jumano" as traced by Scholes (Scholes and Mera 1940:271-276). Their dress is said to have been scant, the men wearing loincloths and the women deerskins at the waist.

Suma social organization is described as similar to that of neighboring Apache groups. To judge from the size of bands, there may have been band organizations with talented headmen rising to the level of petty chieftains or with individual leaders whose charismatic personalities and abilities enabled them to attract followers from surrounding local groups (see the discussion of tribal leaders in Sahlins 1968). The local groups were probably under the leadership of the most prominent head of one of the component extended families; his power over his followers was, from all evidence, persuasive rather than coercive, as was that of the band leaders.

One of the band leaders, a petty chieftain named Joseph Antonio Pastor, led 90 families to settle at San Lorenzo el Real near Paso del Norte in February 1765, where they were given land by New Mexican governor Tomás Vélez Cachupín. The chief was granted permission to wear Spanish garb and carried a baton of office. Succession to the office of chief was said to be patrilineal in 1779, although this may have been a recent adaptation in response to Spanish expectation. In this particular case of succession at San

Lorenzo, it is interesting to note that because Joseph Antonio Pastor's only son died before taking office, the position passed to his son-in-law, Juan Domingo, who was recognized by the Spanish Commander General of the Interior Provinces (*Expediente;* Naylor 1969:5-6).

Naylor (1969:5) suggests that the band ranged in size from 50 to 75 persons, but the evidence I have suggests considerably larger sizes. Assuming that most of the groups that settled more or less voluntarily at missions were under the leadership of a single chief and hence constitute a band, the band in the 1692 conversion of San Diego de los Sumas, located seven leagues from Paso del Norte and two from Socorro, contained 300 individuals (Walz 1951:288). Three groups, presumably bands, were settled by Rivera (1946: 53,66) at San Lorenzo, "the place of Guadalupe" (below Paso del Norte), and at Carrizal in 1726, and 70 other families, persumably from another band, were settled at Janos the following year; none of these sites was occupied long, however. Sixty families settled at the mission of Nuestra Señora de las Caldas some eight leagues below Paso del Norte on the Rio Grande in 1730 or shortly before and remained there until 1749 (Hackett 1937:407; Adams 1954:107-108). The band under Joseph Antonio Pastor, mentioned above, consisted of 90 families when they settled at the unoccupied site of San Lorenzo in 1765, and shortly after the old chief's death in 1778, there were 72 adult males and a total population of 191 persons (Hackett 1937: 460; *Expediente; Estado de la Misión,* quoted in large part in Bandelier 1890:87, fn. 1, who errs in his arithmetic, however). Using the conservative figure of 2.5 persons to a family, the following band sizes may be suggested from the figures given above: 300,175,150 and 225. The average size of these bands, as derived above, is just over 200 persons.

Nothing is known of Suma marriage and kinship customs, although it may be assumed that monogamy was the rule since the priests make no mention of polygamous families, although many other transgressions are bewailed. Bandelier (1890:87) infers from evidence given by a Manso informant at Paso del Norte in 1883, and from tribal designations of children of mixed marriages in the baptismal records at Paso del Norte, that the Sumas were matrilineal in descent.

Medicine men, shamans or diviners, existed among the Sumas, and there is some indication that they may occasionally have wielded considerable influence on the band (Bandelier 1890:87;

Bannon 1955:105). The possibility that some of these were prophets of messianic cults has not yet been investigated sufficiently.

The technology of the Sumas was relatively simple before they acquired Spanish arms, horses, and horse trappings. They used the bow and arrow and lived in flimsy brush shelters called *jacales* that they covered with skins in winter and furnished with beds of grass (Bandelier 1890:87; Naylor 1969:4-5). After settling at the missions, they seem to have readily adapted to the use of European type agricultural implements--hoes, hatchets, plough-shares, teams of oxen, etc. (*Expediente*). As noted above, Chief Joseph Antonio Pastor of San Lorenzo was granted the privilege of wearing Spanish clothing, and presumably his followers and others were encouraged to acquire the dress of their mentors. They were expressly discouraged from leaving the pueblos to hunt (*Estado de la Misión*) for the purpose of acquiring food or hides for clothing.

The principal sustenance of the Sumas under aboriginal conditions is said to have been mescal, mesquite beans, prickly pear fruit, roots, seeds, fish, and animals. Domesticated plant and animal foods were utilized after they became commonly available from Spanish settlements in the area (Naylor 1969:4).

Very little of the ideology of the Sumas can be reconstructed. They had medicine men or shamans, as noted above, who presumably aided in interpreting the will or action of the supernatural, but the nature of their beliefs concerning the supernatural is unknown. One shaman is reported in 1662 to have attracted large followings as a result of his ability to perform such unexplained feats as walking on hot coals and blowing flames from his mouth. These performances were accompanied by dances and the use of an unidentified intoxicant. An incident of ritualistic cannibalism reported during this time period in the same general area of northeastern Sonora indicates a belief that some of the qualities of an individual, in this case bravery, could be acquired by eating bits of his flesh (Naylor 1969:6).

Peyote was employed in some of their religious rituals which terminated in "the greatest impurities and obscenities", and while under the influence of the peyote they are said "to have become furious" (*Estado de la Misión*). In general, the ideology of the Sumas living along the Rio Grande may be judged, from their numerous revolts against Spanish imposed sedentism, to have been such as to equip them for the relatively independent life of the hunter-gatherer. It is difficult, therefore, to accept Bandelier's interpretation of Spanish missionary reports which maintain that Sumas inhabiting the Casas Grandes area were "...different from their brethren who roamed near the Rio Grande, [and that they were] ... described as docile, even as a sedate stock, whom it became easy to accustom to the culture of the soil after the methods in vogue among the Spaniards of the seventeenth century" (Bandelier 1890:90). The record of late 17th century warfare between Sumas and Spaniards in the area does not support this perspective. As a matter of fact, most Spanish records concerning Sumas refer to their raiding activities or to the recent truces and subsequent reduction to missions, as the following chronology of contacts indicates.

The earliest mention of an Indian group under the name "Suma" is in the Benavides Memorial of 1630 (Benavides 1965:12) and probably refers only to the group living along the Rio Grande. The term "Jumano" was used earlier by Espejo in 1582 (Hodge, Hammond, and Rey 1945:111) and referred to people living in this same area. Western Sumas were first mentioned in 1645 as being on the war path around Teuricachi in northeastern Sonora where they endangered the lives of pioneering Franciscan missionaires (Bannon 1955:87). In 1651, a Jesuit missionary in northeastern Sonora persuaded a group of about 100 Sumas with their families to accept a peace offer at Opotu. This was followed by several requests by Sumas for missionaires to instruct them. In 1653, a rancheria of about 60 Christian Suma families was being administered at Carretas in northwestern Chihuahua (Bannon 1955:104-105). In 1659, the mission of Nuestra Señora de Guadalupe was founded at El Paso for Mansos and "Zumanas" (Hughes 1914:306-307,390). About 1663, Sumas living at Casas Grandes asked for priests to teach them about Christianity (Bancroft 1884:364), and in this same year the mission Santa Ana del Torreon was established for Sumas in northwestern Chihuahua (Bancroft 1884:365; Hughes 1914:363). Sometime between this date and 1667, at least one other mission, named Nuestro Padre San Francisco de los Sumas, was established near El Paso for Sumas recently settled in that area (Hughes 1914:310; Scholes 1929:56-57).

Suma and other mission Indians in northern Chihuahua were reported ready to revolt with the Pueblo Indians of New Mexico in 1680, but the swift action of the Spaniards forestalled them. Another mission for Sumas, Santa Gertrudis, was established in 1683 at Samalayuca, 35 miles south of El Paso (Hughes 1914:329,

334) but it was short-lived. Almost all of the Indians of the Chihuahau area rose in revolt in 1684, destroying most Spanish habitations and missions in northern Chihuahau except some of those at El Paso and the convent at Casas Grandes (Bancroft 1884:365-366; Bandelier 1890:91, fn. 2; Hughes 1914:342,363). Some Sumas then formed an alliance with Jano, Jocome, Apache, Sobaipuri, and other groups and resumed raiding of the sedentary Indians to the west in northeastern Sonora (Bolton 1936:247, fn. 3; Bancroft 1884:253, fn. 27). Little evidence is available on Suma-Jumano activities east of El Paso because there were few Spanish entradas and no settlements in possible Suma territory there, until much later.

Some groups, particularly Sumas at Casas Grandes, settled down after the revolt of 1684 and began to till their fields again, but unrest continued, and they were frequently accused of plotting revolt. At one time, Spaniards executed by clubbing 52 of the conspirators at Casas Grandes and 25 more in Sonora (Sauer 1934:72-73). The Spaniards succeeded in splitting an alliance between Sobaipuris, Janos, Jocomes, Apaches and Sumas in 1687 (Bolton 1936:264, fn. 3) and, as a result of battles fought between the former allies and the Spanish-Suma encounters, most of the Sumas remaining at war were forced to ask for peace and to settle in the various missions and presidios once again. One of these hostile bands of Sumas entered into peace negotiations with Captain Juan Fernandez de la Fuente of Janos presidio in 1698, but as early as 1689 the Sumas seem to have begun losing their leading place among the marauders of western Chihuahua to the Janos and others (Sauer 1934:73,75).

In the Paso del Norte area, however, Sumas continue to appear in the historic record as alternating between rebellion and peaceful settlement at their missions. In 1691, 20 Sumas, survivors of a rebellion at the conversion of Guadalupe somewhere down the river from Paso del Norte, were reported to have been living for some time with the Piros of Socorro. The following year a new mission with 300 converts was established for Sumas at San Diego de los Sumas, seven leagues from El Paso, and an irrigation ditch was opened and a church built for them (Walz 1951:285-286, 288).

A severe smallpox epidemic is said to have swept through the settlements in northern Chihuahua between 1693 and 1709 and to have taken a terrible toll of the Indians, Sumas included (Bandelier 1890:87, fn. 1), but the records of vital statistics have not yet been found that reflect this catastrophe. In 1706, a new mission for Sumas, Santa María Magdalena, is mentioned in the Paso del Norte area, but it was apparently short-lived as no other mention of it has been found; San Lorenzo el Real was a small settlement of Spaniards with no Indians at this date (Hackett 1937:377-378). Pedro de Rivera encountered several bands of Sumas during his inspection of the Spanish garrisons in the area that is now northern Chihuahua and succeeded in settling three groups at San Lorenzo el Real, at the place of Guadalupe below Paso del Norte, and at Carrizal in 1726, and a fourth group of 70 families at Janos in 1727 (Rivera 1946:53,66).

Eight leagues along the river below Paso del Norte and near an hacienda with sheep and cattle, a mission named Santa María de las Caldas was founded for Sumas in 1730 or shortly before. The priest's house and the dwellings of the Indians were built, but no separate church building was constructed. In 1745, these Sumas revolted and killed one Spaniard but settled down in their pueblo again. Another dispute in 1749 led to the destruction of the hacienda, the priest's quarters, and the Indian dwellings. The mission was not refounded thereafter (Adams 1954:107-109).

Mission San Lorenzo el Real held 50 to 58 Suma families in 1744 (Bandelier 1890:87, fn. 1; Hackett 1937:406) and 150 Spaniards and 150 Indians in 1749 (Ocaranza 1934:146), but in 1754, it is described as a poor community of six or eight Spanish families and no Indians, these Sumas having revolted and abandoned the site (Hackett 1937:460). The revolt apparently resulted from the summary execution of the Suma sacristan at the mission by soldiers from the garrison at Paso del Norte, acting on the orders of their captain (Hackett 1937:428). The mission at San Lorenzo was revived in February 1765 when 90 families of Sumas from the Diablo and Eagle Mountains of west Texas settled there under their chief, Joseph Antonio Pastor. Governor Tomás Vélez Cachupín of New Mexico had contacted these Sumas the previous September and promised to give them land at San Lorenzo, which he says he did, but agricultural implements and seeds were not provided until 1768 (*Expediente*). This mission continued until some time after 1784, 191 Sumas being there in 1778 or thereabouts (*Estado de la Misión*), and 30 "Indians" and 205 Spaniards there in 1784 (Juarez Archives, Reel 39:304).

There are several records of Sumas serving as auxiliaries or scouts for the Spaniards. Chief Joseph Antonio Pastor and some of his

9

men went with the Marques de Rubí expedition to New Mexico (*Expediente*); and others may have accompanied Rivera in the Chihuahua area in 1726-7 (Rivera 1946); a Suma captain was killed and others wounded along with several Spaniards in an encounter with Apaches in 1774 (Bucareli y Ursua 1774), and they were being used regularly at presidios in 1773 (Thomas 1932:199).

Indian ethnic identity became unimportant during the 19th century, and only in the relatively pure Indian towns are there records that distinguish between Indians and non-Indians. In 1883, Bandelier found that Sumas were remembered as having lived around San Lorenzo el Real, but they were reported to have "confounded themselves with the Spanish population." At the old mission of Nuestra Señora de Guadalupe in Paso del Norte, Bandelier was told that most of the Sumas were wiped out in a smallpox epidemic in 1780 and that the last Suma, a man, had died some 14 years before, leaving only one son (Lange and Riley 1970:161, 163).

The mission Sumas did not become genetically extinct, of course; they merely lost their tribal identity through intermarriage with other tribes such as the Tiguas, Mansos, and Piros (Lange and Riley 1970: 240-1). The Suma hunting and gathering mode of existence was often likened to that of the Apaches (see the two documents translated below), and it is entirely probable that many Sumas who did not settle in the El Paso area missions and towns became progressively more closely allied with Apache groups until they eventually lost their identity as Sumas.

The dossier (*expediente*) below, in substantiation of a Suma Indian's claim to chieftaincy, is a copy prepared by Antonio Bonilla, secretary to Commander General of the Interior Provinces, Teodoro de Croix, in Chihuahua City on August 1779. It is owned by the Harvard College Library, Cambridge, Massachusetts. I am indebted to Dr. Stephen Williams, Director of Peabody Museum, and to the staff of the Harvard College Library for assistance in obtaining microfilm pertaining to this and related research.

The document covers various events relating to the Suma chief Joseph Antonio Pastor, his son-in-law Juan Domingo, and their followers who settled at the town of San Lorenzo about four miles east of Mission Guadalupe in El Paso del Norte. The time period covered ranges from 1764 to 1779.

At the beginning of this period a Suma band of 90 families under chief Joseph Antonio was living in two local groups under subordinate leaders in the Eagle and Diablo Mountains in extreme eastern Hudspeth County and western Culbertson County near the center of the Trans-Pecos area of Texas. At this time, members of this band or other Sumas were residing on the Rio Grande at the small settlement of Tiburcios on the present site of San Elizario, Texas. In 1779, it is evident that there were still Sumas pursuing their traditional hunting and gathering mode of existence outside the settlement.

It is manifest that this particular Suma chief, and presumably others as well, was only a spokesman and war leader for his followers and had little or no coercive authority over them. The discrepancy between the Spanish legal model of Indian political organization and the actual organization of the Suma is clearly spelled out by Pedro Galindo Navarro, Commander General Teodoro de Croix's assessor general. For this and other reasons this document is of great importance to our understanding of Suma lifeways.

COPY OF THE DOSSIER ADVANCED BY THE INDIAN JUAN DOMINGO ASKING THAT HE BE NAMED CHIEF GENERAL OF THE SUMA NATION
(Translation)

[Letter, Viceroy Antonio Bucareli y Ursua, Mexico City, 30 Aug. 1775, to Treasurer Manuel Antonio de Escorza]

In a letter of the past July 25 Your Honor tells me of having been advised by Commander Inspector Don Hugo Oconor to pay the Indian Joseph Antonio the salary of a soldier which yearly has been assigned him by my predecessor, the Marquis [Carlos Francisco] de Croix. This is accompanied by a certified copy of the dossier advanced in this matter, of which Your Honor sends me a copy. In its fulfillment you delivered to the aforementioned Indian the two hundred and ninety pesos which he earned the past year of seventy-four, that being the same amount a soldier of the presidio earns at present.

With this understanding, and with what was told me by the Royal officials on this matter, I have decided that Joseph Antonio shall continue to earn the salary of a soldier, according to the new Royal Rule of Presidios and, therefore, I let Your Honor know, so that with this knowledge, and knowing that I have approved the payment you made to him of the two hundred and ninety pesos, all these provisions will be carried out. May God give Your Honor many years. Mexico, August 30, 1775 – Don Antonio Bucareli y Ursua [to] Señor Don Manuel Antonio de Escorza. –

[Letter, Commander Inspector of the Interior Provinces, Hugo Oconor, Presidio de Carrizal, 8 March 1775, to Treasurer Manuel Antonio de Escorza]

My dear Sir: By the attached warrant, Your Honor will see the favor granted by the Superior Government of New Spain to the Chief of the Suma nation, of the salary earned yearly by a soldier of a presidio; and since this is a delicate matter, in case the Chief should become irritated by some demurrer that could be avoided in the paying of the salary assigned to him, I enclose for Your Honor the warrant, so that you may order that through the treasury under your care the interested Chief be paid the salary he earned last year, of 1774, under the usual formalities; and of this action Your Honor can give account to the Viceroy using as testimony the original warrant drawn up in favor of the aforementioned Chief, which I include for Your Honor. May our Lord keep Your

Honor many years, Presidio de Carrizal, March 8, 1775. I kiss the hand of Your Honor, your most faithful servant-- Hugo Oconor [to] Don Manuel Antonio de Escorza.

[Cover Letter, Viceroy Carlos Francisco de Croix, the Marquis de Croix, Mexico City, 25 March 1768, to Pedro del Barrio.]

At the request of the Chief of the Suma Indians of the Province of New Mexico, I pass on to Your Honor the enclosed certified copy of decisions reached so that the part pertaining to Your Honor will be promptly carried out and you will report to me upon its execution. God keep Your Honor many years, Mexico, March 25, 1768. The Marquis de Crois [to] Don Pedro del Barrio.

[Attorney Juan María Ramirez de Arellano to Joachin Antonio Guerrero y Tagle.]

BRIEF----Most Excellent Sir, Joachin Antonio Guerrero y Tagle: [As] procurator of Indians for the Chief Captain of the Suma nation of Christian and gentile Indians, congregated and established in the town of San Lorenzo el Real, jurisdiction of the presidio of El Paso del Norte of the government of the kingdom of New Mexico, and in due form I appear before Your Excellency and say: On behalf of my client and the whole [Suma] nation, I say that when making his general inspection in the jurisdiction of said presidio [in] the year of seventy-[sic., sixty-] four, with the good will of my client and of his whole nation, as will be evident, Don Tomás Vélez Cachupin, Governor of that kingdom finding it best for the comfort of the aforementioned and of his nation, congregated them in said town of el Real at a distance of a league from the mentioned presidio and assigned them good farm land for their subsistence and that of their families. They are very happy in that place but lack the necessary implements for working their land and for this reason they lack the necessary grain for their support. Because of this it is difficult to keep some families of his people from wandering among the other towns begging for the necessary sustenance. They are also liable to abandon their own town and land, and to desist from their intention of becoming Christians. In order that my client and all his nation remain in the town assigned to them start Christianizing themselves, and converting others, it is worthwhile to both majesties to assign and give them the necessary implements, and worthwhile for their conservation, since with these things they feel themselves permanent and occupied by the protions of land assigned them. They will obtain that which

13

is necessary for their food and that of their families and they will avoid changing their mind and returning to their infidelity. In this respect and to cover the expressed needs of my client and those of his nation, and because it is proper and agreeable to the above, it may please Your Excellency to order that from the account of the Royal Treasury as is customary, there be given to my client and his companions the corresponding implements [consisting] of picks, hoes, hatchets, plough-shares, and teams of oxen for the tilling of their land, as it is done by His Majesty to new establishments and congregations of Indians. In this way they will obtain the relief they wish for their future permanent residency. For the solicitation of this, and the relief of his nation, my client claims to have come with two others, hoping that the Catholic piety and Catholic zeal of Your Excellency would grant him this benefit.

In addition, although they have enough land, many of them lack the waters of Holy Baptism, especially the mentioned Chief Captain, my client, and because he wishes this Christian Catholic benefit, he implores Your Excellency's greatness to help him and to take the necessary measures to obtain this. And with the character of a Christian, serving God and our Catholic monarch, he offers to do all he can to urge those of his nation to attain the same end which is above all else to serve Your Excellency. Therefore, please take the necessary measures, and pass on the Assessor General this Brief together with the notebook of said inspection. For these reasons, I beg of Your Excellency that you do all I have asked, which is just and necessary. – Juan María Ramirez de Arellano [Attorney at Law], [to] Joachin Antonio Guerrero y Tagle.

[Decree of the Viceroy, the Marquis de Croix, Mexico City, 13 Jan. 1768.]
DECREE—Mexico, January 13, 1768. – [Send] To the General Council with the bound record mentioned. – de Croix.

[Opinion of Assessor General Diego de Cormide, Mexico City, 25 Jan. 1768, to the Viceroy, the Marquis de Croix.]
OPINION—Most Excellent Sir: With respect to finding himself in this city, Don Tomás Vélez, who was governor of New Mexico, himself executed the enclosed inspection. This presumption is passed on so that it will inform with complete justification, and with clarity on that which may be offered from his inspection so that you may take steps concerning the claim of these natives.

14

Your Excellency will decide what pleases him. Mexico, January 25, 1768. – Don Diego Cormide.

[Decree of the Viceroy, the Marquis de Croix, Mexico City, 25 Jan. 1768.]
DECREE----Mexico, January 25, 1768.--As it appears to the Assessor General -- de Croix.

[Former New Mexico governor Tomás Vélez Cachupín, Mexico City, 27, Jan. 1768, to the Viceroy, the Marquis de Croix.]
REPORT---Most Excellent Sir--With respect to the higher decree of Your Excellency, which precedes, emanating from the claim recorded above, made on the Higher Administration of Your Excellency by the Chief Captain of the Suma nation, on which Your Excellency orders him [Vélez] to inform himself of its content, specifically and with clarity: I must explain to Your Excellency that, as is evident in the report of the inspection which is inserted and which I performed in the Presidio of El Paso, I brought together said Suma nation in the town of San Lorenzo el Real, a league away from the mentioned presidio, because the families of this nation found themselves dispersed among the other neighboring towns. Great damage resulted to all that jurisdiction, because without land for their support they were almost beggars and this made them offensive and exposed, because of their need, to desertion and alliance with the enemy Apache nation. Considering that the land of the town of El Real is very capacious and of such corresponding usefulness as to be enough to support the whole nation, at my prompting, this nation, part of which was gentile, reduced itself to a permanent establishment in which it has been for three years. Many of the persons who, at the time of the congregation were gentiles, are already catechised and Christians, as is stated in the letter of the religious missionary charged with their administration. The letter is found on page eight of the report of inspection.

Although I surveyed and granted them enough good land for the planting of all types of seeds, all under irrigation, I did not give them the agricultural implements and contrivances which the Chief asks of Your Excellency, inasmuch as in that kingdom [of New Mexico the governor] is not empowered to do this on behalf of His Majesty, without the order of the Higher Administration of Your Excellency, since new settlements and congregations of natives have always been given the corresponding farming im-

15

plements on His Majesty's behalf. Because of the poverty of the Indians, it appears that the Sumas are equally deserving of His Majesty's charity especially now that they have the special merit of making war with the enemy Apaches of Gila, Faraones, and Natages in consortium with the Presidio of El Paso. The latter makes successful campaigns against these barbarians accompanied by the Sumas led by this Chief, a man of courage and prudence. It is he who has subjected and reduced to our devotion his entire nation. These actions could be facilitated by giving them the help they ask for in planting their crops. This would greatly help the jurisdiction of El Paso, since the Sumas will be able to support themselves, and thus increase their crops without leaving their settlement. They will then be in a position to have supplies to go out on campaigns without doing it at the cost of the King as is the custom in the Administration of New Mexico. And they will justify the royal good will with which His Majesty looks upon the natives of these his dominions.

Up until now they have done their planting with the help of the neighboring Spaniards of the town of El Paso and of El Real who lend them their plows and oxen but in this way they cannot extend their planting so that it will be sufficient to support them during the year. The neighbors give them this aid, in spite of its being troublesome in a way for them, in consideration of the utility they obtain from the tranquility, peacefulness, and permanent settlement of this Suma nation. When this nation was unsettled and made war with us, it caused in that country many damages, so that the government of New Mexico applied the most active means to pacify this nation, and to bring it under the vassalage of the King and of the Catholic religion. There would be grave risk of dissipating the state of peace and piety as happened in all the preceeding administrations were not that which they ask granted by Your Excellency's great mercy, especially when this Chief came so far [to Mexico City] to make his petition.

The number of families that constituted this nation at the time of congregating and establishing them in the town of El Real, was ninety including Christians and gentiles, for whom I consider a sufficient supply to be one hundred and fifty hoes, with an equal number of *coas* [type of hoe], fifty axes, ten ploughshares, and ten teams of oxen which, regulated by the market price of today, adds up to four hundred pesos, the purchase being made in this city with the exception of the oxen (which may cost one hundred and fifty pesos bought in the government of New Mexico, not including in this price the transportation cost to the Presidio of El Paso which is two pesos and six reales per *arroba* [ca. 25 pounds]).

To assure that the Sumas receive these implements they ought to be sent to the Captain of the presidio, Don Pedro del Barrio, with superior orders from Your Excellency so that he will make the delivery to the Suma nation congregated in the Real of San Lorenzo with the compliance of the Chief and religious missionary. The implements should not be distributed to each family except at the time of going out to do the work on their land, and at the end of the afternoon before the prayer all the tools should be picked up, each individual returning the one he took out in the morning to the Chief with the knowledge of the missionary and the Minister of Justice whom the Captain places in the town, so that the tools will not get lost. Such loss would quickly occur if distribution were made amongst the families, and no relief or utility would be obtained.

It is equally true that the Chief, who is present, has not been Christianized and that he voluntarily asks for the holy waters of baptism. It would be sad for him to leave this capital without that for which he asks, imploring the pre-eminent support of His Excellency. It would be very much in keeping with the high dignity and piety of His Excellency to favor this individual in his intentions, in the form that your merciful judgment may find convenient. And he will return to his country, obliged and endeared by the equitable and noble acts of His Excellency, to be a faithful subject of the King, and to employ himself in his royal service.

This is all I can present with which to inform His Excellency's superior intelligence so that above all His Excellency may decide what is most pleasing to Him. Mexico, January 27, 1768.–Tomás Vélez Cachupín.

[Decree of the Viceroy, the Marquis de Croix, Mexico City, 28 Jan. 1768.]
DECREE––Mexico, January 28, 1768.–[Send] To the Assessor General--de Croix.

[Opinion of Assessor General, Diego Cormide, Mexico City, 3 Feb. 1768.]
OPINION––Your Excellency–So that this despatch may become

17

formal as should please Your Excellency, give the Fiscal Agent a chance to say if he wants to make some change in the matter--as concerns the two petitions presented. Your Excellency will decide what he likes. Mexico, February 3, 1768 -- Don Diego Cormide.

[Decree of the Viceroy, the Marquis de Croix, Mexico City, 4 Feb. 1768.]
DECREE----Mexico, February 4, 1768--as it appears to the Assessor General – de Croix.

[Fiscal Agent Velarde's response, Mexico City, 12 Feb. 1768, for the Viceroy, the Marquis de Croix.]
FISCAL'S RESPONSE: Most Excellent Sir--The Fiscal Agent has no objection that the Indians of the Suma nation congregated in the town of San Lorenzo el Real, jurisdiction of the Presidio of El Paso del Norte in the kingdom of New Mexico be given by the Exchequer the contrivances and implements mentioned by Don Tomás Vélez Cachupín, who was governor of said kingdom, under the rules which are proposed in the preceding report. What he does point out is that similar erogations have always been decided upon in a meeting of the War and Treasury Departments, and this practice having been approved by His Majesty, as evidenced by many despatches of similar nature of which the Fiscal has been told, he must make it known to Your Excellency so that, if it pleases him, he will order that the business be taken to said meeting, and the corresponding decision taken there. As concerns the baptism requested by the Chief Captain of the mentioned nation, the Fiscal Agent considers it befitting the Christian piety of Your Excellency that he place this Indian under the care of a person of his liking, so that with sufficient instruction in the Catholic dogmas he will be prepared to receive it. Mexico, February 12, 1768–Velarde.

[Decree of the Viceroy, the Marquis de Croix, Mexico City, 21 March 1768.]
DECREE----Mexico, March 21, 1768. There is no objection, by the Fiscal Agent or others, to giving the town of the Suma nation the implements for which its chief asks; reports by the Marquis de Rubí whom they accompanied on his trip to New Mexico indicate that they deserve being encouraged and taken care of by my Higher Administration; and furthermore, the Inspector General who has

18

examined this despatch is of the same opinion. Therefore, let orders be given the Commanding Captain of the missions and frontiers of Nueva Vizcaya, Don Lope de Cuellar, that he hand over to this chief seven Indians of his nation whom he says are detained in a workshop.

So that there may be a clear understanding with the Captain of the Presidio of El Paso, there will be supplied to the said nation and town, and in the manner and method proposed by Don Tomás Vélez Cachupín, the implements the latter mentions in his report. Orders will also be given the same Captain of the Presidio of El Paso to advance credit to the chief of the Sumas and to honor it to an amount equivalent to a salary [of a soldier] of that Presidio. I bestow upon the chief in recognition of his courage and fidelity permission to bear the baton [of chief of office] and to wear the clothing of a Spaniard, under the conditions that he and his Indians make war against the Apaches.

In order that he may receive the holy water of baptism I charge the same Captain of the Presidio and the religious of that mission with the responsibility of taking care of this matter with all possible haste, but under no circumstances must the Chief be treated like the young catechumens as regards to the methods with which they are castigated for carelessness or lack of application. To this end two testimonials will be taken for the two captains mentioned and they will be registered with the Royal Tribunal of the Exchequer in the Royal Treasury.--De Croix.

[Certificate of Joseph de Gorraez, Mexico City, 27 March, 1768.]
In accordance with the originals that remain in the records of the matter and official documents of administration and war of this kingdom under my care, and as proof, for the Captain of Presidio of El Paso del Norte, of the things ordered by his Excellency, the Viceroy of New Spain, I offer this testimonial. Mexico, March 27, 1768.--Joseph de Gorraez.

[Petition of Juan Domingo, Suma Indian, to Commander General of the Interior Provinces, Teodoro de Croix, 1779?]
Brigadier and Commander General -- Sir -- [I am] Juan Domingo, Indian of the town of San Lorenzo el Real of the Suma nation. I appear before you in the best possible way, and I say, that in the year of sixty-four, in the month of September, being in the last town of this jurisdiction which is that of El Socorro, the governor

of this kingdom, Don Tomás Vélez Cachupín, as noted in his general inspection, became aware that there was, in a wooded area, a temporary settlement of Sumas of my nation down the river far from the town they called Tiburcios, which is at the southeast corner of this jurisdiction. Said governor sent a call to the Chief of this settlement who within a few days arrived with his people from the mountains they call Sierra del Diablo and Cola de la Aguila. When he received the message from said governor, this chief, whose name was Joseph Antonio Pastor, set himself on the road with the important men of his settlement. This man, was as an infidel, Chief of the entire Suma nation, and after becoming a Christian he was still Chief.

The governor having delivered to them an eloquent discourse for the purpose of reducing them to the pale of our Holy Catholic Faith, was answered by said chief that of course they would subject themselves with the qualifying condition that they be given the depopulated town of Las Caldas. The said governor answered them that this was not advisable, that the town of El Real was better because of better and more dependable lands, that he would give him as much land as the chief wanted. This he did and said Chief was satisfied and happy. The governor had three oxen killed for them in the town of Socorro to be distributed among the Chief's people and they were distributed in the governor's presence. After the distribution he asked the Chief when he would move to the town of El Real and he told him that it would be in February of sixty-five, upon which they agreed. The Chief told the governor that he needed some wagons and oxen to move their implements and wood to said town to make their houses, and all was furnished by the governor. He left orders for Lt. Joseph Horcasitas, to move them and settle them in said town and to give them the land His Majesty ordered, all of which was done in said year of sixty-five.

In the year of sixty-six said Chief went to the city of Santa Fe, capital of his kingdom, to see the governor who gave him four teams of oxen so that they could begin work and black blankets for his wife and daughters.

In the year of sixty-seven, in September, the governor left his governorship for Mexico, and having arrived at this town of El Paso he called to him said Chief and asked him if he wanted to accompany him to Mexico to see the Viceroy. The Viceroy at the time was His Excellency the Marquis de Croix who attended to and looked upon said Chief with much love and fondness, and who gave him the title of General of the Sumeria, and the more beneficial position of soldier which post, as is publicly and widely known, he filled both as an infidel and as a Christian until his death. In addition His Excellency Viceroy and Captain General Marquis de Croix gave him a uniform, a baton, and sixty pesos for the road because of his good service which was publicly and widely known, His Excellency being informed of such by the Marquis de Rubi'who was inspector of the interior presidios, and by the governor. In like manner His Excellency the Viceroy ordered that the said town be given oxen, ploughs, picks, axes, and hoes which Captain Cuellar delivered to said Chief.

This Chief, Joseph Antonio, having died, left a married son, and the latter was killed by the Apaches in the presidio of San Eleceario in this year of seventy-eight and left no sons. Consequently, the chieftainship belongs and falls upon me since I am married to the eldest daughter of the deceased Chief, and I have sons who are heirs, but in the interim they are not in a state to obtain their inheritance. So that I can deliver it I humbly ask and beg Your Excellency that he issue orders in my favor granting me the same faculties that my deceased master had. The whole town acclaims that I become Chief. It is the custom in this kingdom that in all towns there is a Chief, and when one dies, his son takes over. The commission of the deceased Chief which was given him by His Excellency the Viceroy is in the treasury. Therefore, I ask and beg of Your Excellency to please do as I have asked, and I swear in the proper form that there is no malice in my petition. By request of Juan Domingo -- Joseph de ....[incomplete.]

[Certificate of Fray Cayetano Joseph Bernal, Socorro, 29 Dec. 1778.]

I certify, in the best form I can and must and that the law permits, that Juan Domingo, Suma Indian, is married to Mariá Antonia, daughter of the deceased Joseph Antonio, Chief and General of the Suma nation, who died in the month of February of this year of one thousand seven hundred and seventy-eight. I give this petition on his behalf because I myself made said Chief aware of this when I was Minister of the Mission of San Lorenzo del Real, and as proof I sign, on December 29, 1778. -- Fray Cayetano Joseph Bernal. Doctorate Minister of Socorro.

[Certificate of Fray Antonio de Galfarsora, San Lorenzo el Real,

4 Jan. 1779.]

The aforementioned certification agrees with the book of funerals which is in my hands, and as proof I sign on January 4, 1779 -- Fray Antonio de Galfarsoro, Doctorate Minister of [San Lorenzo el] Real.

[Endorsement of Commander General of the Interior Provinces, Teodoro de Croix, 29 Jan. 1779.]

Chihuahua, January 29, 1779 -- [Send] to the Assessor General. --de Croix.

[Opinion of the Assessor General, Pedro Galindo Navarro, 9 April 1779, to Commander General de Croix.]

Commander General: Regarding the documents pertaining to the matter of this petition which is in the Royal Treasury and which has been given to me by Don Manuel Antonio de Escorza so that with more instruction and knowledge I can carry it out, it happens that on January 13 of the past year of sixty-eight the Chief and Captain of the Christian and gentile Indians of the Suma nation applied for help from the Superior Administration of Mexico, stating that at the inspection made in the year of sixty-four the governor of the province of New Mexico, Don Tomás Vélez Cachupín, had them gathered in the town of San Lorenzo, jurisdiction of the presidio of El Paso del Norte. But because he had not given them the necessary implements for the cultivation and planting of the land which he distributed, they lacked the seeds needed for support of themselves and their families. This forced many to go as vagrants, searching out food in the other towns, and this made the settlement and subjugation of other Sumas more difficult. In order to obtain peace, the Chief asked that they be assigned and given, in accordance with the Law, the implements necessary for new settlements and congregations of Indians. And since the mentioned Chief captain, who with two men of his nation had gone to Mexico City, was still a gentile, he asked to be baptized and offered to do all he could so that all those of his nation would ask for baptism.

Attached to the despatch is the notebook of the inspection made by Governor Vélez Cachupín, the report which was asked of him when he was found to be in Mexico, and which he furnished, and also that which was made by the Marquis de Rubí. With full

22

knowledge of all this and of the opinion presented by the fiscal agent, His Excellency, the Viceroy Marquis de Croix issued a decree on 25 March 1768, that conformed with the opinion of His Excellency, Don Joseph de Galvez, who was inspector general at the time. The Viceroy ordered that Don Lope de Cuellar, Commanding Captain of the missions and frontiers of Vizcaya, hand over to the Chief seven Indians of his nation who he said were being held in a workshop; and reminded the captain of the Presidio of El Paso that he would furnish the same Chief, and those of his nation and towns, the implements that Governor Vélez Cachupín mentioned in his report and in the form and according to the method he proposed.

An order was also given to the Captain of the Presidio of El Paso to advance credit to the said Chief and to honor it to an amount equivalent to the salary of that presidio. This was awarded him because of his courage and loyalty, and he was allowed to have a baton and to wear a suit like a Spaniard, all under the condition that, with his Indians, he make war against the enemy Apaches. And finally the same Captain and the religious of the mission were charged to proceed with the most speed possible to see that he receive the baptismal water, without for any reason, treating him like the young catechumens, as far as the corrective methods used to punish them for neglect or lack of diligence. For the fulfillment of this order, testimonies were to be drawn up for the aforementioned Captains and those registered with the Royal Tribunal of the Exchequer of the Royal Treasury.

On the 25th of March the aforementioned official transcript was forwarded with the corresponding order for its effective compliance to the Captain of the Presidio of El Paso, who was at the time Don Pedro del Barrio now transferred to that of Carrizal. After this and with a date of 8 March of '75 Don Hugo Oconor sent another testimony to the treasurer, Don Manuel Antonio de Escorza, there accompanying the originals one from the Most Excellent Marquis de Croix and official transcripts directed to Don Pedro del Barrio, so that through the treasury entrusted him, he give the interested Chief under the usual formalities, the salary, which was accumulated in the previous year of '74; and because of the new regulation, which was now in practice, the maximum wage set for each military position was reduced to that of 290 pesos which was paid by the treasurer to the Chief, who at the time was named Joseph Antonio, in consideration of this assignment. He gave an account to His Excellency the Viceroy, who approved it, by the order which he sent on 30 August of '75, ordering him to continue paying under the same method according to the documents, which accompany the dossier and must be returned to the treasury where they belong.

The Chief, Joseph Antonio, passed away without leaving a male successor other than a son who was killed by the Apaches in the Presidio of Carrizal in the previous year of '78. There remain some daughters, the eldest named María Antonia, and she is married to Juan Domingo, Indian of the same tribe and town of San Lorenzo del Real, as is documented in the certificate of the ministers, Fray Cayetano Joseph Bernal and Fray Antonio de Galfarsoro, who have served successively at that mission. Juan Domingo claims that, as her husband, he should be issued a commission with the same rights that his deceased father-in-law had, stating it to be the general custom of the kingdom that once the father dies, the son becomes Chief, and that the whole town acclaims it, in order that it may be verified in this way.

By the laws of Title 7, Book 6, of the Code of Laws of these kingdoms, it is provided that those Indians, who in their time of infidelity were chiefs, retain their rights after their conversion and settlement. The courts in doing justice to those that, because of being principal descendants of the leaders, try to succeed them in the chieftaincy, must restore their jurisdictions, rights, and income, that were owed them, or were taken away, and the possession and custom introduced since the discovery of the Indies must be recognized. In the chieftaincy, the sons succeed the fathers, with explicit prohibition against the introduction of innovations, or of taking from some to give to others and that for no criminal cause may the common justices deprive them of it, because the knowledge of this matter is reserved to the courts and circuit judges of the district. It is also prohibited that the mestizos be chiefs or that the latter call themselves gentlemen of the towns. And it is ordered that all the natives be settled in their towns, and that they pay the chiefs their tax services and vassalage, which may derive from antiquity. The chiefs should not be tryants nor excessive, for in such a case they must fix a regimen for themselves and temper themselves to what is just. Finally, there are pointed out the exemptions, enfranchisements, and jurisdiction that the casiques exercise and to which they are entitled.

It is confirmed by the referred documents, that while a pagan, the deceased Joseph Antonio was chief of the Suma families that settled and congregated in the town of San Lorenzo. And there is no doubt that his eldest daughter, María Antonia, succeeded to the chieftaincy and that her husband, Juan Domingo, rightfully enjoys and exercises that post.

The Sumas, during the time when they were pagans, lived little differently from the Apache nation now. It is noted that they have a head or chief that rules them and directs them in war functions and usually it is he that is most outstanding among them. In other matters, however, they don't recognize him as being superior, nor do they offer him obedience, vassalage, tributes, nor anything else, and even the temporary settlements are dispersed in the hills, moving from one place to another when and however they please, without recognizing any other head but the common father of all, or of the greatest number of families of which they are composed.

From this principle arises the observation that during the time of his paganism, the deceased Joseph Antonio Pastor was nothing more than the head or chief of the Sumas of his settlement and his followers contributed nothing to him. Nor did he exercise any superiority or jurisdiction over them. The same practice has continued after his subjection and must continue henceforth with his successor. It is true that through His Excellency the Viceroy, he was conceded the enjoyment of a position as a soldier of that Presidio, but it is also true that this favor was personal and due to his fidelity, and his offers that through him his entire nation would be converted and together would wage war against the Apaches. But these hopes have not been carried through. On the contrary, there is no lack of indications and perhaps proof, that many of them have united and banded together with the others and have helped them to commit hostilities. There seems to be no reason, justice, or rational motive to explain why this gratuity that is perjudicial and a burden to the Royal Treasury should be transmitted to his heirs.

But it must be kept in mind that the Suma nation is one of those esteemed throughout the country for its bravery and bellicosity and that rewarding the Casique in some way might result in attracting and converting all his compatriots, so that thus united, they may truly make war on the Apaches. In order to avoid the contributions which the Indian generals of the Tarahumara asked of those of their nation, I set before your lordship in another dossier the suggestion that they may be given a moderate salary that is considered sufficient for the expenses of trips that they make to visit the towns of their district, and some campaign sallies. With regard to everything I believe your lordship may, if you wish, declare the Indian Juan Domingo, as husband and personal associate of María Antonia, his wife, Chief and general of the Suma nation; and order that he be given the corresponding title with the same gifts, facilities, provisions, and responsibilities as are contained in the orders sent to the generals of the Tarahumaras and Tepehuanes. Decided thusly, there will no longer be a need to continue the salary of the position of a soldier, that his deceased father-in-law enjoyed, giving him, if you think it convenient, the moderate salary that is given the said generals of the Tarahumara; but your lordship will resolve it according to your wishes. Chihuahua, April 9, 1779 -- [Assessor General] Don Pedro Galindo Navarro.

[Decree of Commander General Teodoro de Croix, Chihuahua, 14 April, 1779.]

Chihuahua, April 14, 1779 - As it appears to the assessor-general in his preceeding report, and as a result send forth the corresponding title to the Indian Juan Domingo, with the assignation of one hundred pesos per year, which will be paid in this treasury where an account will be taken; and inform His Majesty-- [Teodoro] de Croix.

[Certification by de Croix's Secretary, Antonio Bonilla, Chihuahua, 30 August 1779.]

Copy of the original dossier which remains in the office of the general command in my care of which I certify. Chihuahua, August 30, 1779.

/s/ Antonio Bonilla

Rubric

The document that follows, "State of the Mission of San Lorenzo el Real, Town of Zumas," is taken from a copy in the Peabody Museum Library, Harvard University, collected by Adolph Bandelier during the latter years of the last century. Neither the date of writing nor the author is known, but from internal evidence it can be placed in the latter part of the 18th century with a probable date between February 1778 and April 1779. The mention of Hugo Oconor, who was Commander Inspector of the Interior Provinces between February 17, 1772 and March 16, 1777 (Gerald 1968:7), limits the possible time of writing to this period or slightly later. Chief Joseph Antonio Pastor brought his band of Sumas to settle at San Lorenzo in February 1765, and was chief until his death in February 1778. This document was apparently written after his death but before his son-in-law, Juan Domingo, was recognized as chief by Viceroy de Croix on April 14, 1779 (see dossier above). It also is improbable that the document was written after the 1780s because the mentioned settlement of Tiburcios was known after that time as Presidio de San Elceario (on the site of the present San Elizario, Texas), the garrison having been ordered transferred to that locality on February 14, 1780 (Gerald 1968:25). Construction apparently began in the early 1780s. Evidence is lacking as to its completion date, but additional structures were being built or old ones repaired in mid-1790 as is indicated by a list of persons from Ysleta, Socorro, and other towns in the El Paso area who participated in the construction during June of that year (Juarez Archives, 40:unnumbered exposure).

Fray Francisco Atenacio Dominguez was in the El Paso area at this time, and it is tempting to regard this document as a portion of his lost visitation report on the El Paso missions, or an addendum. He wrote his superior that he had finished his report by August 1777, and remained in the El Paso area until shortly after October 1778 (Adams and Chavez 1956:xviii).

The archive from which Bandelier obtained his copy is unknown at present, but the original has not been found in either the Santa Fe or the Ciudad Juarez archives. Large portions of the Spanish are quoted by Bandelier in his *Final Report* (1890:87 fn. 1, 89 fn. 1), but this translation by Edward Elias and the present writer is the first that is known to have been made available.

STATE OF THE MISSION OF SAN LORENZO EL REAL,
TOWN OF ZUMAS
(Translation)

Said mission is formed by seventy-two male Indians, and seventy-two female Indians--married and single--33 indoctrinated boys and 14 girls. Among these there are six pagan men and seven pagan women, all of which are of age.

There are some Christians, in name only who were baptized by order of Captain Muñoz, without any catechism or the slightest bit of instruction upon what they were receiving. There are others whom the laborers in the fields baptize when in danger of death, but it is impossible to convert either these or the pagans. The whole nation is composed of people without political organization or subordination to justice and the minister; they always aspire for independence. This is proved by the type of life they lead, similar to that of the Apaches and by more than fourteen uprisings credited to them since their reduction, during which time allied with the pagans they have been the cause of most of the hostilities experimented by those towns.

In their last uprising their insolence came to such a degree that they killed all those defenseless people they found on the roads and in the towns: in Carrizal they did the same thing, and entering the church they desecrated the images and sacred vestments dressing themselves with them, carrying the patens hanging from their neck and the little spoons from their hair.

Because there are in the town that is called Tiburcios, two families of pagans of that nation, which is the focal point of their evil doings, male and female Indians are continually running off, living the way they please for months and years, and at present there has been for more than a year among those pagans a proselyte who was baptized as an adult, who goes alone into the mountains and sustains himself by hunting, which is why they have surnamed him "Cazador" [the hunter], and no efforts on the part of the minister have succeeded in bringing him in and settling him at the mission, not even his going out personally to bring him in.

They observe their own brand of religion; they use an infinite number of superstitions and abuses as they are able to in heathenism. The principal diviners among the Christians are three named Santiago Chicama, Antonio Colina, and Felipillo. It would be very advisable to separate these together with all the heathens from the

28

townspeople before they end up corrupting the rest, as well as the two families of heathens in Tiburcios as I have mentioned, who are called Muilo and Carbon, who are their leaders and accessories to all iniquity.

The Chief [cacique] died, and it would be better not to permit them to name another one, since he has amongst them a kind of sovereignty in which all that he commands is executed without repugnance; he alone do they obey, preferring his judgment on any matter over that of any justice or minister, and even their governor, who is appointed by the Royal Judge, is subordinated completely to the Chief.

They are very wicked people given to drunkenness, and the worse kind is not that from wine and brandy [aguardiente], but that from the plant they call Peyote, this entralls them to the point that they end up in a state of fury. They consider it a mysterious plant and use it in their religious meetings which usually end up in the greatest impurities and obscenities. They congregate in these meetings at night and with little light. Everybody incenses [with the smoke of a pipe?] everyone else and those others [the diviners] explain the main dogmas of their religion, and end as I have said.

These and many other disorders have been made known to the principal Justice of this jurisdiction, as well as to Don Hugo de Oconor, both of whom being fearful of another uprising (as they claim) did not dare to remedy these excesses, although they did ask the Minister to endure them. There is no missionary who can tolerate them. In four years, five different Ministers have been placed in office, and the one that is at said mission now conveys to our Reverence his distress and the causes that motivate it, so that for the love of God you will assist in finding a remedy.

[End of Document]

BIBLIOGRAPHY

ADAMS, ELEANOR B.

1954   *Bishop Tamaron's Visitation of New Mexico, 1760.* Historical Society of New Mexico Publications in History XV, Albuquerque.

ADAMS, ELEANOR B. and ANGELICO CHAVEZ

1956   *The Missions of New Mexico, 1776.* University of New Mexico Press, Albuquerque.

BANCROFT, HUBERT H.

1884   *History of the North Mexican States and Texas.* Vol. 1, 1531-1800. A.L. Bancroft & Co., San Francisco.

BANDELIER, A.F.

1890   *Final Report of Investigations Among the Southwestern U.S. Carried on Mainly in the Years from 1880 to 1885.* Part I. Papers of the Archaeological Institute of America, American Series III., Cambridge.

BANNON, JOHN FRANCIS

1955   *The Mission Frontier in Sonora 1620-1687.* United States Catholic Historical Society, Monograph Series XXVI, New York.

BENAVIDES, FRAY ALONSO DE

1965   *The Memorial of Fray Alonso de Benavides: 1630.* Translation by Mrs. Edward E. Ayer, annotated by Frederick Webb Hodge and Charles Fletcher Lummis. Horn and Wallace, Albuquerque. (Reprint).

BOLTON, HERBERT EUGENE

1908   *Spanish Exploration in the Southwest, 1542-1706.* Barnes and Noble, Inc., New York.

1936   *Rim of Christendom.* A biography of Eusebio Francisco Kino, Pacific Coast Pioneer. The MacMillan Company, New York.

BUCARELI y URSUA, ANTONIO

1774   Acompaña extracto de las últimas novedades acahecidas en las Provincias internas. México 27 de Octubre 1774. Archivo General de Indias, Sevilla. Copy in Bancroft Library, University of California, Berkeley. Chapman 2753.

CHAPMAN, CHARLES E.

1919   *Catalogue of Materials in the Archivo General de Indias for the History of the Pacific Coast and the American Southwest.* University of California Publications in History, Vol. VIII. University of California Press, Berkeley.

Estado de la Misión de San Lorenzo el Real Pueblo de Zumas.

n.d.   Harvard College Library Manuscript, Cambridge: (Translated herein.)

Expediente Promovido por el Yndio Juan. Domingo Solicitando se le Nombrase General Cazique de la Nación Suma. Copia

1779   Harvard College Library Manuscript, Cambridge: (Translated herein.)

FORBES, JACK D.

1959   Unknown Athapaskans: The Identification of the Jano, Jocome, Jumano, Manso, Suma, and other Indian Tribes of the Southwest. *Ethnohistory* 6 (2) : 97-159.

GERALD, REX E.

1968   *Spanish Presidios of the Late Eighteenth Century in Northern New Spain.* Museum of New Mexico Research Records No. 7, Museum of New Mexico Press, Santa Fe.

HACKETT, CHARLES WILSON

1937   *Historical Documents relating to New Mexico, Nueva Vizcaya and approaches thereto, to 1773.* Vol. III, Publication 330, Carnegie Institution of Washington, Washington, D.C.

HODGE, FREDERICK W., GEORGE P. HAMMOND, and AGAPITO REY

1945   *Fray Alonso de Benavides's Revised Memorial of 1634.* University of New Mexico Press, Albuquerque.

HUGHES, ANNE E.

1914   *The Beginnings of Spanish Settlement in the El Paso District.* University of California Publications in History, Vol. 1, No. 3, University of California Press, Berkeley.

JUÁREZ ARCHIVES

Municipal Archives of Ciudad Juarez, Chihuahua.
Microfilm in Library, The University of Texas at El Paso.

KELLEY, J. CHARLES

1955   Juan Sabeata and Diffusion in Aboriginal Texas. *American Anthropologist* 57 (5): 981-995

KROEBER, A.L.

1934   *Uto-Aztecan Languages of Mexico.* Ibero-Americana 8, University of California Press, Berkeley.

LANGE, CHARLES H. and CARROLL L. RILEY

1970   *The Southwestern Journal of Adolph F. Bandelier, 1883-1884.* University of New Mexico Press, Albuquerque.

McLAUGHLIN, WALTER U., JR.

1962   First Book of Baptisms of Nuestra Señora de Guadalupe del Paso del Norte. M.A. Thesis in History, University of Texas at El Paso.

31

NAYLOR, THOMAS H.

1969   The Extinct Suma of Northern Chihuahua: Their Origin, Cultural Identity and Disappearance. *The Artifact* 7 (4) : 1-14, Journal of the El Paso Archaeological Society.

NEWCOMB, W.W., JR.

1961   *The Indians of Texas.* University of Texas Press, Austin.

OCARANZA, FERNANDO

1934   *Establecimientos Franciscanos en el Misterioso Reino de Nuevo Mexico.* Privately published, Mexico.

OROZCO y BERRA, MANUEL

1864   *Geografía de las Lenguas y Carta Etnográfica de Mexico.* Privately published, Mexico.

RIVERA, PEDRO DE

1946   *Diario y Derrotero de lo Caminado, Visto y Observado en la Visita Que Hizo a los Presidios de la Nueva España Septentrional el Brigadier Pedro de Rivera.* Con una introducción y notas por Vito Alessio Robles. Secretaría de la Defensa Nacional, Dirección de Archivo Militar, Archivo, Histórico Militar Mexicano, No. 2, Taller Autográfico, Mexico, D.F.

RUDO ENSAYO BY AN UNKNOWN JESUIT PADRE, 1763.

1951   Republished from Buckingham Smith. Translation, American Catholic Society, Philadelphia, 1863. Arizona Silhouettes, Tucson.

SAHLINS, MARSHALL D.

1968   *Tribesmen.* Prentice-Hall, Englewood Cliffs, N.J.

SAUER, CARL O.

1934   *The Distribution of Aboriginal Tribes and Languages in Northwestern Mexico.* Ibero-Americana 5, University of California Press, Berkeley.

SCHOLES, FRANCE V.

1929   Documents for the History of the New Mexican Missions in the Seventeenth Century. *New Mexico Historical Review* 4(1):45-58; 4(2):195-201.

SCHOLES, FRANCE V. and H.P. MERA

1940   *Some Aspects of the Jumano Problem.* Contributions to American Anthropology and History VI, Publication 523, Carnegie Institute of Washington, Washington, D.C.

SCHROEDER, ALBERT H.

1962   A Reanalysis of the Routes of Coronado and Oñate into the Plains in 1541 and 1601. *Plains Anthropologist* 7:2-23.

1969   Spanish Entradas, the Big Houses and the Indian Groups of Northern Mexico. *The Artifact* 7(4):15-22. Journal of the El Paso Archaeological Society.

SPICER, EDWARD H.

    1962   *Cycles of Conquest.* University of Arizona Press, Tucson.

SWANTON, JOHN R.

    1952   *The Indian Tribes of North America.* Bureau of American Ethnology Bulletin 145, Washington, D.C.

THOMAS, ALFRED B.

    1932   *Forgotten Frontiers:* A Study of the Spanish-Indian Policy of Don Juan Bautista de Anza, Governor of New Mexico, 1777-1787. University of Oklahoma Press, Norman.

WALZ, VINA

    1951   History of the El Paso Area, 1680-1692. PhD. Dissertation, University of New Mexico, Albuquerque.

Rex E. Gerald, Director of the El Paso Centennial Museum and Assistant Professor of Anthropology at the University of Texas, El Paso, obtained his B.A. degree at the University of Arizona in 1951 and his M.A. at the University of Pennsylvania in 1957. Currently he is a Ph.D. candidate at the University of Chicago. Mr. Gerald is a member of a number of professional and honorary societies and has published in a variety of journals. He has worked in the field of physical anthropology, served as consultant in ethnology and ethnohistory to the Tigua Indians of Ysleta del Sur before the Indian Claims Commission, and has undertaken archeological field work in the Hudson's Bay Trading Post at Fort Vancouver, Wash., in Spanish missions and presidios in the greater Southwest, in prehistoric Southwestern sites, and took part in an underwater study of Classic-Post Classic deposits in the Sacred Well of the Maya at Chichén Itzá, Yucatán. He is currently interested in testing hypotheses relating social systems of Indian groups to the encompassing ecosystems, using demographic, economic, technological, and social data derived from archeological and documentary sources.

33

SOME ECONOMIC ASPECTS OF INDIAN CONTACTS IN THE SPANISH SOUTHWEST

S. Lyman Tyler

The Indian adapted himself to his environment very well. This would imply that if he were a nomad it was because the climate, the vegetation, and the animal life were favorable to a migratory existence. If he were sedentary, this also resulted from a long period of adaptation to his surroundings. He may not have been completely sedentary or entirely nomadic until contacted by Europeans. A possible exception is the Indian of the Great Plains.[1]

The economy of the nomadic and the sedentary Indians complemented each other. In historic times, conflict often occurred between these two groups, yet commerce existed. Cotton mantas and corn were exchanged for tanned hides brought by the nomads. Utes are known to have traded at Taos; Querechos or Vaqueros (Apaches) traded with Pecos Pueblo.[2] Castañeda's account of the Coronado expedition states that the nomadic tribes

> ...went there to spend the winter under the wings of the settlements. The inhabitants do not dare to let them come inside, because they cannot trust them. Although they are received as friends, and trade with them, they do not stay in the villages overnight, but outside under the wings. The villages are guarded by sentinels with trumpets, who call to one another just as in the fortresses of Spain.[3]

The Indians of the buffalo plains would take these hides to the pueblos nearest them. Some went to Pecos, others to the sedentary tribes of Quivira, and still others were said to trade with the settlements in the southeastern part of the present United States within the area designated "La Florida." Wherever they went to trade, these nomads might be allowed to winter outside the settlements if they desired. During the winter months, a kind of truce prevailed.[4] When the so-called wild tribes left the shelter of the pueblo in the spring, the truce might be broken.

Pueblo Indians, as farmers in the fields, generally were not favored by strategic location. Their normal activities could be

35

hampered by the nomads. A few of these marauders were able to keep an entire pueblo of several hundred inhabitants on the alert. No one knew when they would strike next. Raids were part of the nomadic way of life. Pueblo Indians had their crops to care for and their land to till, and working alone or in a small group in the field, they never knew when a superior force of nomads might attack to appropriate their crops, carry them off as captives, or leave them dead in their fields.[5]

Trade in Captives

The Indian custom of taking captives appears to be of long duration. The "Turk", who told the stories of Quivira that led Francisco Vásquez Coronado to the buffalo plains, was a captive of the Pecos Indians. Cabeza de Vaca began his experience among the Indians of the southern United States as a captive. Many of the stragglers from the early Spanish expeditions were captured and held. Jusepe, an Indian who escaped from the 1595 Humaña expedition on the plains at the time of the murder of Francisco Leyva de Bonilla by Antonio Gutierrez de Humaña, was held captive by Apaches, later escaping to return to New Mexico where he acted as a guide for Zaldivar and Oñate in their expeditions to the buffalo plains.

It was customary for the Utes, Apaches, Navajos, Pawnees, Comanches, and other nomadic tribes to take captives in their raids upon each other and upon the more sedentary Indians. The aged might be put to death, the most desirable women and the finest young men kept by their captors, and others sold or traded to the sedentary tribes. Some of the women were taken as wives and adopted into the tribe. A particularly able young man might become a leader of the band that was responsible for his capture.

The traditions of the Utes recall the arrival of the Spaniards in New Mexico. Some of their earliest memories are linked with Spaniards who entered their territory in search of small groups of people who could be captured and taken to the Spanish settlements.[6] From there the captives might be sent to work in the mines at Parral, to Mexico City, or to one of the other provinces of New Spain.

In the years that Captain Don Bernardo Lopez de Mendizabal was governor of New Mexico, 1659-61, it was estimated that he had sold from 70 to 80 Indians as slaves to the mines of Parral alone.[7] He also held slaves as personal property and probably sold others in New Mexico and other parts of New Spain.[8] Indians who had come to the pueblos for food were reported to have been seized and sent to the mines at Parral to be sold into forced labor.

A missionary report carries a description of the way some female captives were treated when they were brought to the settlements to be traded.

> Among other infamies there is one of such nature that if I did not so desire a remedy I would remain silent, since it is so obscure and unfit for chaste ears. It is the truth that when these barbarians bring a certain number of Indian women to sell, among them many young women and girls, before delivering them to the Christians who buy them, if they are ten years old or over, they deflower them and corrupt them in the sight of innumerable assemblies of barbarians and catholics (neither more nor less, as I say), without considering anything but their unbridled lust and brutal shamelessness, and saying to those who buy them, with heathen impudence: "Now you can take her--now she is good."[9]

Another situation that made it difficult for the missionaries in their efforts with both Pueblo Indians and nomads was the practice engaged in by government officials of mixing with the wives and daughters of non-Christian Indians, reportedly violating them shamelessly. This was done so openly, according to the friars' reports, that when the Indian husbands learned of these acts they often refused to have anything more to do with their wives, for it was known that they had been corrupted by the Spanish officials. The following incident is given as an example of this practice.

> A certain governor was in conversation with some missionaries, and an Indian woman came into their presence to charge him with the rape of her daughter, and he, without changing countenance, ordered that she should be paid by merely giving her a buffalo skin that he had at hand.[10]

The value of a buffalo skin was between two and three pesos.

In the pueblo of Cochití in 1663, Don Diego Dionisio de Peñalosa Briceño y Berdugo, governor of the province from 1661 to 1664, had attempted to take a Pueblo girl when her father interfered. Don Diego said he would not take the girl, but if he did not the father must pay him for her. The Indian agreed to give 26 pesos for the privilege of keeping his daughter. This was the value of an Apache woman bondservant. To pay for the girl, three cows, antelope skins, buckskins, and cotton mantas were accumulated to the sum of 26 pesos.[11]

In the mid-17th century, large antelope skins or buckskins were worth two pesos each. Small antelope skins were valued at two for one peso. A horse was worth three pesos, and the saddle, bridle, stirrups, and spurs for one horseman brought 12 pesos, or were worth as much as four horses. A month's salary for convict labor or for a common soldier was 15 pesos. A sergeant's salary was 17 pesos per month, and a commander of 50 men was given four Castilian ducats per day or about 165 pesos per month. In the 18th century, salaries were considerably higher for presidial soldiers and officers. A free man doing a responsible job was given a salary of one peso per day. With such a set of values, an Apache slave woman, worth eight horses, almost two months labor by a common soldier, 12 large buckskins, or several cows, was a valuable property.[12]

Inter-tribal Exchange

Trade between various nomadic tribes probably always existed. Exchange between Havasupais or Yavapais, south and east of the lower Colorado River, with Paiutes across the river from them indicates that intercourse between these peoples is of long duration. The Havasupais and the Yavapais were called Coninas and Cruzados in Oñate's time and retained these names until much later during the Spanish period. They were Yuman in their linguistic affiliation.[13]

It is known that there was frequent contact between Utes and Hopis at an early date, and Ernest Beaglehole gives an insight into the nature of trade carried on between these two peoples.

> In place of present Hopi-Navajo trade, in the old days the Hopi villages appear to have traded fairly extensively with the Paiutes. These people, according to informants, at one time lived very close to the villages, frequently bringing wood and piñon gum, horses and meat, to be exchanged for food, water, bread and corn mush. The Paiute also brought bows and arrows-self bows, which the Hopi backed with sinew or with Yucca bindings over a coating of piñon gum. Sometimes they brought children to trade for food. These the Hopi sometimes kept, but more often they traded them on to the Mexicans in return for blankets and horses.[14]

Buffalo skins and other articles acquired by Hopis through trade were often re-traded to Paiutes, Havasupais, or Navajos at an exchange rate of one buffalo skin for a good horse.[15]

Navajo Indians and various Ute groups have a long history of both war-like and friendly relations. It should be remembered that Navajos and the people known collectively to the Spaniards as Utes were made up of many bands under separate chiefs and that only a very loose identification existed for either of these peoples as a whole. Sometimes an unusually powerful leader might make his influence felt over several bands, but usually the fact that there was peace between Navajos and Utes in a certain sector did not mean that the two as a whole were at peace.

Native testimony by both Navajos and Utes gives evidence of the existence of trade between the two peoples over a long period of time.[16] According to W.W. Hill, "Aside from the Pueblo, the most intensive trading activities with the Indian peoples were between the Navajo and the Northern and Southern Ute." There was also extensive trade between Paiutes of southern Utah and Navajos. The bands on the periphery of Ute and Navajo country would, through inter-tribal trade, exchange goods they obtained for items they lacked. This important inter-tribal exchange resulted in a wide selection of both finished products and raw materials.[17]

Certain Ute and other unidentified Shoshonean groups merged with Navajos. An example of this is the *Notadine* clan of the Navajos. These are "Ute people."[18] Some Navajo hunting methods and weapons are similar to those of Utes. The communal rabbit, deer, and antelope drives, stalking, the use of pits to capture game, the encircling of game by fire, ritual and taboo killing of bears, and the trapping and keeping of eagles are hunting methods used by both Navajos and Utes.[19] Traditions of Navajos inform us that "Ute people" brought good weapons of all kinds; two kinds of shields, one round and one having a crescent-like cut in the top.[20] Navajos also had a form of embroidery work which, according to their legends, they stole or purchased from Utes.[21]

Utes furnished Navajos buckskins and buckskin clothing, elk hides and elk-hide storage sacks, buffalo robes, saddle bags, horses, bandoliers, and beaded bags. There were also certain ceremonial objects used by Navajos such as otter skins, buffalo tails for rattles, buffalo genital organs, and pitch for ceremonial whistles that were supplied by Utes.[22] Navajos supplied blankets, goats, sheep, corn, pinyon nuts, moccasins, and other items to Utes.[23] Their location and way of life resulted in Utes generally supplying raw materials while Navajos frequently traded finished products.[24]

It is not certain just when Navajos acquired the art of weaving. If they were not weaving before the Pueblo Rebellion of 1680, there was plenty of opportunity to learn then. During the 12 years that the Spaniards remained out of New Mexico, from 1680 to 1692, and immediately afterwards, there were many expert Pueblo weavers living among Navajos. Navajo flocks and herds grew rapidly during this period.[25]

The Navajo blanket became an important item of manufacture and trade. Both Apaches and Utes were eager to obtain these blankets.[26] According to Hill,

> The trade article most in demand by the Ute was the so-called "Chief blanket." These were not ordinarily used by the Navaho but were manufactured almost entirely for commercial purposes and almost exclusively for the Ute. According to informants, in earlier days this item commanded a price of five buckskins or a dressed buffalo robe, or one good mare. As they became more numerous they dropped in value to four buckskins and finally to three, two, or in some cases even one, depending on the size. Blankets other than "Chief" were also traded, one of good size being the equivalent of two buckskins. Otter and beaver skins were cut in lengths two finger-widths wide by the Ute. Such strips were highly prized by the Navahos.[27]

Utes, customers of long standing, always favored blankets with a bold black and red pattern.[28] Navajos kept themselves informed concerning Ute, Christian, and Pueblo ceremonial calendars and used this knowledge to good advantage in their trading expeditions.[29]

When Utes and Navajos came together to trade, they selected a "friend" from the other tribe. If an individual was trading for the first time, he would go about the camp until he found someone having the articles he desired; that person became his "friend." When subsequent trading expeditions were made, these two men would continue the relationship that had been formed. There was no evidence of trading in the sense that we know it, that of bargaining. Navajos and Utes looked upon the transaction as an exchange of gifts. When a "friend" was selected, the Navajo would give him the blankets or other items he might have to trade. The Ute "friend" would then reciprocate by giving a horse, buckskins, buffalo robes, and other items.[30] In trading with Pueblo Indians a different relationship existed.

> When you first arrive at the Pueblo to trade they see you coming and ask you to come to their houses. They will look to see what you have brought and will take what they want. They do not do as the Utes; if you

are not careful they will give you only food in return. The Pueblos are greedy; they are not like the Utes. If you want turquoise beads or buckskin, you have to "buy" it from the Pueblos.[31]

The Indian trading areas were of wide scope. When Fray Marcos de Niza was on his way to the Seven Cities of Cibola (Zuni) with the Negro Estevan in 1539, he encountered Indians enroute to Mexico to exchange hides for the goods of Mexican Indians. Montezuma is said to have had a buffalo bull as part of his zoological collection in Mexico City.[32]

Spanish Influence on Indian Trade

When the Spaniards arrived in New Mexico, they soon learned the routine that was followed in trade between Pueblo and nomadic tribes and ascertained means by which they could best profit from this trade. When the friars reported the evils of slave trade to their superiors in Mexico and informed the viceroy of the practice by which New Mexican governors were enriching themselves, laws were promulgated that banned human traffic. This type of trade did not stop, however, in spite of numerous proclamations from the viceroy and the governor of New Mexico declaring it to be illegal. As long as there was a demand for Indian slaves and a supply was easily obtained, the practice continued.[33]

The governor of New Mexico attempted to regularize the trade in skins, blankets, horses, corn, salt, and other items between the Pueblos and nomads and Spaniards and nomads by setting a particular date and place for these tribes to come with their goods. It was said of Utes:

> Every year in the month of October they come to trade with us, and they come to the fair in the boundaries of Pecos. They bring much chamois skin, and cured buffalo hides that they are permitted to trade for animals, corn meal and other items. [34]

Utes and Plains tribes also came to Taos to an annual fair held there. The governor would try to be present at these general fairs to see that justice was done to all parties involved. The tribes also used the Taos fair as an opportunity to exchange prisoners they had taken from each other in their battles on the plains or in raids upon enemy rancherias. Trouble often ensued in the bargaining, and the governor and the military had to be present to avoid the possibility of differences breaking out into open warfare. The following is a description of one of the fairs.

> When the Indian trading embassy comes to these governors and their Alcaldes, here all prudence forsakes them, or rather I shall say that they do not guess how completely they lose their bearings, because the fleet is in. The fleet being, in this case, some two hundred, or at the very least fifty, tents of barbarous heathen Indians, Comanches as well as other nations, of whom the multitude is so great that it is impossible to enumerate them. Here the governors, Alcaldes, and Lieutenants gather together as many horses as they can; here is collected all the ironware possible, such as axes, hoes, wedges, picks, bridles, "Machetes," "Belduquen," and other knives ("for the enemy does not lack iron and these other commodities.").
>
> Here, in short, is gathered everything possible for trade and barter with these barbarians in exchange for deer and buffalo hides, and, what is saddest, for Indian slaves, men and women, small and large, a great multitude of both sexes, for they are gold and silver and the richest treasure for the governors, who gorge themselves first with the largest mouthfuls from this table, while the rest eat the crumbs. Here only God can so confuse this innumerable multitude of Indians--barbarians, cannibals, armed and mixed with numerous apostates from our holy faith.[35]

There was an abundance of animal skins to be used for clothing by Pueblo Indians and New Mexicans when these were brought to the annual fair.[36]

Although they were careful to protect themselves by making it illegal for settlers and Pueblo Indians to acquire the trade goods except at the fairs, some of the governors sent parties of men to the plains at other than the specified times, when, without competition, they could obtain hides at better prices. Governor Mendizabal sent Diego Romero with five other men and a chief of the nation called "Apaches of the Plains" to trade for buffalo and antelope hides in August 1660. They were away on this trip about a month.

When they arrived at the rancheria of Plains Indians, Romero told them he had come to trade. They brought a bundle of antelope skins and a bundle of buffalo hides to him. Romero asked them if they did not remember his father who had come among them and left a son by an Indian woman. He declared that he wished to do the same. The Indians brought a new tent and set it up, placed a bed of new antelope skins in the middle of it, and called Diego Romero to sit upon the bed. A wedding dance was then begun, and when it was finished a young maiden was brought to him. The next morning the Indians came, annointed his breasts with her blood, and then made them man and wife. A feather was placed in

Romero's hair, and he was proclaimed one of them. The bundle of antelope skins, and that of buffalo skins, and the tent were given to Diego Romero by these "Apaches of the plains."[37]

Another means used by surrounding tribes and New Mexicans to carry on trade at times other than the scheduled fairs is explained by Pedro Tamaron y Romeral. Nomads would plant small crosses along the road. From these they would suspend a leathern pocket with a piece of deer or other fresh meat inside. At the foot of the cross a buffalo hide would be stretched out. The Indian indicated by these signs that he wished to trade with those who adored the cross. He offered the Christian travellers a hide for provisions which could be supplied according to the generosity of the Christian trader. Soldiers of the presidios, who understood these signs, would take the hide and leave some salted meat in its place.[38]

It seems evident that exchange between Indian tribes of the Southwest and other natives on the northern frontier existed before the arrival of the Spaniards. Spanish governors attempted to regularize and control this trade in captives, hides, blankets, corn, and horses so they could realize a profit from it.

NOTES

1. A.F. Bandelier, *Final Report of Investigations Among the Indians of the South-western United States...1880 to 1885* (Papers of the Archaeological Institute of America, American Series, 2 vols. John Wilson and Son, Cambridge, 1890-92) i:26-27.

2. *Ibid.*:164.

3. George Parker Winship, *The Journey of Coronado* (American Explorers Series, New York, 1904):105.

4. *Ibid.*:111.

5. Frank C. Lockwood, *The Apache Indians* (The Macmillan Company, New York, 1938):4-6.

6. Marvin K. Opler, The Southern Ute of Colorado, in *Acculturation in Seven American Indian Tribes*. Ralph Linton, ed. (Appleton-Century Company, New York, 1940):171.

7. France V. Scholes, *Troublous Times in New Mexico, 1659-70* (Historical Society of New Mexico, Publications in History, Vol. II, Albuquerque, 1942).

8. Charles W. Hackett (ed.), *Historical Documents Relating to New Mexico, Nueva Vizcaya, and Approaches Thereto to 1773*. 3 vols. (Carnegie Institution, Washington, 1923-37) 3:26.

9. *Ibid.*:487. These reports were sometimes given to embarrass the civil authorities and could not always be taken at face value.

10. *Ibid.*:427-428.

11. *Ibid.*:244.

12. *Ibid.*:249,291,312,316.

13. A.L. Kroeber, *Cultural and Natural Areas of Native North America* (University of California Publications in American Archaeology and Ethnology 38, Berkeley, 1947):35-41.

14. Ernest Beaglehole, *Notes on Hopi Economic Life,* Yale University Publications in Anthropology (1937) 15-83.

15. *Ibid.*:84.

16. W.W. Hill, Navajo Trading and Trading Ritual, *Southwestern Journal of Anthropology* (1948) 4:371.

17. *Ibid.*:375.

18. Clarles Avery Amsden, Navajo Weaving (University of New Mexico Press, Albuquerque, 1949):181; Washington Mathews, *Navaho Legends* (Houghton Mifflin, Boston, 1897):32, 146.

19. W.W. Hill, *The Agricultural and Hunting Methods of the Navaho Indians,* Yale University Publications in Anthropology (1938) 18.

20. Mathews 1897:146.

21. Hill 1948:377.

22. *Ibid.*:377.

23. *Ibid.*:376.

24. *Ibid.*:392.

25. Amsden 1949,129.

26. *Ibid.*:180-181.

27. Hill 1948:380.

28. Amsden 1949:192.

29. Hill 1948:382.

30. *Ibid.*:389.

31. *Ibid.*:388-389.

32. Frederick W. Hodge, George P. Hammond and Agapito Rey, *Fray Alonso de Benavides' Revised Memorial of 1634* (University of New Mexico Press, Albuquerque, 1945):230.

33. France V. Scholes, Civil Government and Society in New Mexico in the Seventeenth Century, *New Mexico Historical Review* (1935) 10:81-86.

34. Nicolas de Lafora. *Relación del viaje que hizo a los Presidios Internos* (P. Robredo, Mexico, D.F., 1949):102, 104-105.

35. Hackett 1937, 3:486-87.

36. *Ibid.*:449.

37. *Ibid.*:156,161-162.

38. Pedro Tamaron y Romeral. Demonstración del Vastisimo *Obispado de la Nueva Vizcaya* (Biblioteca Historica Mexicana, Mexico, 1937):342-347.

S. Lyman Tyler, presently director of the Center for American Indian Programs and of Studies of the American West, has served as professor of history at Brigham Young University and the University of Utah. In addition, he has been or is serving in the capacity of director, chairman, member, consultant, expert witness, or officer in various organizations, societies, and research endeavors relating to the field of western history, education, and Indian affairs. His articles, technical reports, and books exemplify his wide interest in western history.

TRADITIONS OF NORTHERN PLAINS RAIDERS IN NEW MEXICO

Paul M. Raczka

Historians and ethnologists have been notably concerned with the interactions of the Plains Indians with the Pueblo and Spanish settlements of the Southwest. The majority of these efforts have been centered upon the Southern Plains Indians, specifically the Comanches, Kiowas and Utes. Recent evidence has focused attention in another direction--that of the Northern Plains and Plateau regions. The evidence presented in this paper is not intended to imply any conclusion on cultural interactions. The main purpose is to make researchers aware that these events did take place and to consider them in future evaluations.

While archeology has shed some light on the extent of Pueblo materials upon the plains, the reverse is beset with problems. This is due possibly to the non-distinctive nature of most of the prehistoric Plains Indians' artifacts. Considering the present material uncovered within the field of Plains Archeology, we can arrive at a somewhat stable date-range of contact. Identifiable Pueblo potsherds dating A.D., 1525-1650, of the Pueblo IV glaze-decorated type, appeared within the state of Kansas at various sites. These same sites yielded turquoise, obsidian, and occasional glass beads and objects of iron. "These last items can probably be regarded as of Spanish origin, obtained directly or indirectly through contacts with white men in, or operating from, the Rio Grande Valley" (Wedel 1942:106-107).

Turning to historical documents, we can establish the existence of certain trade routes dating to the pre-horse days of both regions. By this is meant the *use* of the horse by the American Indian and not merely the knowledge of its existence.

Reports of the Coronado expedition in 1541 stated that the Que-rechos and Teyas, nomads of the Southern Plains, journeyed to the Pueblos for trade purposes during the winter (Winship 1896:528). In addition, the use of Pueblo guides by the expedition would imply a familiarity with the Plains area by these people. In 1599, Vicente de Saldívar Mendoza also encountered Plains Indians since identi-

47

fied as Apaches (Querechos,) returning from trade with Picuris and Taos Pueblos (Bolton 1916:226). It should be noted that both of these episodes predate Ewers' suggestion of 1630 for Plains Indians becoming horsemen. In the 1690s, Vargas recorded that a band of Apaches called Chiyenes (Chipaynes in the original document--ed.) arrived at Picuris Pueblo for trade (Curtis 1925: vol. 16:36). Identification as Cheyennes is questionable since at this date they were supposedly located along the middle course of the Minnesota River (Mooney 1907:358). Dating of the appearance of the horse among the Cheyennes is estimated at about 1750.

The Cheyennes in their Northern Plains location have been documented as visitors to New Mexico. Lewis and Clark recorded that they frequently stole horses from Spanish settlements in 1804-06, while John Bradbury in 1809-11 stated that the Cheyennes, Poncas, and Pawnees often raided the Spanish settlements (Jablow 1950).

Due to the relatively late isolation of the Plateau tribes, our information from that area is sparse. Rigsby's informants stated that the Yakimas traveled to New Mexico early in the 19th century for the express purpose of horserading and trading (Rigsby and Silberstein 1969: fn. 12, 50).

Clark (1966:216) recorded Nez Perce legends of travels into the Southwest and Mexico. Perhaps further investigation would yield more conclusive evidence in this direction.

Our most reliable evidence of raids from the north concerns the Blackfoot and Gros Ventre Indians. For those who find it difficult to accept the oral traditions of these tribes, accompanying statements by white participants or observers are included. James Willard Schultz was perhaps one of the most prolific recorders of Blackfoot life during the late 1800s. While some of his personal tales are suspect, his adherence to the Blackfoot culture caused a faithful recording of tales related to him. The earliest contact was related by Many-Tail-Feathers, historian of the Blackfoot tribe in Montana.

> Then, we know not how long ago it was, a war party of the Pikunis (Piegans), travelling into the far south, the Always-Summer-Land, made a very strange discovery, so very strange that they could hardly believe what they saw; enemies of some kind were riding animals (horses) as big as elk and leading others packed with their belongings.

After observing for several days, they attacked and took many of these strange beasts back to their people. Seeing the advantages of this new animal, war parties of all three tribes (Blackfoot) began

48

going down to Always-Summer-Land to obtain some of the elk-dogs. "They took them from different Indian tribes and from a different kind of white man living there." They also took "very long big-knives (swords); long, iron, pointed spears; and iron shirts (shirts of mail) ...Well, the time came when our three tribes had so many elk-dogs that they no longer went into the Always-Summer-Land for more of them" (Schultz 1962:312). This tale contrasts markedly with Ewers' speculation that the Blackfoot obtained horses from the Plateau tribes and casts some doubt on his dates of the late 18th century (Ewers 1955:19).

Let us add two more statements to this source of supply. The Assiniboines were eastern neighbors of the Blackfoot and "always in want of horses" (Thompson 1916:265). Yet Henry in 1776 records, "The horses of the Osinipollos (Assiniboines) were originally procured from white people, with brands, who live to the southward; that is, the Spanish colonists, in New Mexico" (Henry 1901:304). Drawing again on Thompson, we have his record of a Blackfoot war party consisting of 250 warriors under Kootana Appe. In 1787, the early part of September, they proceeded southward near the east foot of the mountains in search of Snake Indians. Not finding any, they continued south until they sighted a long file of horses and mules led by Black men (Spaniards). When they attacked, the Spaniards rode off leaving the horses and mules. They were loaded with silver which they threw off. "The place this war party started from is in about 53°20′N (Edmonton, Alberta), and the place where they met the Spaniards conveying the silver from the mines is about the latitude of 32°N (southern border of New Mexico) a distance of 1500 miles in a direct line" (Thompson 1916:370-371).

An interesting cross-check is related by Andrew Garcia, a native of New Mexico, who traded in the Plateau area. He met an old Blackfoot named White Grass, who stated that he and some of his people often went down and stayed with the Utes while raiding the Pueblos and "blackhaired white men". This coincided with Garcia's grandfather's tales of "red devils from the north" who were worse than the Comanches (Garcia 1968:165,167).

The reports by the expeditions of Josiah Gregg and Captain Sublette relating to attacks by Blackfoot and Gros Ventre parties near the Oklahoma-Colorado border on the Cimarron River are too conclusive to be claimed as mis-identification (Gregg 1926:72, 85). Jedediah Smith claimed the Santa Fe Trail to be harassed by Gros Ventres (Morgan 1964:328), and Charles Bent, traveling with Col.

49

Viscarra along the Santa Fe Trail, had a skirmish with some Gros Ventres on the Cimarron (Lavender, 1954:104). The approximate date of these events was 1830. All of the individuals cited had conducted trade on the Northern Plains and thus were familiar with the Blackfoot and Gros Ventres.

We are presented an insight to the whys and wherefores of these northern people in the manuscript of George Bent. He stated that in 1825 the Cheyennes and Arapahos were living north of the Platte River near the Black Hills. The Gros Ventres came to visit their kinsmen, the Arapahos. With them came 20 Blackfoot, fleeing from a raid on a Canadian fort. Shortly thereafter the Blackfoot made up a war party and headed south. There they ran off Kiowa and Comanche horses and on their return told of great herds of buffalo and wild horses between the Arkansas and Platte. Part of the Cheyennes and Arapahos moved to this area south of the Platte and in this way divided the tribes into the northern and southern Cheyennes and Arapahos. The Gros Ventres eventually returned to Canada, but the Blackfoot married into the Cheyenne Tribe. The last one died in 1880, and the children and grandchildren are still living near Colony, Oklahoma (Hyde 1968:32-33). Evidently the Gros Ventres were still in the south in 1834. Colonel Henry Dodge, during his conference for peace in the Southern Plains, reported that Blackfoot and Gros Ventres came in with Arapahos (Lavender 1954: 161).

In an isolated incident, James Doty, in 1854, wrote that ten years prior, five Blackfoot followed the eastern slope of the Rocky Mountains until they reached Taos and towns between there and Santa Fe. (Doty to Stephens).

James Bird, one-time employee of the Hudson Bay Company, returned in 1846 with a Blackfoot war party from the far south, the Always-Summer-Land, with a large band of horses taken from the Mexicans. The story associated with this adventure brings forth a few more details. It concerns mainly Bear Head, owner of a sacred albino otter bow case, and Skunk Cap, a Cree who also claimed the bow case. In 1845, a war party went south to raid the Mexicans.

> In a fight that the party had down there with the Many Bracelets people (the Navajos), Bear Head was mortally wounded ... So poor Bear Head died, and with some difficulty the party got his body and belongings up into a house of the ancient and vanished Cliff Dwellers and came home with the horses that they had taken from the Mexicans.

Shortly after, Skunk Cap organized a war party of Assiniboines to raid the Mexicans. In reality, he was after the sacred otter bow case buried with Bear Head. The Assiniboine party was wiped out except for Skunk Cap. He was killed by Bear Head's brother, Far-Off-In-Sight, while he was in the Cliff Dwellers' houses looking for the bow case. James Bird was with Far-Off-In-Sight's party and thus a witness to this tale (Schultz 1962:179-180).

The last reported Blackfoot adventure in the Southwest was in 1856 and was related by Charles Rivois. Far-Off-In-Sight, who led the Bow Case war party, asked Rivois to join a war party to the far-south tribes for horses. Far Pine, a Tewa who had been living with the Piegans for two years, was to go with them. Fourteen days from Ft. Benton, they reached Taos. Far-Off-In-Sight and Talks-With-The-Buffalo had been there before. After the Taos chief, Tua (Bear[?]), feasted them, they rode to nearby Taos town to meet Little Chief (Kit Carson), a friend of Far Pine's. Afterwards they visited with the Picuris, and then their adventures led them to Pawnee country and eventually home.

Thus it appears the Northern Plains people were not strangers to New Mexico. As mentioned previously, this paper is not definitive but hopefully will cause closer investigation of the interactions between New Mexico and the Northern Plains.

BIBLIOGRAPHY

BOLTON, HERBERT E. (ed.)

1916   *Spanish Exploration in the Southwest, 1542-1706.* In Original Narratives of Early American History. Barnes & Noble (Reprint), New York.

CLARK, ELLA

1967   *Indian Legends from the Northern Rockies.* University of Oklahoma (Reprint), Norman.

CURTIS, EDWARD S.

1970   *The North American Indian, Vol. 16.* Johnson Reprints (Reprint), New York.

DOTY, JAMES TO STEVENS, ISAAC I.

1854   December 20, Indian Office Records, U.S. National Archives.

EWERS, JOHN C.

1955   *The Horse in Blackfoot Indian Culture.* Bureau of American Ethnology Bulletin 159, Washington.

GARCIA, ANDREW

1968   *Tough Trip Through Paradise.* Bennet H., Stein, ed., Ballantine, New York.

GREGG, HOSIAH

1926   *The Commerce of the Prairies.* University of Nebraska, Lincoln.

HENRY, ALEXANDER

1901   *Travels and Adventures in Canada and the Indian Territories.* Geo. N. Morange & Co., Ltd., Toronto.

HYDE, GEORGE

1968   *Life of George Bent.* University of Oklahoma Press, Norman.

JABLOW, JOSEPH

1950   *The Cheyenne in Plains Trade Relations 1795-1840.* American Ethnological Society Memoir 19, New York.

LAVENDER, D.

1954   *Bent's Fort.* Doubleday, New York.

MOONEY, JAMES

1907   *The Cheyenne Indians.* American Anthropological Association Memoirs I, Washington, D.C.

MORGAN, DALE L.

1964   *Jedediah Smith and the Opening of the West.* University of Nebraska, Lincoln.

RIGSBY, BRUCE AND MICHAEL SILVERSTEIN

1969   Nez Perce Vowels and Proto-Sahaptan Vowel Harmony. *Language* 45 (1).

SCHULTZ, JAMES WILLARD

1962   *Blackfeet and Buffalo: Memories of Life Among the Indians.* University of Oklahoma Press, Norman.

TYRRELL, J. B. (ed.)

1916   *David Thompson's Narrative of His Explorations in Western America, 1784-1812.* The Champlain Society, Toronto.

WEDEL, WALDO

1942   Archaeological Remains in Central Kansas and Their Possible Bearing on the Location of Quivira. *Smithsonian Miscellaneous Collections* 101 (7), Washington.

WINSHIP, GEORGE PARKER

1964   *The Coronado Expedition.* Rio Grande Press (Reprint), Chicago.

Paul M. Raczka, Executive Director for the Napi Friendship Association, Pincher Creek, Alberta, received a Bachelor of University Studies Degree from the University of New Mexico. A great portion of Mr. Raczka's youth was spent on the Six Nations Reserve, Ontario and Tonawanda Seneca Reservation, New York. His interest in Native Culture has involved him in New Mexico radio program work presenting American Indian music and information, in managing the sales desk at the Maxwell Museum of Anthropology, University of New Mexico, and in publishing several articles on the ethnohistory of various native peoples, including articles on the Northern Plains Indians and on Plains-Pueblo Indian relationships.

SOME ECONOMIC
CONSIDERATIONS OF
HISTORIC RIO GRANDE
PUEBLO POTTERY

David H. Snow

It probably is safe to assume that Pueblo Indian pottery has attracted as much attention, scientific and otherwise, as any single aspect of Pueblo culture. Pueblo Indians have been making pottery for about 1,500 years, but surprisingly little is known about its role in Pueblo economy. It is unusual, in the voluminous archeological and ethnographic literature, to find more than a casual discussion of pottery beyond the descriptive level. Archeologist have religiously reported trade wares from their sites but have generally ignored the systems of socio-economic interaction implicit in their use of the concept. With few exceptions, ethnographers too have neglected the implications of the manufacture and distribution of pottery in Pueblo economy. In fact, E.P. Dozier has consistently denied the Rio Grande Pueblos an economic life beyond that of subsistence farming. According to Dozier,

> There are no indications of craft specializations either by village or by families or individuals within the village. Likewise there is no evidence of intra-village markets or even extensive trading between villages. Economic activities had hardly developed beyond reciprocal gift exchanges between pueblos and between Pueblos and nomadic tribes (1961:102-103).

More recently, referring to nearly 300 years of association between the pueblos and an "Hispanicized population," Dozier noted that both groups were subsistence farmers; and he implied specifically that *because* of this "There was no specialization either in products of the land or in manufactured items; hence there was no opportunity for the development of complex trading activities". "Pueblo economy", according to Dozier, "until the closing of the last century was subsistence farming" (1970:9).

To deny economic specialization by the Pueblos in the manufacture of goods or in the cultivation of certain products, and a role for these in inter-community and inter-regional exchange systems, is to ignore a substantial body of evidence to the contrary. The exchange of pottery, for example, has played a considerable economic role in Rio Grande Pueblo culture since at least the 15th century (Warren 1969; Kidder and Shepard 1936).

55

The discussion presented here is a preliminary attempt to show that the exchange of pottery was a fully developed pattern whose existence for more than 300 years of Pueblo history implies an economic complexity somewhat above the level of gift-exchange and subsistence farming. Furthermore, the production of Pueblo pottery, for inter-village and inter-ethnic use was an economic specialization of considerable importance, considering the fact the Spaniards were dependent upon the Pueblos for the bulk of their household ceramic utensils.

On the whole, the conquest of the Pueblo world by the Spaniards and the subsequent development of Spanish Colonial culture had very little overall effect on Pueblo ceramic traditions. In some cases, of course, physical disruption of Pueblo populations by Spanish authorities adversely effected some pottery centers. The Pueblo Revolt had disastrous results for the pottery centers in the Galisteo Basin, and it may well be that the abandonment of these pueblos was the reason for the disappearance of the glaze-paint tradition.

Several new vessel types introduced by the Spaniards, the handled cup, the soup-plate, pitchers with handles and pouring spouts, and a few other miscellaneous forms, became part of the repertoir of the Pueblo potter. Nevertheless, the gradual evolution of form in traditional vessel types (such as the olla and bowl) throughout the 17th, 18th, and 19th centuries, seemingly owes nothing to Spanish or other influences. The only major change in style, aside from the loss of the glaze-paint technique and subsequent return to carbon paint in most of the Rio Grande pueblos, was an increase in the popularity of plain-surfaced vessels. These usually were red-slipped and polished, often smudged black, and are the forerunners of the popular red and black polished wares of the modern Tewa villages. Infrequently, non-pueblo design motifs and elements are found on vessels from the pre-railroad period but are so rare as to be of little concern.

Over the long run, however, these changes were no different in kind than those observable throughout this nearly 2,000 year old Southwestern tradition. The major Spanish impact on this most traditional of Pueblo crafts, a major contribution to its evolution, was to perpetuate it and, at the same time, to leave it virtually unchanged.

A.H. Schroeder (1972;68-69) recently asked whether Pueblo culture survived because of the physical and cultural isolation of

56

the New Mexico religious and civil administration on the northern edge of the Spanish Colonial frontier. He suggested that this isolation prevented the Pueblos from becoming Hispanicized, and this, in turn, allowed them to continue to view Spanish culture as alien to their own. Isolation was clearly a factor in the Spanish dependence on the Pueblos for pottery. Throughout the Spanish Colonial and Mexican periods, it was never feasible to ship, over the long distance from Mexico, large enough quantities of pottery to supply a variety of frontier needs.

On a different level of interpretation, the concept of ethnicity is a two-way proposition. The Spanish colonists in turn saw Pueblo culture as alien, and it is worth considering that the manufacture and sale or exchange of pottery in the frontier situation, where miscegenation and culture mixing were rife, was a symbol of ethnic, cultural, or perhaps class, differences. Making pottery was the Indian thing to do. Along with the kiva and its associated ceremonies, a distinctive mode of dress, and language, it was an obvious symbol of Indianness.

Similar criteria have operated in the recent past in parts of Mexico to maintain a clear distinction between Indian and Mexican (or Spaniard). Spanish women, or those who chose to consider themselves Spanish rather than mestizo or Indian, regardless of their particular genetic makeup, did not customarily make pottery in Mexico or elsewhere in Latin America. In frontier New Mexico, it is doubtful that the "Hispanicized population" referred to by Dozier ever produced sufficient pottery, if indeed they ever made any, to supply the demands of inter-community, local, or even household needs (see discussions by Hurt 1939; Hurt and Dick 1946; and Dick 1968; for comments on Spanish-American pottery). Spanish women in New Mexico had nearly 300 years in which to become proficient potters. Their failure to do so belies the self-sufficiency ascribed to them by Dozier and suggests the existence of ethnic values and attitudes on the Spanish Colonial frontier which might help to explain the persistence of Pueblo culture in terms other than passive resistance to acculturative forces or the weakness of them.

In the recent past, at least, making pottery was one means of supplementing the Pueblo family income, through barter or sale, but as production for the Anglo market increased, the circulation of pottery within the barter system all but ceased. By 1900, increasing demand by tourists for souvenirs and increasingly stiff competition from mass-produced stoneware, ironstone "china", and hotel crockery from the east had rendered most Indian pottery unserviceable and had reduced it to the status of bric-a-brac. Today, most Pueblo pottery is produced solely for the cash income derived from its sale; and even though it is no longer serviceable, the economic gain to the potter continues to motivate production. Whether pottery is to be exchanged within a barter system or sold for cash, the need (or desire) to supplement basic subsistence techniques has always been an integral part of Pueblo life. The Spanish colonists and their Spanish-American decendents benefited from and supported, out of necessity, this traditional Pueblo activity. Prior to the arrival of the railroad, both Indians and Spaniards (and to the lesser extent, Anglos) obtained, through an inter-community exchange system based on barter or outright cash purchase, tremendous quantities of Pueblo ceramics for domestic use. Dependent on this traditional source of ceramics, Spanish-Americans were all but eliminated from the market by the Anglos' penchant for pottery knick-knacks.

In the early 1900s, according to Spanish-American informants in the upper San Juan River area, "Utes, Jicarilla Apache, and Navajo came...each summer to trade baskets, pottery, and moccasins for wheat, corn, beef, and mutton" (Dittert 1961:257). With reference to San Juan Pueblo pottery prior to the revival during the 1930s, G.D. Schroeder (1964:47-48) said that it

> ...was a trade item directed towards the neighboring Spanish-American market. Since most pueblo women knew how to make pottery, the ability to do so did not create special prestige in the village. During the latter part of the nineteenth century and early part of the twentieth century the Jicarilla Apache traded in the San Juan area, taking pottery from San Juan and Picuris to the Spanish-Americans living near the Chama and the upper San Juan Rivers. The non-Indians, especially those near Rosa, New Mexico, for years used as much pueblo pottery as stoneware.

Spanish-American demands for cooking utensils were not limited to Pueblo products. In 1846, it was reported that the Jicarilla Apaches manufactured a "species of potters ware...much used by them and the Mexicans for culinary purposes. This, they barter with the Mexicans for the necessaries of life, but in such small quantities as scarcely to deserve the name of traffic" (Abel 1915:6).

Certain vessel forms and pottery styles were in demand on an inter-pueblo exchange level. As late as the 1950s Lange (1959:154) noted the Cochiti preference for Zia, Acoma, and Zuni water jars obtained through trade, while most of the Cochiti production was directed toward the tourist market. During the middle to late 1880s, Matilda Cox Stevenson recorded her observations at Zia Pueblo.

> The Sia women labor industriously at the ceramic art as soon as their grain supply becomes reduced, and the men carry the wares to their unfriendly [Spanish] neighbors for trade in exchange for wheat and corn. As long as the Sia can induce the traders through the country to take their pottery they refrain from barter with their Indian neighbors. The women usually dispose of the articles to the traders, but they never venture on expeditions to the Santa Ana and the Jemez. Each year a period comes, just before the harvest time, when no more pottery is required by their Indian neighbors, and the Sia must deal out their food in...limited portions...(1894:11-12).

In 1881, Captain J.G. Bourke noted that the pottery in use at both Taos and Picuris came from San Juan Pueblo (1936:278; 1937:47). Speaking of Pueblo pottery in general, Bourke observed that "A strong family resemblance runs through it all...but it would not always be safe to trust the judgement of a white man in this respect because the different Pueblos trade so much with each other that models of any given style are likely to be encountered in almost every one of the villages" (1936:268).

"By the beginning of the twentieth century", according to Dozier (1970:9, "trade became a convenient way [for the Pueblo Indians] to procure food and materials otherwise difficult or impossible to obtain". In view of the ethnographic, historic, and archeological data concerning inter-village and inter-ethnic exchange of pottery and other items during the past 300 years, his statement is difficult to assess.

It is perhaps unfair to blame ethnographers for their lack of interest in Pueblo pottery. In spite of continuing small-scale manufacture of functional vessels by some potters, the decline in serviceable pottery production eliminated this traditional craft from ethnographic consideration since the more recent products no longer represented aboriginal art. As early as 1889, for example, W.H. Holmes of the Smithsonian Institution's Bureau of American Ethnology cautioned his scientific colleagues against the current trends in Pueblo pottery and warned that "The country is flooded with cheap and, scientifically speaking, worthless earthenware made by Pueblo Indians to supply the tourist trade...". He concluded that

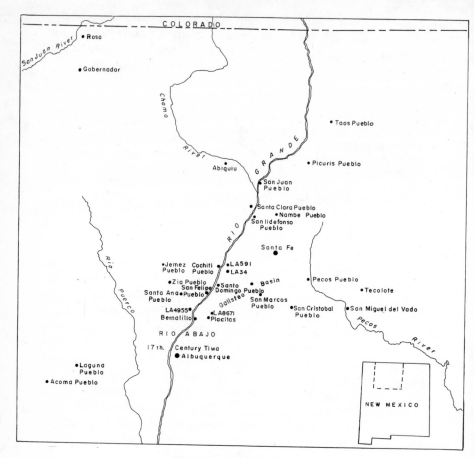

Rio Abajo and Santa Fe Area Sites

60

"only those persons who happen to be familiar with the refined and artistic wares of the ancient Pueblos can appreciate the debasement brought about by contact with the whites" (1889:320). In the railroad station at Rito, New Mexico in 1881, Bourke described a scene which became a familiar one to tourists during the next 50 years or more.

> The sugar bowls and salt cellars were bric-a-brac that would have set Eastern collectors crazy with envy; they were of ornamental ware, made by the pueblos of Laguna, six miles distant. A dozen or more of the Indians were hanging around the door, waiting to sell their wares to the passengers (1936:106).

Fallen from a state of aboriginal grace, Pueblo ceramics suffered a 20th century revival which resulted in their current status as objects d'art, a category which even today most anthropologists are unwilling to tackle.

Spanish explorers from the beginning were impressed with Pueblo pottery. The Coronado expedition noticed "earthenware glazed with antimony and jars of extraordinary labor and workmanship, which are worth seeing" (Winship 1896:522). Hernan Gallegos, chronicler of the 1581 Chamuscado-Rodriguez *entrada,* was lavish with his praise of Piro and Tiwa pottery. He commented that the vessels he saw were "of better quality than the pottery of New Spain"; and that they were equal to, "and even surpass, the pottery made in Portugal" (Hammond and Rey 1966:82,85). Less than 20 years later, the Spanish colonists found themselves almost entirely dependent on this pottery for their household and other needs. There is no indication of this fact from the documents of the period until 1694 when Governor Don Diego De Vargas noted in his journal that some Pecos Indians had arrived in Santa Fe "with glazed earthenware to sell." (Espinosa 1942:198). During the intervening years, nearly all of the pottery used by the Spaniards was either purchased or bartered from their Pueblo neighbors, a fact which is amply demonstrated in the archeological record.

The degree to which Spanairds were dependent on Pueblo ceramics during the 18th century is known almost entirely from archeological evidence. Documents seldom mention the ubiquitious Pueblo pottery recovered from archeological sites of this period, perhaps because it was such a familiar household item. The use of locally made vessels in churches and *conventos* testifies to the general scarcity of imported Mexican ceramics, a fact also emphasized by documentary and archeological data. In 1776, Fray Francisco Atanasio Dominguez inventoried the contents of the *convento* at Nambe Pueblo, where he recorded "6 plates, 6 cups, 2 jars, and 4 candlesticks, all these of clay and manufactured in the pueblo". At Laguna church he found "An earthenware cup for an incense boat, and a spoon of the same"; and at Zuni he noted a "Spoon and incense boat for a clay censer made by the Indians". At nearly every mission and *convento* he noted the use of pueblo-made bowls and pots for baptismal fonts and holy water containers (Adams and Chavez 1954).

In the inventory of estates at Abiquiu in 1806, at Agua Fria in 1830, and at Santa Fe in 1832, six earthen jars and three large earthen bowls are the only ceramic items of presumed Pueblo manufacture listed in nineteen inventories and wills during the period 1727 to 1839 (S.A.N.M.). In Santa Fe, expenses incurred by the government "for replacing the clay utensils" used for entertaining visiting Plains Indians amounted to 4 pesos, 2 reales in 1807 (S.A.N.M., 2:Oct. 31,1807).

Not until nearly the mid-19th century does some indication of the magnitude of the pottery market become apparent from historical sources. Discussing the Pueblo Indians in the 1830s, Josiah Gregg remarked that they

> ...manufacture...both for their own consumption, and for the purposes of traffic, a species of earthenware...[these] are the universal substitutes for all the purposes of cookery, even among the Mexicans...(Moorehead 1954:193).

According to Davis, in 1857, "The peasantry also make earthenware for domestic use, and carry considerable quantities of it to the towns to be sold" (Davis 1938:83). In another passage he observed that the Pueblos [the "peasantry"]

> ...devote the greater part of their time to the manufacture of earthenware, which they sell in quantities to the Mexicans. This ware is in universal use in the territory, and there is considerable demand for it in the market (Ibid.:327).

It is unfortunate that these observers failed to mention the specific sources of this universal commodity, for it is apparent that not every pueblo was engaged in its manufacture and distribution. The very fact that some pueblos made little or no pottery indicates that others specialized in its production. The failure of anthropologists, generally, to recognize this fact reflects a stereotype which A.V. Kidder faced after petrographic analyses of Pecos pottery.

It has always been assumed that potting was one of the regular household tasks of every Pueblo woman; that each town was in this regard self-sufficient. But if whole classes of pottery---were imported, we must postulate an extraordinary volume of trade and allow for a compensating outward flow of other commodities. Furthermore, we must believe that the production of vessels at the source of supply was much greater than was needed for home consumption, in other words, that rudimentary commercial manufacturing was practised (Kidder and Shepard 1936:xxiii).

Each pottery-making pueblo today has its own style, or type, for which it is famous, highly polished black wares of Santa Clara and San Ildefonso, Picuris micaceous ware, and so on, but these specializations were not always so restricted, and it often is difficult to pinpoint the source of archeological specimens with desirable accuracy. For example, the polished black ware was made, according to Bourke in 1881 (1936:268), "by a number of Pueblos, but after conventional patterns, almost if not absolutely, identical". Bourke noted also that the San Felipes made black and white pottery (1938:214). Almost certainly they were copying the familiar Tewa Polychrome types in the same manner that the Santo Domingos and Cochitis did. Bourke was told also that the Picuris "know how to make [pottery] and to color it red, black, and white", but he added that "they were not making any while I was there" (1936:278). It is well-known that the Jicarilla Apaches specialized in the manufacture and trade of pottery for which Picuris is now famous (Gunnerson 1969; see above, pp. 4-5).

From every Spanish Colonial and 19th century Spanish-American ruin investigated, Pueblo pottery has been recovered in varying quantities. Collections of potsherds from 16 Laboratory of Anthropology (LA) sites used for this study indicate that about 99% and 97%, respectively, of the total from 17th and 18th century sites were from Pueblo Indian vessels. The remainder were imports from Mexico. Pueblo pottery sherds comprised 78% of the total from those Spanish sites occupied during the period 1800-1850 and about 39% from sites occupied between 1850 and about 1900. In general, the Spaniards obtained most of their pottery from pueblos nearest them. During the 17th century, however, vessels from the Rio Abajo area, south of Santa Fe, were in common use in the general Santa Fe area, and the Tewa pueblos north of Santa Fe supplied a considerable number to the Rio Abajo. After the Pueblo Revolt, when the manufacture of glaze-paint decorated wares had ceased, Tewa ceramics were traded to the south in even larger quantities, but the remaining southern pueblos seldom traded their wares north of La Bajada, 15 miles south of Santa Fe.

The loss of the glaze-decorated pottery tradition created, apparently, a gap in the production of painted ceramics which was not filled completely by the return to non-glaze mineral paint by Zia and Santa Ana potters, or to carbon paint decoration by other pueblos. Decorated sherds from a 17th century site near Cochiti Pueblo comprised about 50% of all Pueblo pottery. Of this category, 64% were glaze-decorated; and 54% of the decorated sherds from another nearby 17th century site were also glaze decorated. Petrographic analysis of these two glaze-ware assemblages indicate the major sources shown in table 1. The origins of the matte-painted and plain-surfaced sherds (not including cooking-ware sherds) from these two sites are shown in tables 2 and 3. On the other hand, decorated sherds from 18th and 19th century sites combined made up only 25% of the total assemblage and almost all were from the Tewa villages.

From about 1700 to 1850, the percentage of Tewa pottery from sites of that time period near Santa Fe, Cochiti, and at Placitas (near Bernalillo) is 98%, 99%, 75%, and 64% respectively. The two higher figures represent Santa Fe area sites closest to the source. The authors of the report of the excavations at the Placitas site, where 64% of the pottery recovered was Tewa in origin, remarked that

> The relatively high proportion of these wares may be explained as a matter of taste preference, and may indicate a focusing of trade from the Placitas area toward Santa Fe or testify to the aggressiveness of trade carried on by the northern pueblos. In either case, it would seem that the manufacture and sale or trade of polished black wares was of importance to the economy of the northern pueblos during the middle part of the 19th century (Brody and Colberg 1966:17).

Three varieties of modern wares (post-1700) were recovered by Kidder from excavations at Pecos Pueblo: plain red, plain black, and painted. The great majority of the painted vessels, according to Shepard (Kidder and Shepard 1936:541-546), contained tuff temper and were traded to Pecos from the Tewa villages. Tuff temper, indicating the same source, occurred in about one-half of the

TABLE 1

PROVENIENCE	BOWLS		JARS		SOUP PLATES		MISC. FORMS	
	LA 591	LA 34	LA 591	LA 34	LA 591	LA 34	LA 591	LA 34
COCHITI/RIO ABAJO	91	86	77	92	90	100	46	
PECOS	9	1	22	7	10		53	
SAN MARCOS							1	
ZIA			1					
ACOMA		13		1				

Table 1. Percent of glaze-decorated sherds from 17th century Spanish Colonial sites near Cochiti Pueblo, New Mexico.

65

TABLE 2

PROVENIENCE	BOWLS		JARS		SOUP PLATES	
	LA 591	LA 34	LA 591	LA 34	LA 591	LA 34
COCHITI/RIO ABAJO			50			
TEWA	43	48	50	88		100
ZIA	2	52		12		
HOPI	55					

Table 2. Percent of matte-painted sherds from 17th century Spanish Colonial sites near Cochiti Pueblo, New Mexico.

Table 3

PROVENIENCE	BOWLS		JARS		SOUP PLATES		MISC. FORMS	
	LA 591	LA 34	LA 591	LA 34	LA 591	LA 34	LA 591	LA 34
COCHITI/RIO ABAJO	84	36	9	5	90	5	95	
TEWA	16	64	46	84	10	95	5	
ACOMA			30	11				
HOPI			15					

Table 3. Percent of plain-surfaced sherds from 17th century Spanish Colonial sites near Cochiti Pueblo, New Mexico.

plain black specimens while its occurrence in the plain red category was "very exceptional". The majority of the plain red ware was sand tempered and Shepard believed that most of it was manufactured at Pecos Pueblo. At San Miguel del Vado, occupied from 1794 to the present, collections from the earlier section of the village indicate considerable business with the pueblos, recalling Bandelier's observation near Tecolote, New Mexico in 1881 that "the Indians of today sell [smudged pottery] to the people" (Lange and Riley 1966:346). Pottery from the Tewa villages, including Nambe and possibly San Ildefonso, predominates, but Zia, possibly Santa Ana, and either Cochiti or Santo Domingo, are represented in small numbers (Warren 1971). By contrast, three sites occupied in the 17th century in the Bernalillo and Cochiti areas contained small percentages of Tewa pottery: 7% and 30% from the latter and 13% from the Bernalillo site.

A sharp decrease in the number of jars is discernable from the 17th to the late 19th century. For approximately the first half of this period, 61% of all forms recovered were jars compared to 28% during the last half. These figures include cooking-ware vessels, which are almost exclusively jar forms.

The decrease in the number of jar forms through time is related to a decrease in the number of cooking-ware vessels at Spanish sites. This ware made up 35% and 52% of the 17th century sherds at Cochiti area sites. The combined cooking-ware sherds from 16 sites occupied from the mid-18th through the 19th century, comprised only 19% of all the pottery recovered from surface collections. Whether this decrease signified changes in the manner in which food was stored or prepared (or both) is a matter of conjecture at this point.

The brief presentation of archeological data adds substance to the written sources. Taken together, there can be no doubt that Pueblo economic pursuits were somewhat more involved than primitive gift-exchange and subsistence farming. When it is remembered that pottery can only be made during the summer (agricultural) months, that the pueblo potters were supplying enough vessels to support the needs of an estimated 40,000 people (not including the Pueblo Indians themselves; Dozier 1970:91) just prior to the American period, then some idea of the magnitude and importance of this activity in Pueblo life can be appreciated.

Unlike the modern situation, in which the individual potter or craftsman produces for a highly competitive market, in the past specialization most likely was by the community. G.D. Schroeder has pointed out, as mentioned above, that particular prestige did not accrue to the individual potter at San Juan Pueblo since most women were proficient at this task. San Juan Pueblo was the unit of specialization, and within it, individual craft production was merely an aspect of a pattern of community specialization. The archeological distribution of historic period Pueblo pottery, indicated briefly above, suggests that this pattern is an old one in Rio Grande Pueblo economy.

The economic system within which the Pueblos and their agricultural Spanish neighbors operated was based on the needs common to social units of equivalent, or nearly equivalent, status. Cash usually was scarce or absent except at the upper levels of frontier society. Goods and services rendered at the domestic level of necessity were normally exchanged on a reciprocal basis. This type of exchange is, nevertheless, an economic one and certainly warrants more than the ritual bobbing of anthropological heads in the direction of Pueblo economics.

The railroad era finished the domestic pottery market. Where Spanish influence had minor effects on some attributes of Pueblo pottery, and perhaps increased the market demand somewhat, the Anglos irrevocably altered the very structure of the market. Not only did they interject cash into a barter system, but their entry into the market upset the equilibrium of the volume and the kinds of pottery required in the market. Consequent shifts in the market structure eliminated the traditional Spanish-American buyers and very nearly eliminated Pueblo pottery.

BIBLIOGRAPHY

ABEL, A.H.

1915   *The Official Correspondence of James B. Calhoun.* Office of Indian Affairs, Government Printing Office, Washington.

ADAMS, E.B., and FRAY ANGELICO CHAVEZ

1956   *The Missions of New Mexico, 1776.* University of New Mexico Press, Albuquerque.

BOURKE, J.G.

1936   Bourke in the Southwest. *New Mexico Historical Review* 11:77-122, 217-282.

1937   Bourke in the Southwest. *New Mexico Historical Review* 12:41-77.

1938   Bourke in the Southwest. *New Mexico Historical Review* 13:192-238.

BRODY, J.J., and ANNE COLBERG

1966   A Spanish-American Homestead near Placitas, New Mexico. *El Palacio* 73 (2):11-20.

DAVIS, W.W. H.

1938   *El Gringo or New Mexico and Her People.* Rydal Press, Santa Fe.

DICK, H.W.

1968   Six Historic Pottery Types From Spanish Sites in New Mexico. In *Collected Papers in Honor of Lyndon Lane Hargrave,* Albert H. Schroeder, ed., pp. 77-94, Papers of the Archaeological Society of New Mexico 1, Museum of New Mexico Press, Santa Fe.

DITTERT, A.E., JIM J. HESTER, and FRANK W. EDDY

1961   *An Archaeological Survey of the Navajo Reservoir District, Northwestern New Mexico.* Monographs of the School of American Research and the Museum of New Mexico 23, Santa Fe.

DOZIER, E.P.

1961   Rio Grande Pueblos. In *Perspectives in American Indian Culture Change,* Edward H. Spicer, ed., University of Chicago Press, Chicago.

1970   *The Pueblo Indians of North America.* Case Studies in Cultural Anthropology, George and Louise Spindler, ed., Holt, Rinehart, and Winston, Inc., New York.

ESPINOSA, J.M.

1942   *Crusaders of the Rio Grande.* Institute of Jesuit History Publications, Institute of Jesuit History, Chicago.

GREGG, JOSIAH

1954   *Commerce of the Prairies.* Max L. Moorehead, ed., University of Oklahoma Press, Norman.

GUNNERSON, J.H.

1969   Apache Archaeology in Northeastern New Mexico. *American Antiquity* 34:23-29.

HAMMOND, G.P., and AGAPITO REY

1966   *The Rediscovery of New Mexico, 1580-1594.* University of New Mexico Press, Albuquerque.

HOLMES, W.H.

1889   Debasement of Pueblo Art. *American Anthropologist* (new series) 2:320.

HURT, W.R.

1939   Indian Influence at Manzano. *El Palacio* 46/11:245-254.

HURT, W.R., and HERBERT W. DICK

1946   Spanish-American Pottery from New Mexico. *El Palacio* 53 (10-11):280-288, 307-312.

KIDDER, A.V., and ANNA O. SHEPARD

1936   *The Pottery of Pecos.* Vol. II. Papers of the Southwestern Expedition, Department of Archaeology, Phillips Academy, Yale University Press, New Haven.

LANGE, C.H.

1959   *Cochiti, A New Mexico Pueblo, Past and Present.* University of Texas Press, Austin.

LANGE, C.H., and CARROLL L. RILEY

1966   *The Southwestern Journals of Adolph E. Bandelier, 1880-1882.* University of New Mexico Press, Albuquerque, and the School of American Research, Museum of New Mexico Press, Santa Fe.

SCHROEDER, A.H.

1972   Rio Grande Ethnohistory. In *New Perspectives on the Pueblos,* Alfonso Ortiz, ed., pp. 41-70, University of New Mexico Press, Albuquerque.

SCHROEDER, G.D.

1964   San Juan Pottery: Methods and Incentives. *El Palacio* 71/1:45-51.

SPANISH ARCHIVES OF NEW MEXICO (S.A.N.M.)

n.d.   New Mexico State Records Center, Santa Fe.

STEVENSON, M.C.

1894   *The Sia.* Bureau of American Ethnology Annual Report 11, Smithsonian Institution, Government Printing Office, Washington.

WARREN, A.H.

1969   Tonque: One Pueblo's Glaze Pottery Industry Dominated Middle Rio Grande Commerce. *El Palacio* 76 (2):36-42.

1971   Unpublished Laboratory notes, Museum of New Mexico.

WINSHIP, G.P.

1896   *The Coronado Expedition, 1540-1542.* Bureau of American Ethnology Annual Report 14, Smithsonian Institution, Government Printing Office, Washington.

David H. Snow is Curator of Archeology at the Museum of New
Mexico's Laboratory of Anthropology. He obtained his BA in Anthropology from the University of New Mexico in 1964, and attended Brandeis University to complete graduate studies in the
Department of Anthropology. He has conducted archeological field
work, in both prehistoric and historic sites, in New Mexico, New
England, and in British Honduras. He currently is preparing a series
of research reports on the Museum of New Mexico archeological
salvage work at Cochiti Dam and is finishing requirements for a
PhD in Anthropology.

THE MYSTERIOUS A
TRIBE OF THE
SOUTHERN PLAINS

Marc Simmons

In historical accounts of Western America, the Plains Indians have received a conspicuous amount of attention from both serious scholars and popular writers. The spectacular and bloody series of military engagements during the second half of the 19th century readily engages interest, as does the singular mode of life pursued by these tepee-dwelling, buffalo-hunting nomads. As a result, Plains Indian history for the short period from 1825 to 1900 has been subjected to microscopic examination with investigation producing a virtual avalanche of books and articles. Further research doubtless will bring to light some new particulars, even on such meticulously studied events as the battle of the Little Bighorn and the Cheyenne campaigns, but for the greater part the facts have already appeared and the story has been told.

The case, however, is altogether different for the 18th century when activities of the Plains tribes were reported upon only infrequently by French traders and explorers from the east and Spaniards from the southwest. The few whitemen who penetrated the Indian domain possessed only the vaguest ideas concerning the identification, languages, and blood relationships of the tribes they encountered, and their chronicles are often confused and spare on the kind of details necessary to reconstruct a coherent historical picture. Notwithstanding, colonial archives, particularly those of the Spaniards, can prove a rich source of information on early Plains Indians, provided a researcher will pursue the scraps of scattered datum with diligence.

Much has already been gleaned from Spanish documents about Apaches and Comanches for the years after 1700, although nothing resembling a comprehensive history has yet appeared. For other groups, especially those east and northeast of New Mexico, serious survey and compilation of information has scarcely begun.

One fact that seems to be emerging from Spanish documentary

MAP

The Souther
Plains

MONTANA

Yellowstone R.

NORTH   DAKOTA

SOUTH   DAKOTA

Missouri R.

WYOMING

NEBRASKA

Loup R.

Platte R.

Republican R.

COLORADO

KANSAS

Arkansas R.

Wichita
Villages

Abiquiu   • Taos

• Santa Fe

El Vado

OKLAHOMA

NEW   MEXICO

Pecos R.

Rio Grande

Red R.

Spanish
Fort

TEXAS

El Paso

Nacogdo

74

sources with increasing clarity is that, beginning at an early date, members of remote tribes from the central and even northern plains made direct contact with colonial New Mexican settlements. On occasion, Crows, Gros Ventres, Shoshones, Blackfeet, Arikaras, Osages, and other peoples who dwelled hundreds of miles from New Mexico appeared along the Rio Grande to raid and trade. The majority of anthropologists and historians have generally been unwilling to admit these aboriginal travelers ranged so far, but the evidence now appears irrefutable.[1]

The tribes of the southern plains known to the Spaniards most intimately in the latter 1700's were the Comanches, Kiowas, Kiowa-Apaches, Mescalero and Lipan Apaches, plus the Utes and Jicarilla Apaches who clung to the western periphery of the plains. In addition, the New Mexicans had occasional contact with Pawnees, Jumanos (Wichitas), Arapahos, Cheyennes, and a group referred to in contemporary documents as the A or sometimes as Aa or Aaa.

Identification of these mysterious A people has posed a vexing problem for scholars. Actually Spanish-New Mexican documents from the later colonial period are filled with unrecognizeable names of Plains tribes or bands--a welter of tags applied by the Spaniards willy-nilly to Indians they knew imperfectly or scarcely at all. But of those names still unidentified, none perhaps appears more frequently and consistently, or through the documents over a longer period of time, than that of the puzzling A.

The earliest reference to an A Indian in the Southwest thus far discovered dates from 1742, a burial mentioned in the Catholic Church records of New Mexico.[2] David M. Brugge, who closely studied the ecclesiastical sources, has shown that in the century from 1740 to 1840, A women and children were widely distributed as servants throughout the Spanish settlements and Rio Grande Pueblos. The largest number he finds occur in the decade of the 1790s: 24 As baptized in the parishes of Taos, Picurís, San Juan, Santa Clara, Nambé, San Ildefonso, Santa Fe, Jémez, Sandía, Belén, and Tomé.[3] These baptisms, representing infants, children, and adult females, were performed upon captives purchased by the Spaniards from Comanches during the annual trading fairs at Taos, Picurís, and Pecos.

Comanches roamed widely across the southern half of the Great Plains, fighting, horse stealing, and taking slaves that could be sold in New Mexico. At least by 1700, the Spanish king had decreed that as a humanitarian gesture Indian captives, whenever possible, should be ransomed by colonial officials, placed in citizens' homes, and educated as Christians. In this way, significant numbers of Pawnees, Wichitas, Apaches, As, and others (called collectively *genízaros)* became members of Spanish households, performing domestic chores in exchange for their board and education. Reference to these Indians as *esclavas* or slaves was punctiliously avoided since they were by law free men.

Joseph Antonio de Villaseñor in his descriptive *Teatro Americano,* published in 1748, mentions the As, Cuampes, and Pawnees as enemy tribes living on the New Mexican frontier. The latter two groups, as will be demonstrated shortly, figure prominently in identification of the As.

In 1750, the New Mexican Governor, Vélez Cachupín, heard some disturbing news from Felipe de Sandoval, a Spaniard who had been living in French Louisiana and who reached Santa Fe with a small party after a journey across the plains. The Jumanos (Wichitas) had made peace with their long-time foes, the Pawnees, and had drawn them into an alliance with the Comanches and the A tribe, the latter two having been enemies until 1749. The Jumanos at this time were residing in two large villages of grass lodges, surrounded by stockades and moats, situated on the banks of the Arkansas River in present northern Oklahoma. The Pawnees dwelled farther north in a series of towns along the middle Missouri and its tributaries, but no mention was made at this date of the region inhabited by the As.[4] The alliance apparently had been encouraged by the French who desired to trade unmolested among Plains Indians and believed that conditions of peace were more conducive to advancement of their mercantile interests. Spanish alarm arose out of fears that the confederated tribes might unite their warriors to attack New Mexico or at the very least give safe passage to any French expedition that had designs on the Province.

Additional references to A Indians crop up sporadically in the years after 1750. Two French traders reached Santa Fe in August of 1752 and related that an Indian woman of the Aé tribe guided them. "She had fled from the house of her master here [Santa Fe] four months before and was following the road to her country. On the other side of the Rio Napestle [Arkansas], they met the woman and were easily able to persuade her to conduct them to these parts from a northern direction."[5]

A more curious note on the As by Governor Manuel Urrisola

76

asserts that they chased some Comanches who were fleeing from a camp in the Taos Valley during December 1761.[6] It is not clear whether these As were from the plains or from among the A *genízaros* living in New Mexico. The church records, as previously cited, unquestionably indicate the presence of As in the northern New Mexico villages, as does a detailed census report of 1752 that refers to the "Genízaros of Abiquiú composed of Aes, Pananas (Pawnees), Quituches (Kichai, a division of the Wichitas), Apaches, Cuampis, and Yutas (Utes)."[7]

At least by 1787, if not before, the As were definitely at war again with the Comanches. In the summer of that year, a large force of Yamparica Comanches made an attack upon an A village, destroying 200 teepees, killing five chiefs, and taking numerous prisoners.[8] Apparently the As along with Wichita friends, and in spite of the Comanche menace, made periodic trips to Santa Fe to confer with Spanish officials. Governor Fernando de la Concha, for example, reported in 1791 that he expected members of the A and Jumano nations to come in for gifts and rations during the summer.[9]

A report in the Spanish Archives of New Mexico for 1795 speaks briefly of three Apache prisoners being transferred by the governor in Santa Fe south to El Paso, accompanied by "an Indian of the A nation who is also being sent because of his perverse habits."[10] Of what crime this A was guilty, no mention is made, yet his perverse conduct was a harbinger of a more serious situation involving fellow tribesmen just a few years later.

In early fall of 1800, a combined force of 400 to 500 Pawnees, Kiowas, Abajoses, and members of the A tribe attacked the Abiquiú district. As the war party withdrew, it was pursued by a small troop of Spanish soldiers led by Lt. Don Antonio de Arce who feared to attack the raiders because of their strength. The governor at once put detachments in the field to patrol the frontier and give warning should the enemy return to renew hostilities.[11]

The ease with which these marauders had entered the Abiquiú area bewildered Spanish authorities, for the district was on the northwestern frontier of the province rather than on the east facing the plains. A possible explanation was obtained from friendly Comanches who reported that an A captive raised among them had earlier deceived six of their warriors by convincing them to accompany him on a raid against his own people. Once in the field, the captive had led the luckless Comanches into a trap prepared by the A nation and all were killed. It was this traitorous individual, according to the Comanche story, who, knowing the entrances and exits of New Mexico, had guided the huge party of Pawnees, Kiowas, Abajoses, and As against Abiquiu.[12] The comanches attempted to settle their own scores with the Kiowas and As in the summer of 1803 when a formidable army led by the head chief spent 96 days scouring the plains in a fruitless search for the enemy.[13]

Another tale of A perfidy appeared in New Mexico a short time afterward. About 1799, the village of El Vado (either the present San José or San Miguel) was founded on the Pecos River, and the governor sent there "an Indian of the A Nation" Josef María Gurule to serve as interpreter for Plains Indians when they came to visit or trade. Gurule had been raised as a captive among the Comanches but evidently later came to live in the Rio Grande settlements, hence his knowledge of languages. In carrying out his assignment, he proved utterly faithless. He spuriously claimed to be the son of Guanicaruco, chief of the Yamparicas; he mistreated the residents of El Vado; and whenever Comanches appeared, he deceived them and stole their animals. His misconduct continued for several years until the Comanches vociferously demanded action against him. So in early 1804, the governor removed the offending A from El Vado and replaced him with Alejandro Martín, a reliable interpreter well-known to the Indians.[14]

Either as a result of transgressions at El Vado or subsequent mischief elsewhere, within a year criminal charges were brought against Gurule. In January 1806, the governor recorded that four Indians named Francisco El Comanche, Francisco Javier of the A Nation, Josef María Gurule, also of the A Nation, and Antonio María [unidentified] had all been subjected to a judicial investigation conducted by the assistant alcalde of Pecos, and as prisoners they were being sent under escort to the jail in El Paso. Through their misconduct, they had so enraged the Comanches that the governor felt they should be removed from the up-river settlements to avoid trouble.[15]

At about this same time, Governor Real Alencaster advised his superior in Chihuahua, Commandant General Nemesio Salcedo, that Cuampes, Sayanas, and As had been coming to Santa Fe regularly in recent years asking for an alliance with the Spaniards and the opening of trade relations. The three tribes, he noted, were allied with one another.[16] The Sayanas it is clear were Cheyenne, but the Cuampes, who appear in the documents of the 18th and early

19th centuries almost as frequently as the As, offer no easy iden-tification. In 1805, according to a statement of one of their chiefs, the Cuampes were living on a tributary of the Platte River.[17] Without entering into a detailed analysis of the "Cuampes problem", it is suggested here that this tribe was the Arapaho. The fact that use of the term Arapaho has not been found in any Spanish or Mexican document prior to 1840, even though this tribe in asso-ciation with the Cheyennes must have been known in New Mexi-co long before that date, in part leads to this conclusion. [18]

Don Pedro Bautista Pino, New Mexico's representative to the Spanish Cortes, in his *Exposición* of 1812 included in his enumer-ation of the "wild tribes" surrounding the province, the following: Cuampes, Cahiguas (Kiowa), Aas-orejones, Jumanes, and Panana.[19] Father Juan Guevara's report to the Bishop of Durango in 1820 in the same context also lists Orejones and Aaas.[20] Why the term Orejones (Big-eared People) became associated with the As at this period is unknown. A Coahuiltecan tribe of south Texas bore this name, as did on occasion a division of the Faraon Apache, but so far as can be determined neither or these had any connection with the As.

According to archival sources, a party of 28 As from the vicinity of the Yellowstone River visited Santa Fe in July of 1819 and was questioned by Governor Facundo Melgares concerning the rumored presence of Americans in that area. The As declared they had seen no whitemen.[21] That their range extended as far north as the Yellowstone, however, is a startling revelation and supports the point emphasized earlier: the Plains tribes wandered much greater distances than most scholars have been willing to concede.

The latest mention of the As to appear until now is found in an 1840 report of Mexican Governor Manuel Armijo that includes them among the nomad tribes inhabiting New Mexico's frontier. After this date, As vanish from the record. At first glance, the explanation would seem to be either that Anglo-Americans con-ferred upon them some other name, or that they became extinct as a tribal entity through reduction of numbers in warfare, by epidemic disease, or through merging with some other group.

The foregoing discussion establishes several points. First, the A Indians were known to the people of New Mexico for at least 100 years, from approximately 1740 to 1840. During this period, mem-bers of the tribe traveling from their domain on the Great Plains made peaceful visits to the Province, but on occasion also, as in

79

the case of the raid upon Abiquiú in 1800, they participated in hostilities against the Spaniards. Second, the As were generally on friendly terms and often associated with Pawnees, Wichitas, Cuampes (Arapahos), and Cheyennes, and except for brief interludes of peace seem to have been antagonistic toward the Comanches. Finally, a significant number of acculturated As lived in the Spanish settlements as *genízaros* and doubtless contributed their blood to the mestizo population.

The mystery remains, however. Precisely who were the As, and from whence derived their curious name. Scholars treating Southwestern history have addressed the problem only in passing, and their cursory attempts at identification in the main appear unsatisfactory. Writers most persistently suggest the As may have been one of the numerous sub-tribes of the Plains Apaches and that, in fact, use of the single letter represents an abbreviation of the word Apache. Some Spanish accounts actually rendered the name thus: Aa, the superior bar being the standard symbol used by colonial scribes to indicate the shortening or abbreviation of a word.[22] If indeed the name A or Aa was the abbreviated form of a longer term, there is no evidence to confirm that it represented the word Apache.

Albert H. Schroeder, who has dealt exhaustively with the Plains Athabascans, hypothesizes that the As may well have been Kiowa-Apaches and this to be sure is an attractive suggestion.[23] Although this small tribe is known to have been present on the southern plains during the 18th century, reference to it in contemporary Spanish documents, at least under this name, is scarce. I find only a single mention of the term in the colonial records: a *genízaro* of Belén in 1746 made an official statement that he was a native of the *nación apache caigua* (Kiowa-Apache Nation).[24] Thus, the name for this people was current at a relatively early date, although it does not preclude confusion on the part of the Spaniards, leading at other times to designation of the same group by some other label. In any event our picture of A history, fragmentary though it be, does not seem to coincide with what is known about the early Kiowa-Apaches.

Other researchers less versed in the complexities of colonial history have made wild stabs in the dark, attempting to link the As with such tribes as the Arapahos, Osages, or the Eyeish of east Texas. Previous discussion has demonstrated that the Arapaho (Cuampes) were allied with the As at the end of the 18th century, and hence the two groups were distinct. As for the Osages, who occasionally appeared along the New Mexico border, the Spaniards knew them by the name Guazas or Guasases.[25] The Caddoan Eyeish, sometimes written as Ays, who lived near Nacogdoches, Texas, at once seem the most likely candidates for the elusive As. But this dwindling tribe by 1795 was said to contain only 90 persons, and according to a report of 1805 the total had dipped to 20 survivors.[26] Nor were the Eyeish ever known to venture upon the plains; certainly they never traveled north of the Arkansas River as the As were accustomed to do, nor did they visit New Mexico.

These speculations concerning the identity of the As have been presented to show the fog that has enveloped this problem. Further illustrations may be dispensed with since, as the remainder of the present discussion will demonstrate, it is possible to identify the As with fair certainty.

The entire question may be resolved by reference to a letter written in 1778 by Athanase de Mézières, a Frenchman serving as Spain's Indian agent on the Texas frontier. In a statement to his superior the Commandant General of the Internal Provinces, De Mézières referred to a commission handed him by the governor of Texas to visit "the Avages nation (this is the one that the French call Ayoues, and the Spaniards Aas), or Mahas, who last year came down from the banks of the remote Missouri River, on which they had their town, in order to unite with these [i.e. the Taovayas or Wichitas]."[27] This explanation, with some elaboration, unravels the entire A enigma.

The Mahas were the Panimahas or Skidi Pawnees, also known as the Wolf or Loup Pawnees because their traditional home was on the Loup River in Nebraska. These Mahas constituted one of the four principal branches of the Caddoan speaking Pawnees, the remaining three being the Republican, the Grand, and the Tapage or Noisey Pawnees. The Panimahas or Skidis were often considered a separate tribe since they spoke a dialect distinct from other Pawnee divisions. Obviously this fact was recognized by the early Spaniards and Frenchmen who therefore distinguished this group by name from the Pawnee proper.

But why did the Spaniards employ the strange term A or Aa for a people they also knew as Mahas or Panimahas? The answer seems to be that they picked up this designation from the French in the early 18th century. Father José Antonio Pichardo, in compiling a treatise on Spain's northern American frontier prior to 1803, declares that the French first gave these Pawnee the name Avoyelles

82   Pawnee Warriors

(meaning Aa vowels). As reason, he cites classical sources that define "Aa", taken from the Greek, as the confluence or meeting of several waters or streams. Since the Panimaha, when initially encountered by French traders, were living along the Missouri and its tributaries, a land full of rivers Pichardo says, it occurred to them to call these Indians Aas, and within time Avoyelles.

Most of Father Pichardo's reasoning and his reference to antiquity should perhaps be dismissed as pure fantasy. But not his contention that the French first knew the Panimahas by the term Avoyelles or Aa vowel people. The Caddoan name for the Pawnees was Awahis which shows obvious similarity to Avoyelles, and its numerous variations: Aavage, Aguages, Aoiages, Aaovage, Aaovajes, Avajes, and Ayoues, all of which were applied at one time or another to the Panimahas. The most promising explanation then would seem to be that the vanguard of French explorers heard the Panimahas identified by the Caddoan term Awahis which sounded to their ears enough like Avoyelles or "A vowels" that they called them the Aa Indians. Only in this context does De Mézières's statement that "the Avages nation is the one the French call Ayoues and the Spaniards Aas or Mahas" appear comprehensible.

Once the As are tied to the Panimahas, more concrete discussion is possible since the latter name occurs with some frequency in the later colonial period. When they were first contacted by white men, the Panimahas and the Pawnees proper inhabited the forks of the Loup River in central Nebraska, their villages extending northward to the Missouri where they mingled with their linguistic relatives the Arikara. According to their own tradition, the Panimahas possessed more of a roving nature than other Pawnees, and early maps show them distributed over a wide section of the north central plains. Some bands were designated as Maha Errante, or Wandering Maha. [29] De Mézières, in the letter previously cited, describes them as "docile, honest, devoted to the cultivation of the soil, to hunting, and to war. [They] are indefatigable, as is shown by the laborious marches on foot to which they have been reared . . . . They dress in long garments, their weapons are firearms and sabers, and they are somewhat swarthy in color."[30]

The Panimahas' history was evidently closely tied to that of their Caddoan kinsmen, the Wichitas, who in the early 18th century, as mentioned, occupied the valley of the Arkansas. Bernard de la Harpe, a French agent from Louisiana, established outposts among the Wichitas in 1719 at which time they numbered nine villages,

Pawnee Earth Lodge

but, by 1749, warfare with the Little Osages had reduced their population and caused them to concentrate in two adjacent towns. Eight years later, Osage pressure forced the Wichitas to migrate south where they founded new villages on the Red River (near present Spanish Fort, Texas).[31] The Spaniards in Texas referred to the Wichitas on the Red by the name Taovaya, although they continued to be known to the New Mexicans by the older and more general term, Jumano.

The Panimahas and other Pawnees also experienced prolonged warfare with the Osages of Missouri, although as early as the 1680s, Mahas were reported to be trading Apache slaves to that tribe.[32] From the onset, the Osages possessed a clear advantage in the conflict because their proximity to French settlements in the Mississippi Valley gave them ready access to firearms. Later, however, the Panimahas made contact with Englishmen on the upper Mississippi from whom they obtained weapons and trade goods.

At least by 1772, and probably sooner, itinerant Panimaha traders were at the Taovaya or Wichita settlements on the Red River bartering English articles and guns and causing alarm among the Spaniards of Texas who feared their own commerce with this tribe would be disturbed.[33] As De Mézières mentions in the quotation above, Panimahas in 1777 took the road south, moving down to join the Taovaya villagers on the Texas frontier. This migration may have been prompted by a desire to escape from the Osages and also by friendly overtures made by Spanish officials who hoped to pull the Panimahas away from English contact and into their own commercial orbit.

In 1778, Commandant General Teodoro de Croix observed that the Aovages or Panimahas, numbering about 800 men, had located themselves next to the Taovayas, and other Wichita sub-tribes.[34] If this figure for adult males is correct, it would suggest a total population of at least 2,500 for the Panimahas on the Red. Notwithstanding, it is certain that other Panimaha bands remained in the north in their old homeland. This would account for the New Mexican reports of As near the Platte, As allying with the Cheyennes and Arapahos, and As visiting the vicinity of the Yellowstone.

It is probable that the division of the Panimahas mentioned as Wandering Pawnee (Maha Errante) was the group most often met by Spaniards from New Mexico. Pedro Vial, who made several expeditions across the plains, reported in 1805 seeing or hearing news of the Pananas, Lobos (Wolves), Otos, and others in the neighborhood of the Missouri, and the Cuampes, Caiguas, Aas, and Sayanas farther west. The Pananas would be the Pawnee proper, the Lobos those groups of Panimahas or Skidis settled permanently along the Missouri, and the Aas in this case (if our thesis is correct), the Maha Errante.[35] A Spanish soldier from New Mexico accompanied by three Taos Indians scouted north in 1810 as far as the Rio Chato (either the Republican or Platte River) where he met tribes of As, Orejones, Kiowas, Cuampes, and Gros Ventres, further confirmation that As as well as Orejones were situated in the region known to be frequented by the Panimahas.[36]

The evidence compiled here established fairly conclusively that the mysterious As were in reality the Panimahas or Skidis. Since Pawnee history for the 18th century is so poorly known, this fact should aid in enlarging our body of information for this important Plains tribe. Moreover, this discussion suggests that further careful survey of Spanish documents is needed to unravel the tangled threads of the Plains Indians' story during the 18th century.

NOTES

1. The Osages, for example, who ranged through Missouri and Arkansas, raided Santa Fe in 1790, stealing 800 head of horses. In the same year the governor of Louisiana commented: "The said nation [Osage] is extremely unfaithful [making] various incursions against the establishment of Santa Fe, capital of the kingdom of New Mexico" (Noel M. Loomis and Abraham P. Nasatir, *Pedro Vial and the Roads to Santa Fe*, University of Oklahoma Press, Norman, 1967:24). In 1821, the last Spanish governor in New Mexico, Don Facundo Melgares, complained of Osage depredations, saying: "They steal our horses and murder our people, and the Americans sell them the arms and ammunition which they use in war upon us" (Thomas James, *Three Years Among the Indians and Mexicans*, J. B. Lippincott Co., Philadelphia, 1962:85).

    A report of Governor Manrrique, Mar. 3, 1809, doc. no. 2206 in the Spanish Archives of New Mexico, State Records Center, Santa Fe (cited hereinafter as SANM), mentions a visit to Santa Fe in 1809 by a delegation of Barigones (i.e. Gros Ventres). It is not clear whether these were Siouan-speaking Hidatsas, known as Gros Ventres of the Missouri, or the Atsina branch of the Arapahos who were called Gros Ventres of the Plains. In 1829, Gros Ventres from the Upper Missouri reputedly attacked a caravan of Mexican traders from Santa Fe near the Cimarron Crossing of the Arkansas (James F. Meline, *Two Thousand Miles on Horseback*, Hurd and Houghton, New York, 1868:293-294).

    Bands of Gros Ventre, Crow, and Shoshone Indians from Wyoming were seen near Taos and around Bent's Fort during the decade of the 1830s. Apparently they had been visiting this region for some time (David Lavender, *Bent's Fort*, Doubleday, New York, 1954:133, 151). A war party of 250 Blackfeet from Canada allegedly raided a Spanish pack train in the Southwest in the year 1787 (J.B. Tyrell, ed., *David Thompson's Narrative of His Explorations in Western America*, 1784-1812, Champlain Society, Toronto, 1916:370). About 1826, according to a story collected by George Hyde in 1910 from a Cheyenne, a war party of Blackfeet and Gros Ventres (Atsinas) raided south to the Red River and carried off a large herd of Comanche and Kiowa horses. One clan of Blackfeet subsequently settled permanently among the Southern Cheyennes and Arapahos (George E. Hyde, *Life of George Bent*, University of Oklahoma Press, Norman, 1968:32-33).

2. David M. Brugge, Some Plains Indians in the Church Records of New Mexico, *Plains Anthropologist*, (1965) 10(29):181.

3. *Ibid.*:182.

4. John Francis Bannon, ed., *Bolton and the Spanish Borderlands* (University of Oklahoma Press, Norman, 1964):159, 163.

5. Alfred Barnaby Thomas, *The Plains Indians and New Mexico, 1751-1778* (University of New Mexico Press, Albuquerque, 1940):109-110.

6. Eleanor B. Adams, ed., *Bishop Tamaron's Visitation of New Mexico, 1760*, (University of New Mexico Press, Albuquerque, 1954):62. See also Albert H. Schroeder, A Study of the Apache Indians: Part II, The Jicarilla Apache, 1959, Mimeo, MS, Prepared for Jicarilla Lands Claim Hearing, U.S. Dept. of Justice.

7. Estado General y Particular del Reyno del Nuevo México, 1752, Provincias Internas, vol. 102, pt. 3, Archivo General de la Nación, México (cited hereinafter as AGN).

8. Pedro Ignacio Sanchez to Gov. Juan Bautista de Anza, Rio de Santa Clara, Aug. 22, 1787, Prov. Int., vol. 65, pt. 4, AGN.

9. Gov. Concha to the Count of Revilla Gigedo, Santa Fe, Apr. 20, 1791, Prov. Int., vol. 65, pt. 4, AGN.

10. Pedro de Nava to the Gov. of New Mexico, Chihuahua, Aug. 8, 1795, doc. no. 1340, SANM.

11. Pedro de Nava to the Gov. of New Mexico, Chihuahua, Oct. 1, 1800, doc. no. 1511, SANM.

12. Gov. of New Mexico to Pedro de Nava, Santa Fe, Nov. 24, 1800, doc. no. 1517[4], SANM. Continuing his investigation into this affair, the Governor learned the following summer of a possible alliance of the Jicarilla Apaches with the four raiding tribes, and that these, since they were familiar with New Mexico, may have served as guides (doc. no. 1548, SAMN). The Governor here refers to the Abajoses as relatives of the Llanero Apaches, which means they were probably Kiowa-Apaches, but possibly Navajos. Although angered at the four tribes because of their hostile actions, the Governor nevertheless expressed the hope on March 23, 1801 that they could be brought into alliance with the Spaniards since their position on the plains would make them useful in keeping watch over Englishmen from Canada who, according to rumor, were attempting to unite the tribes of the upper Mississippi for the purpose of attacking Spanish possessions (doc. no. 1533 [9], SANM).

13. Summary of Events Occurring in the Province of New Mexico, from June 29 to Aug. 31, 1803, doc. no. 1673, SANM.

14. Gov. of New Mexico to Nemesio Salcedo, Mar. 28, 1804, doc. no. 1714 [2]. SANM.

15. Governor Real Alencaster to the Commandant General, Santa Fe, Jan. 17, 1806, doc. no. 1931, SANM.

16. This correspondence is mentioned in Nemesio Salcedo to the Gov. of New Mexico, Chihuahua, July 19, 1805, doc. no. 1859 [2], SANM.

17. Loomis and Nasatir 1967:424.

18. An article by Hugh Lenox Scott, The Early History and the Names of the Arapaho, *American Anthropologist* (1907) 9:545-560, makes no mention of early Spanish names for this tribe. Detailed study will be necessary to link the Cuampes firmly with the Arapahos. If this can be done, their presence in New Mexico as early as 1748, as indicated by Villaseñor (see reference above), will alter present thinking concerning the date of Arapaho migration from the north. Major Long, on his expedition to the Rockies in 1820, observed that: "The Arapaho, Cheyenne, and others formerly carried on a limited trade with the Spaniards in New Mexico, with whom they exchanged dressed bison skins for blankets, wheat flour, maize, etc... (Scott 1907:550.)

19. H. Bailey Carroll and J. Villasana Haggard, eds., *Three New Mexico Chronicles* (The Quivira Society, Albuquerque, 1942):128.

20. Guevara to Bishop Castañiza, Oct. 23, 1820, Books of Accounts, Archives of the Archdioces of Santa Fe, Albuquerque.

21. Luís Navarro García, *Las Provincias Internas en el Siglo XIX* (Escuela de Estudios Hispano-Americanos, Sevilla, 1965):100. Another source gives the number of As in this party as 24 (Alfred B. Thomas, ed., An Anonymous Description of New Mexico, 1818, *Southwestern Historical Quarterly* (1929) 33(1):54.

22. See e.g. Trial Record of Genizaros, Santa Fe-Chihuahua, Dec. 9, 1805-Mar. 28, 1806, doc. no. 1931, SANM.

23. Schroeder 1959:67.

24. This document is cited in Silvio Zavala, *Los Esclavos Indios en Nueva España* (El Colegio Nacional, Mexico, 1967):253.

25. Luís Navarro García, *Don José De Gálvez y la Comandancia General de las Provincias Internas del Norte de Nueva España* (Escuela de Estudios Hispano-Americanos, Sevilla, 1964):345n; and Correspondence of Governor Chacón, Santa Fe, Mar. 28, 1804, doc. no. 1714 [11], SANM.

26. Navarro García 1964:494; Frederick Webb Hodge, ed., *Handbook of American Indians North of Mexico,* 2 vols. (Rowan and Littlefield, New York, reprinted 1971):449.

27. The letter is translated in Charles Wilson Hackett, ed., *Pichardo's Treatise On the Limits of Louisiana and Texas,* 3 vols. (University of Texas Press, Austin, 1931-41) 2:243-44.

28. *Ibid.,* 3:71-72.

29. *Ibid.,* 2:map insert.

30. *Ibid.,* 2:224.

31. Elizabeth Ann Harper, The Taovayas Indians in Frontier Trade and Diplomacy, 1719-1768, *Chronicles of Oklahoma* (1953): 273, 279.

32. George E. Hyde, *Indians of the High Plains* (University of Oklahoma Press, Norman, 1959):25.

33. Herbert Eugene Bolton, *Athanase de Mézieres and the Louisiana-Texas Frontier, 1768-1780,* 2 vols. (Arthur Clark Co., Cleveland, 1914) 2:301.

34. Expediente Sobre Comercio Reciproco Entre las Provincias de la Luisiana y Téxas, Prov. Int., vol. 182, AGN; and published in *Boletin del Archivo General de la Nación,* Mexico (1957) 28:210.

35. Gov. Real Alencaster to the Commandant General of the Internal Provinces, Santa Fe, Nov. 20, 1805, doc. no. 1925, SANM.

36. Gov. of New Mexico to Nemesio Salcedo, Santa Fe, Dec. 6, 1810, doc. no. 2363, SANM.

Marc Simmons, Ph. D. has degrees from the University of Texas and the University of New Mexico. For two years he served as a member of the history department of the latter institution. He has written extensively, both articles and books, on the history of the Southwest. Works include *Spanish Government in New Mexico* (1968) and *Yesterday in Santa Fe* (1969), and he is a contributor to the *Handbook of American Indians North of Mexico* and the *Encyclopedia Americana.* Presently he resides near Cerrillos, New Mexico, dividing his time between research and his own horseshoeing and blacksmithing business.

THE PUEBLO OF NAMBÉ
AND ITS LANDS

Myra Ellen Jenkins

The Pueblo of Nambé, located in the foothills of the Sangre de
Cristo Mountains some 16 miles north of Santa Fe along the river
which bears the same name, was in existence when Don Juan de
Oñate occupied New Mexico in 1598. Together with its other
Tewa-speaking neighbors, the small pueblo made its submission to
Spanish sovereignty in that year. A mission had been established by
1613, and a church dedicated to Nuestro Padre San Francisco was
built in 1617. By 1680, the mission included the pueblos of Jacona
and Cuyamungue as *visitas*.[1]

Little else is known of Nambé until August 10, 1680, when the
Indians took part in the bloody, common Pueblo Revolt against
Spanish authority and killed their missionary, Fray Tomás de Torres,
together with his brother and family and a resident of Taos.[2] On
September 12, 1692, reconquering General Don Diego de Vargas
entered the village on his peaceful reconnoissance expedition and
was met by Governor Alonso who quietly rendered his obedience,
and 51 persons were baptized.[3] However, the pueblos, including
Nambé, were not so peaceful during the succeeding four years as
resentment continued to flare over Spanish rule, assignment of
lands near the pueblos to non-Indians, and levies on Indian food
supplies for the starving colonists. Late in 1693, Nambé was abandoned, and the inhabitants fled to San Ildefonso to join other
rebels. Captain Roque Madrid sacked the pueblo of its food supplies
in March of the following year. Gradually, however, the Indians
returned to their village, and when de Vargas arrived at Nambé,
September 25, on his tour of inspection of the reconciled pueblos,
he reported that a cross had been set up in the village, the houses
were being remodeled, and livestock was again grazing along the
river.[4]

Reconciliation was brief. Nambé *cacique* Xenome and another
member of the pueblo known as Diaguillo were leaders of the June
1696 Pueblo revolt during which the Indians again killed three
Spanish residents at the door of the church, then fled to the foothills north of Chimayó to join other dissidents. The missionary,
Fray Antonio Moreno, was killed in San Ildefonso where he was
visiting at the time of the outbreak. Diaguillo was hanged by loyal

91

Indians at Pecos Pueblo, and Xenome was captured and after long interrogation, executed in Santa Fe. By late November, the scattered Nambes had returned to the pueblo, and the final revolt against Spanish rule was over.[5]

Contemporary accounts of the Pueblo of Nambé during the 18th century are also few. On January 12, 1706, Custos Fray Juan Álvarez reported that the church at Nambé was being built,[6] but probably the pre-revolt structure was actually being restored. A larger and more commodious church, constructed through the largesse of Governor Juan Domingo Bustamante, was completed by 1725. This edifice collapsed in 1909, and since that time the pueblo has not had a church building.[7]

The few visitors to Nambé during this period, however, were impressed by the favorable situation of the little pueblo and particularly noted the irrigation system and quality of Indian fields. Fray Manuel de San Juan Nepomuceno y Trigo reported to the Franciscan *Procurador-General,* Fray José Miguel de los Rios in 1754:

> ...setting out from the villa of Santa Fe and travelling north for six leagues, one comes to this mission, which is in a most agreeable location, for it has a beautiful stream which leaps noisily from a leafy mountain. It induces harvests with abundant health-giving waters, and on its spacious fields the Indians sow for the father, their poor minister--since they pay no obvention at all--three *fanegas* of wheat and one *almud* of corn...[8]

Bishop of Durango Pedro Tamarón noted briefly in 1760: "This pueblo is very pleasant, with many plantings and a river that always has water, and this delicious for drinking. An irrigation ditch is taken from it."[9]

The best description of the pueblo was given by the meticulous *visitador* Fray Francisco Atanasio Domínguez in his official 1776 report of New Mexico missions:

> The site, or hole, in which the pueblo of Nambe is established, which I mentioned when I began the account of my visitation, has the Sierra Madre first noted at Santa Fe on the east-northeast. To the northeast, north and northwest are some broken, rugged, red hills, with cañadas here and there. From the point when they begin, which is at the aforesaid sierra, these hills lie in the directions mentioned, forming a very extensive enclosure for the site of the pueblo, which lies near the middle of the site in relation to these hills. To the southeast of the pueblo there is a ridge of hills which, although they are essentially similar to the others, do not curve as they do, but run straight down from the

sierra in the aforesaid direction. These hills are as near, or as close as a musket shot to the pueblo. At their foot a small river with a swift current full of crystalline water comes from the aforesaid sierra... **ITS LANDS AND FRUITS**: They have almost as much land above the pueblo as below it, and it occupies most of the site mentioned, although a great arroyo that arises in the east-northeast and runs to the southwest until it enters the pueblo's river behind the church and convent and in front of the corrals mentioned divides them. They irrigate the upper lands with a mother ditch from well upriver, and they take water for the lower lands from the same ditch a little before the said arroyo empties into the river. The lands are fairly fertile and everything sown in them yields a crop, with a sufficient harvest of everything...[10]

Dominguéz reported that the non-Indian "Rancho de Pojoaque," north of the pueblo of the same name and on the opposite side of the river, contained 25 families with 162 persons.[11] Undoubtedly, most of these belonged to or were servants of the Ortiz family with whom Nambé was to have land difficulties during the next 200 years. The population of Nambé was listed as 50 families consisting of 183 persons.[12] During the 19th century, the numbers decreased rapidly.

This favored location, especially the availability of irrigation water from the Pojoaque-Nambé River and the good pasture lands east and south of the pueblo, made Nambé vulnerable to non-Indian encroachment, particularly as the population declined. Shortly after the reconquest, Spanish settlers moved into the valley between the former Pueblo of Pojoaque and Nambé and were given parcels of land by both Governors Diego de Vargas and Pedro Rodriguez Cubero with little attention paid to the legality of such encroachments on Indian land.[13] Land ownership in the region was complicated by the reestablishment of the Pueblo of Pojoaque by Governor Cuervo y Valdés in 1707. By the end of the century, many families, especially the extensive and powerful Ortiz clan, descendants of Nicolás Ortiz III who was killed by Comanches in 1769 near San Antonio Mountain, claimed much of the land on both sides of the river between the two pueblos in spite of the fact that the Spanish authorities throughout the century attempted to apply the principle that the pueblos were entitled to a minimum of a league of land in each direction from their mission churches.[14] Actually, the distance between the two small pueblos was less than a league, and much of the irrigable land was occupied by non-Indians.

The first formal petition for a grant involving lands recognized as specifically belonging to Nambé appears to be that of Vicente

Durán de Armijo in 1739. Vicente had accompanied his parents, Joseph de Armijo and Catalina Durán, who came to New Mexico with other colonists from Zacatecas in 1695, and lived in the Santa Fe region.15 His brother, Antonio, had secured a small grant near Pojoaque from Governor Cubero in 1701, but had sold the tract back to the Pojoaque Indians when the pueblo was reestablished in 1707.16 In September, 1739, Vicente petitioned Governor Gaspar Domingo de Mendoza for a grant to lands east and south of Nambé, giving as his reasons that his Santa Fe holdings were insufficient to support his family since the river was virtually dry and his crops had failed. To add to his poverty, he stated, he had been able to accumulate some livestock "through a little trade," but hostile Indian attacks on his herds had caused great damage. His petition continued:

> I have seen proper to register a piece of surplus land beyond the lands of the friendly Indians of the Pueblo of Nambé, without disturbing the pastures or waters upon which the herds of this royal presidio or the animals of the said Indians are pastured, nor is any one else using the said lands. They contain about six fanegas for wheat and two for corn, and the boundaries are as follows: on the north, bounded by a dry arroyo, on the south by the lands of Bernardo de Sena, on the east by a mountain, on the west by the lands of the said Indians of Nambé.17

Governor Domingo de Mendoza, on September 24, approved a grant to Durán de Armijo but refused to give him the region requested because of the objections of the Pueblo of Nambé that the donation would be of great injury to them. In taking such action, the governor recognized Indian right to an area larger than a mere league to the east and south. Instead, the petitioner was given two small tracts of land on both sides of the Nambe River west of the pueblo, apparently with the consent of the Indians although this region was well within a league of the village. On October 5, Durán de Armijo was given possession by Alcalde Mayor Juan García de la Mora in the presence of the Indians. After reviewing the governor's decision, the alcalde mayor designated the boundaries and in doing so named various other Spanish land-holders close to the pueblos.

> In view of which his Excellency provides that he shall not have the lands he cites in the said petition, but that which may be selected with the consent of the Indians, and I, the said alcalde mayor, as above, informed of his Excellency's order and of all which had been agreed upon with the

said Vicente in the presence of the said governor and captain general, they said that they would assign and did assign to the said Vicente Durán de Armijo a piece of land to the west of the said Pueblo of Nambé, on the borders of their land on the western side. A small portion is bounded by lands of the Pueblo of Pojoaque which boundary is an arroyo which runs into the Rio Nambé, which is on the south side of the said Rio Nambé, and on the east by a stone marker and a medium-sized cedar tree which is the dividing line between the lands of the pueblo and the said Vicente. On the north, this little piece is bounded by the said river and on the south by an acequia which runs along the foot of some hills, the distance being three *cordels* of fifty varas each from the said river to the said acequia. And the other piece of land which they gave to the said Armijo which is north of the said river, consists of 750 varas in width which is understood to be from east to west, and from north to south it contains 550 varas, the boundaries of which are: on the north, some stone markers along some hills which form the boundary of the lands of General Juan Paéz Hurtado; on the south, it is bounded by the river of the said pueblo; on the east the boundary is a cross on the side of the public road and the lands of the Indians of the said pueblo; and on the west, the lands of General Juan Paéz Hurtado, which boundaries are marked by several stone markers and on one of them is a holy cross which is to serve as a dividing line and boundary, of which two pieces, I gave him royal possession...

There is some evidence that three years later Durán de Armijo again laid claim to the large areas on the east and south which had been denied by Domingo de Mendoza. A document signed by Alcalde Mayor Juan José Lovato on July 21, 1742, stated that Lovato, at the request of Durán de Armijo, had reopened the case since the Nambé Indians had agreed that their original complaint was made only through the "malice of the Indian Juan Xucá and that they thereupon agreed to let Durán de Armijo plant in the area, and kept only the "Salto de Agua", obviously the famous Nambé Falls.[18] While the document itself appears to be genuine, there is serious question as to its legality since it was never deposited in the archives and was only produced before the Surveyor-General in 1873 by claimants of Gaspar Ortiz to lands east of Nambé at the same time as several completely spurious documents were introduced. The matter was not referred to the governor as would have been a requirement if a decision of the chief executive had been reversed in a case involving Indian land, and the document contained no witnessing signatures or marks by the Indians of Nambé who had allegedly agreed to its contents.

There are no other records that Vicente Durán de Armijo actually occupied any land in the area, including the two small tracts. His death occurred in Santa Fe in 1743, and his will, dated November 15, listed his real property as consisting only of his home and piece of farming land on the south side of the Santa Fe River.[19] Before his death, however, Vicente may have conveyed the property to his oldest son, Salvador Manuel De Armijo I, since Nambé church records show that the latter was a resident of that jurisdiction between 1748 and 1754.[20] By the end of the century, the land had apparently come into possession of the Ortiz family.

Documentary information concerning the Pueblo of Nambé is sparse throughout the remainder of the Spanish and Mexican periods. However, the Oritzes continued to petition, and to be denied, land at the pueblo's expense. On September 15, 1842, a Luis Ortiz, resident of the jurisdiction of San Ildefonso, appealed to Governor Manuel Armijo that he and seven others be given a grant to farming lands "halfway between the pueblos of Nambé and Tesuque, which extends from the place called the Arroyo del Venado to the Peñasco." There was no question but that this area was Pueblo land even though Ortiz claimed that it was unoccupied and that he and his partners "would not deprive the adjoining pueblos nor the residents of their pastures and watering places." Ortiz claimed that in 1840 the petitioners had presented their case before the subprefect of the jurisdiction who had informed them that the prefect had agreed that their claim was valid but that nothing had been done to give them possession. Armijo sent the petition to the Prefect of the Northern Jurisdiction, legally-minded Juan Andrés Archuleta, with a notation on the side of the document that a report of the affair should be made to him. Archuleta appended his reply on October 10, stating that the original petition had been investigated in 1840, when the claims of Ortiz were found to be "a fraud" since the Pueblo of Nambé had presented its documents to him showing that the land belonged to the Indians, and he concluded bluntly that "the claim which they make should be silenced." In compliance with further instruction from Armijo for an official settlement of the business, Archuleta appended a brief decision to the original document on October 13 that a complete investigation had been made and that "there is no authority for what this party asks."[21]

With the occupation of New Mexico by the United States in 1846, the long period of official protection of Pueblo Indian land and water right virtually came to an end as entirely different systems of Indian administration and land tenure policy were introduced by the new sovereignty. The Treaty of Guadalupe Hidalgo, signed in 1848, provided that property rights which were valid under Spain and Mexico were to be recognized as valid under the United States, but the courts were unfamiliar with Spanish-Mexican titles under a land grant system which had been more than 150 years in the making in New Mexico. For eight years, the federal government failed to act on land title, and for a much longer period of time it failed to define the status of the Pueblo Indians, and there was no consistent policy of administration. Indian superintendents, agents and other federal officials until after 1876 consistently considered the Pueblos as wards of the government under the Non-Intercourse Act of 1834, but Congress permitted a law passed by the New Mexico general assembly in 1847 incorporating the Pueblos as entities who could sue and be sued to be kept in the statutes.

Until the creation of the Office of Surveyor-General in 1854, confusion in land title reigned. Obviously, the Hispanic residents were particularly troubled lest their grant titles be disturbed. There is evidence that many Anglo speculators moved into New Mexico and conducted a systematic campaign to make the residents uneasy about their land, especially since many of them did not have original grant papers. While the Hispanos were afraid of the new laws, the Pueblo Indians were unaware of them. The problem became so acute that on July 22, 1854, Congress created the Office of the Surveyor-General to investigate the origin and nature of land grant claims, segregate land documents from the official archives for examination and hear the petitions of claimants, both Hispano and Indian. If the Surveyor-General considered that a grant had been legally made under the laws of Spain or Mexico, and in continuous occupation by descendants of grantees or their legitimate successors, he was to recommend that the land be confirmed to the petitioners. Upon congressional confirmation, the land was to be surveyed and patent given. But many genuine papers had been lost; others had been manufactured; old grants long since disallowed as encroachments on Indian land were revived and often conveyed or partly conveyed to speculators, including the attorneys who usually represented their clients for a share of the undivided land in the case of settlement grants, or who bought out the claimants. Grants which were most dubious in the light of Spanish and Mexican laws were often quickly approved as the Surveyors-General were unfamiliar with the laws of the former sovereignties and some of them actually were involved in the speculation. Four-square league grants were made to many of the pueblos on the basis of the so-called "Cruzate grants" of 1689, confirmed by Congress and patent given. But overlapping Spanish grant claims within the Indian patents were sometimes also allowed.

In the cases of "United States vs. Santistevan" and "United States vs. Joseph" in 1874, the United States District Court held that since the Pueblo Indians had been citizens of Mexico, their rights were upheld by the Treaty of Guadalupe Hidalgo, and hence they were not Indian tribes in the sense of the 1834 act, and there could be no federal penalty for settling on their lands. They would, therefore, have to file their cases against trespass in the regular courts. The decision was upheld by the U.S. Supreme Court in 1876.

The Pueblo Indians, now considered as citizens who could hire their own attorneys, were in an even more precarious position when the Court of Private Land Claims was created in 1891 to settle those land grants not completed under the Surveyor-General or confirmed by Congress. In the meantime, reforming Surveyor-General George W. Julian had, in 1886, disallowed many of the decisions of his predecessors on the grounds of illegality or fraud. Again, the encroaching grants which had been disallowed by Julian were revived and some of them approved. Meanwhile, claims of non-Indians in the territorial courts were allowed in greater number. No federal protection was secured until the Sandoval Case of 1914 when the U.S. Supreme Court overturned the 1876 decision and decreed that Pueblo Indians were Indians under the 1834 act and thus under the wardship of the federal government. Unfortunately, however, the pueblos had already lost many of their lands in district courts through unfavorable decisions.[22]

The Pueblo of Nambé submitted a petition before the Surveyor-General on September 29, 1856. She requested only recognition of her minimum four-square league stating that the pueblo was unable to produce any documents as the papers had been surrendered to an acting governor some years before in a case of trespass and had not been returned.[23] If this was the case, the loss must have been at a relatively recent date, since Prefect Juan Andrés Archuleta had notified Governor Armijo in 1842 that Nambé had produced her documents of possession two years before when he had originally investigated the request of Luis Ortiz for a grant between Nambé and Tesuque. The Surveyor-General promptly approved the request of October 2, and Congress confirmed a four-square league grant

98

December 22, 1858. The survey was completed in June 1859, but patent was not issued until 1864, when 13,586.33 acres only were approved, about 4,000 acres fewer than a four-square league.

Meanwhile, also in 1859, descendants of Gaspar Ortiz petitioned for approval of the grant made to Durán de Armijo in 1739, claiming that the land had been sold to Gaspar Ortiz I, but that the conveyance had been lost. They submitted as documentation the original request and decision of the governor allowing the two small tracts west of the pueblo, but denying a larger grant to the east. Ignoring this part of the record, the petitioners laid claim to the larger eastern tract. On July 3, 1859, one month after the Nambé survey, Surveyor-General William Pelham approved the Ortiz petition, following the 1739 decision of Governor Domingo de Mendoza, and allowed the western tracts only, although even this small acreage was an overlap with the Nambé grant.[24] Congress confirmed on June 20, 1860, but the survey was delayed for several years.

During these years, white trespass on lands of all the Pueblos increased. A detailed enumeration of non-Indians on Pueblo lands, prepared by Indian Agent W.F.M. Arny in 1870, showed that there were 175 persons encroaching on the patented lands of Nambé.[25] The Pueblos knew little about attorneys, court procedures, or adverse claims. Nambé was especially vulnerable, since her population was very small and lived even further apart from the white population than many of the other pueblos. Hence, when the rival branches of the Ortiz family presented their petitions to the Surveyor-General in 1872 and 1873 for land east of the peublo, including the "Salto de Agua" or Nambé Falls, no voice was raised in defense of the rights of the Nambé Indians who were then using the land as they had used it for generations.

On September 2, 1872, the heirs of a Juan Luis Ortiz, through attorneys S.B. Elkins and Thomas B. Catron, petitioned for a very large grant to the lands east of the Pueblo, requesting the following boundaries:

On the east by a high mountain called Mosca or the descents of Panchuela; on the west a quarter of a league below the 'Salto de Agua', on the east a small flat hill or a cañada of little springs and some arroyos that run north to west, and on the south by a rocky hill above the Rito Chupadero, or the boundary of the residents of the Rio de Tesuque.

The petitioners claimed that a grant had been made to Juan Luis by

99

Governor Manuel Armijo on June 4, 1846 and that they had been placed in occupation of the tract, which they had continuously occupied, by a José Dolores Trujillo, "supplemental alcalde" of Pojoaque. Surveyor-General James K. Proudfit, without examining any witnesses or investigating the genuineness of the documents, approved the grant October 8, 1872.[26]

On September 27, 1873, however, the Gaspar Oritz heirs, through their attorneys Fiske, Stevens, and Tompkins, filed a new claim for the area originally requested by Durán de Armijo in 1739, claiming that other documents which proved their title had been recently discovered by Jesús María Ortiz y Baca in the effects of his deceased father, Matías Ortiz, executor of the estate of Gaspar Ortiz II, which proved their title. Among these was the alleged Juan José Lovato decision of 1742. They also introduced a set of documents dated 1806, which purported to be a copy of a sale by the heirs of Durán de Armijo to Gaspar Ortiz I of all their lands in the Nambé region and an alleged regrant of the eastern claim made by Acting Governor Joaquín del Real Alencaster on July 21, 1806. A sketch map showed that they claimed over 100,000 acres. These papers were clumsy forgeries. However, Surveyor-General Proudfit approved this "grant" on April 22, 1874, even though it was virtually the same area which he had approved to the Juan Luis Ortiz claimants two years before.[27]

Congressional confirmation was delayed, and on December 27, 1876, Fiske, Stevens, and Tompkins, now part owners of the Gaspar Ortiz claim, reopened the cases before Surveyor-General H.M. Atkinson over the objection of Attorney Thomas B. Catron, a part owner of the Juan Luis Ortiz claim. While several witnesses testified that the signatures of Governor Armijo and Secretary of Government Juan Bautista Vigil y Alarid were genuine, Donaciano Vigil, former military secretary to Armijo, testified that they were forgeries and produced genuine documents signed by Armijo. One of the witnesses who testified that he believed the signatures were genuine was Joab Houghton, former Chief Justice of the territorial supreme court and U.S. trader in New Mexico before occupation, but even he agreed that the signatures were a bit unusual. When queried by Attorney Catron as to whether the apparent difference in handwriting might result from Armijo's use of a steel pen instead of a quill, Houghton reluctantly admitted that while he had introduced steel pens into the region in 1843, he had never known of a Mexican official using one.[28] In addition, Jesús María Ortiz y

Baca produced the alcalde books of Pojoaque which showed that Trujillo had never held the position of supplemental alcalde.

Neither grant was approved, but the two small tracts on the west were surveyed for 57.13 acres in March 1877 and patent delivered to the Gaspar Ortiz claimants.[29]

Surveyor-General George W. Julian, successor to Atkinson, reviewed the many cases approved by his predecessors but not confirmed by Congress, utilizing especially the research of handwriting expert Will N. Tipton. He rejected the claims of both factions of the Ortiz family on the basis that the documents in both cases had been forged.

The Juan Luis Ortiz claim was re-introduced into the Court of Private Land Claims by Catron and a favorable decision rendered on December 1, 1896 for confirmation of a tract not to exceed 11 square leagues. The land claimed was approximately 115,200 acres. Justice Murray dissented, however, on the ground that he considered the 1846 documents fraudulent. The government appealed the case to the United States Supreme Court, which decided against the Catron-Ortiz plaintiffs in the October term of 1899, and the land was ordered returned to the public domain.[30]

Again, Nambé was not represented before the Court of Private Land Claims, and hence no notice was taken of Indian use and occupancy of the land which had been claimed in the Sierra de Mosca grant, although the pueblo was actually leasing a portion of it to non-Indians. In the spring of 1902, one of the lessees, Juan Tafoya, not only refused to pay his rent but was planning to file on the land which had been declared public domain after the Supreme Court decision. Nambé appealed to Special Attorney for the Pueblos, William H. Pope, who strongly recommended to the Commissioner of Indian Affairs that sections in Township 19 North, Range 10 East, on the southeast of the pueblo grant boundary, including Nambé Falls, be withdrawn from public entry and made into a pueblo reservation since "This Pueblo is one of the poorest in the Territory and has been encroached upon by adjoining settlers to an extent such that probably not a third of their Congressional confirmation remains in their possession."[31] He also pointed out that the Indians had been in continuous possession of the land for many years. On the recommendation of Acting Commissioner of Indian Affairs A.C. Tonner,[32] the Commissioner of the General Land Office withdrew the area temporarily while C.J. Crandall, Superintendent of the Indian School at Santa Fe, was authorized by Tonner to investigate the situation. In his extensive report of June 5, Crandall strongly recommended that the area be made into a reservation since "The lands held by these people is less than one half of their original grant." After noting that the Indians had cultivated a portion of the region for many years, he concluded:

> The Indians need this land to better put them in shape to make a living; the simple fact that is will be a reservation, and the title will not be in fee simple, assures to the Indians lands that cannot be taken away from them and lands which they cannot dispose of, as they have done with much of their original grant. As you know, most of the land which Mr. Pope asks to have reserved here, was until recently what was known as a land grant, but the Land Court did not confirm the same, and it therefore > becomes a part of the public domain. The Indians have cultivated or leased this land to other parties for some time, as represented by Mr. Pope, and they have felt that it belonged to them.33

Local opposition, led by New Mexico Territorial Delegate to Congress, Bernard S. Rodey, quickly arose, as other non-Indians were intending to file on the land, especially for mining claims.34 However, the small reservation was given to Nambé in 1902, but it required the presence of U.S. troops to actually remove the lessees who had refused to pay the pueblo rent for the lands they were cultivating.35

Further attempts to secure additional acreage for Nambé, even as executive order reservation, had little success. Indian Bureau officials were keenly aware of the need to secure more grazing lands for all the pueblos, but the failure of the Department of Agriculture to understand the status or needs of the Pueblos and its consistent support of the interests of non-Indians resulted in refusal to surrender to the Department of the Interior grazing lands within the recently created national forests which the Indians sorely needed. The Assistant Commissioner of Indian Affairs, on December 14, 1910, submitted to the Department of the Interior a detailed proposal to eliminate certain lands from the Jemez and Pecos National Forests for proposed additions, to San Juan, Pojoaque, San Ildefonso, Santa Clara, and Nambé. Four years of correspondence, often heated in nature, resulted between the Departments of the Interior and Agriculture, but opposition on the part of the latter caused the plan to be abandoned in 1914.36

The Pueblo Lands Board, created by Act of Congress, June 7, 1924, to settle the question of extinguishment of title on Indian land, issued its final report concerning Nambé August 12, 1926.

The Board determined that Indian title within the Nambé grant had been extinguished to most of the agricultural tracts immediately west of the village but awarded to the Indians several small tracts on the east.[37]

In November 1965, the United States Indian Claims Commission rendered its decision that the Pueblo of Nambé was entitled to payment for 45,000 acres within the Santa Fe National Forest to which it had claim by right of aboriginal use. Some measure of justice for the small pueblo was finally secured four years later when Congress appropriated the necessary funds for compensation.[38]

NOTES

1. For summaries of the early history of Nambé see: Frederick W. Hodge, George P. Hammond and Agapito Rey, eds., *Fray Alonso de Benavides' Revised Memorial of 1634* (University of New Mexico Press, Albuquerque, 1945):236; Eleanor B. Adams and Fray Angelico Chavez, *The Missions of New Mexico, 1776* (University of New Mexico Press, Albuquerque, 1956):52.

2. Charles W. Hackett and C.C. Shelby, eds., *Revolt of the Pueblo Indians of New Mexico and Otermin's Attempted Reconquest, 1680-1682* (University of New Mexico Press, Albuquerque, 1942) 1:10, 96, 109; Charles W. Hackett, ed., *Historical Documents Relating to New Mexico, Nueva Vizcaya, and Approaches thereto, to 1773* (Government Printing Office, Washington, 1937) 3:329, 336, 352.

3. J. Manuel Espinosa, *First Expedition of Vargas into New Mexico, 1692* (University of New Mexico Press, Albuquerque, 1940):138-139.

4. J. Manuel Espinosa, *Crusaders of the Rio Grande* (Institute of Jesuit History, Chicago, 1942):164, 167, 277, 209-210.

5. *Ibid.:*244-247, 250-260, 296.

6. Hackett 1937:375.

7. Adams and Chavez 1956:52.

8. Hackett 1937:466.

9. Eleanor B. Adams, *Bishop Tamaron's Visitation of New Mexico, 1760* (University of New Mexico Press, Albuquerque, 1954):55.

10. Adams and Chavez 1956:58-59.

11. *Ibid.:*60.

12. *Ibid.:*59.

13. For a discussion of grants in this area see Myra Ellen Jenkins, Spanish Land Grants in the Tewa Area, *New Mexico Historical Review* (1972) 47:117-123.

14. For a discussion of land tenure policies of the Spanish government with reference to Indian land see *Ibid.*:113-117.

15. A brief sketch of the Durán de Armijo family is found in Fray Angelico Chavez, *Origins of New Mexico Families in the Colonial Period* (Historical Society of New Mexico, Santa Fe, 1954):36.

16. Jenkins 1972:117.

17. The petition and other documents in this case are in Records of the Surveyor-General, #31, Gaspar Ortiz, State Records Center, Santa Fe, hereafter cited as SG, SRC. The land grant records consisting of the documents listed in Ralph Emerson Twitchell, *The Spanish Archives of New Mexico*, vol. 1, and the records of both the Surveyor-General and its successor, the Court of Private Land Claims, were in the custody of the Bureau of Land Management, Department of the Interior, Santa Fe, until April 10, 1972, when they were transferred to the custody of the State Records Center, Santa Fe.

18. This document is in SG #87, Sierra Mosca Grant, SRC.

19. Spanish Archives of New Mexico, I, #26, SRC.

20. Chavez 1954:137.

21. This document is contained in the papers of one of the attorneys representing the Ortiz family and is in the custody of the State Records Center. It was apparently not utilized or filed in the land grant litigation.

22. For a detailed analysis of the status of Pueblo Indians during these years see Myra Ellen Jenkins, The Baltasar Baca "Grant," History of An Encroachment, *El Palacio* (1961) 68:87-96.

23. SG #R, SRC.

24. SG #31, Gaspar Ortiz, SRC.

25. National Archives, Department of the Interior, Records of the Bureau of Indian Affairs, Record Group 75, Field Papers, Michigan Superintendency, 1854-1871. Hereafter these records will be cited as NA, BIA, RG 75.

26. This case is SG #75, Juan Luis Ortiz or Sierra Mosca, SRC.

27. SG #87, Gaspar Ortiz, also entitled Sierra Mosca, SRC.

28. *Ibid.*

29. SG #31, SRC.

30. Court of Private Land Claims, #87, Sierra de Mosca, SRC.

31. Pope to Commissioner of Indian Affairs, April 4, 1902, NA, BIA, RG 75, Letters Received (LR), File 2328-1902.

32. Tonner to Commissioner of General Land Office, May 9, 1902, NA, Department of the Interior, Records of the General Land Office, RG 49, Miscellaneous Letters Received, File 81142-1902.

33. Included in Tonner to Secretary of the Interior, June 13, 1902, NA, Records of the Office of the Secretary of the Interior, RG 48, LR, File 5262-1902.

34. The objections of Rodey and other opponents are outlined in Crandall to Commissioner of Indian Affairs, August 8, 1902, NA, BIA, RG 75, LR, File 47966-1902.

35. *Santa Fe New Mexican,* November 16, 1903.

36. Correspondence and other documents pertaining to the relations between the Departments of the Interior and Agriculture concerning the proposed reservation are contained in NA, BIA, RG 75, File 4687-1-308.2, S.F., part 3.

37. The final report of the Pueblo Lands Board is in the files of the Bureau of Land Management, the Department of the Interior, Santa Fe Office, Santa Fe, New Mexico.

38. U.S. Indian Claims Commission, "Pueblo of Nambe vs. the United States," Docket 358.

Myra Ellen Jenkins received her B.A. and M.A. degrees at the University of Colorado and her Ph.D. in history at the University of New Mexico. She presently is Chief, Historical Services Division and State Historian in the State of New Mexico Records Center and is a member of the New Mexico Cultural Properties Review Committee. Among her many publications are The Baltasar Baca "Grant," History of an Encroachment, *El Palacio* (1961); The Pueblo of Taos and Its Neighbors, *New Mexico Historical Review* (1966); Spanish Land Grants in the Tewa Area, *New Mexico Historical Review* (1972); *Guide and Calendar to the Spanish Archives of New Mexico* (1967); and *Guide and Calendar to the Mexican Archives of New Mexico* (1970).

MEXICAN INDEPENDENCE DAY AND A UTE TRAGEDY IN SANTA FE, 1844[1]

Ward Alan Minge

In these moments, I saw myself attacked by all the chieftains, taking up their weapons as had the said Panasiyave, who turned on me with an axe in his hand; fortunately, I was able to hit him with the chair in which I had been seated and with which I knocked him to the floor, at the same time two of my orderlies and other officials, who had arrived by accident, restrained not only the remaining five Indians but also other large numbers who started through the window of the room.

Governor Martínez to the Inhabitants
Santa Fe, September 8, 1844

[Author's trans.]

On July 28, 1844, Governor Mariano Martínez de Lejanza appointed a "Patriotic Council" to arrange for celebrating the anniversary of Mexican Independence in Santa Fe. He was new to New Mexico, having arrived the previous fall from Chihuahua and, under the sponsorship of Governor Mariano Monterde of that Department, replaced Manuel Armijo as governor. The elaborate plans and preparations required a month and a half and involved solemn sessions, complex committee arrangements, and donations of money, talent, and labor. The formal and beautifully written minutes of the council meetings testified not only to the Governor's loyalties but also to the popular esteem and enthusiasm for the forthcoming pageant.[2]

During the first session, the Council members selected a president and secretary. The Vicar Juan Felipe Ortiz met their unanimous choice for president and the office of secretary fell to Bernardo Vázquez Franco.[3] Vicar Ortiz then proceeded to name four committees: one to obtain funds, another to organize the public diversions, a third to arrange for firing weapons to achieve the "most glorious effect," and the last to arrange for religious ceremonies. Council meetings were scheduled on Sunday mornings between ten and eleven. The committee for public diversions then asked the Governor to deliver the main address. Within a few days, however, Governor Mariano Martínez turned that responsibility over to the Vicar because his elegant and serious style befitted an occasion recalling the heroes of independence.4

At the August session, they created additional committees and outlined the program. One group was named to receive voluntary subscriptions, and another was formed to invite proprietory citizens to lend their dignity and support to the national fiesta. It was also decided to construct a temple to Mexican Independence. On August 16, the Council members discussed the possibility of a bullfight, after which the committee of public diversions proposed a program for approval.

(1) The eve would open with the customary serenade on the principal plaza, and at nine o'clock the religious buildings would be illuminated inside and out. At eleven, the pealing of bells, artillery salvos, and fireworks would announce "with jubilee the moment when national independence was proclaimed by the immortal Hildago in the village of Dolores."

(2) On the morning of the 16th, the musicians of the garrison would sound reveille (*romperán las Dianas*) in front of the Palace of the Governors; and with artillery salvos, the national flag would be raised on all the public buildings followed by a general pealing of bells. At seven, masses would be celebrated in all the chapels. At nine, the Governor and all the civil and military authorities would pass to the church where the Vicar would celebrate mass in an act of thanks culminating with a solemn *Te Deum*. From there the Governor and the President of the Departmental Assembly with all the company would return to the plaza where they would lay the first stone of a monument to be erected in commemoration of the day's purpose. Then they would proceed to the Palace to hold a reception. In the afternoon, the Governor was to lead the public in a promenade to the Temple in the Alameda to hear a public address for the occasion.

(3) During the afternoon, military musicians, acrobats, and rope walkers worked along the Alameda; and fireworks were scheduled at eight that night. After this there would also be a serenade followed by a retreat ceremony with the musicians. Then there would follow the public dances in the Palace and elsewhere for the public diversion.

(4) Bullfights would be held after the anniversary on days to be designated by the Governor, the President of the Patriotic Council, and the Secretary.5

108

The Vicar Ortiz invited Felix Zubia and Bernardo Franco to discuss with him the matter of constructing the temple and locating a qualified artisan. He also selected members for two more committees. This time one attended to the dances, decorations, refreshments, and music; the other took responsibility for the Plaza de Toros. They also decided that the Pueblo Indians should be invited to dance; and the Vicar addressed formal invitations to the governors of Tesuque, Nambé, San Ildefonso, Taos, Santo Domingo, San Felipe, and Cochití on the same day. Stating the purpose of his request in florid style, he ended by asking the Indians to come dressed in their best adornments, declaring that their acceptance would earn the Council's eternal gratitude.[6]

The seventh session of the Council met on August 5. The second committee announced that all its plans were being put into effect, but the third committee complained that artisans could not be found to operate the fireworks. The sixth committee secured five bulls from Justo Pino and "Señor Montoya." The eighth committee needed to know the date of the fights so posters might be readied to notify the public. The Vicar decided that the fights should be held within three days after September 18, and the Council ended by inviting the Pueblos of Jémez and Santa Ana to dance with the other Pueblos invited earlier.[7]

By August 29, Santa Fe hummed with activity. The temple under construction cost 125 pesos. It would be covered with red, white, and green bunting and illuminated at night.[8]

Earlier in the week, the Governór had granted a request from residents of the First District[9] to trade with Utes. But a few days later, Martínez received bad news from the same district. Colonel Juan Andrés Archuleta reported by *violento* that Utes were collecting in large numbers near Abiquiu. The day before, under escort of Captain José Francisco Vigil and Lieutenant José María Chávez, the Ute Chieftain Panicillo came to Colonel Archuleta to press deep grievances and claims against the Mexican citizens of that region. He claimed the past winter a company of volunteers of *rurales* killed three Ute Indians while making a foray against the Navajo tribe. Later, the same group attacked a *ranchería,* killing seven Utes and taking "members of their families and possessions which they had in their houses and also their horses..." For these trespasses the Chieftain demanded "two small children and two small boys," sons of Ute Indians, in the possession of Mexican citizens. In compensation for the ten men killed, they would be satisfied with ten

109

horses, ten serapes, and ten bridles. Such a settlement, he claimed, would placate his people; and they would "forget all their sorrows and remain peaceful forever." Colonel Archuleta's report ended with a warning that the Indians would wait only two days for an answer and a reminder that there were only a few troops to withstand the multitudes surrounding them.[10]

While Santa Fe went on preparing for the celebrations, Utes moved into the vicinity of Abiquiu to the edges of the fields causing all work to stop. On September 4, the Governor notified the Justice at Abiquiu to do whatever he could to hold off the Utes near that place.[11] The Justice informed Martinez that the Utes were in an ugly mood, that Prefect Archuleta had been unable to settle the problem, and that Panasiyave and his Utes planned to march on the capital the next day, September 5. "I prepared to receive them as customary," the Governor later explained in a manifesto, "placing at their disposal a house for lodging, sheep, bread, and tobacco, along with some other things for their pleasure."[12]

According to Martinez, six Ute chiefs and 108 warriors arrived in Santa Fe on the afternoon of September 5, well armed and mounted on good horses. Their appearance caused uneasiness about the town; and he ordered them to retire for the night, placing a guard around their camp. On the following morning around ten o'clock, they entered the plaza with loaded guns, asked for their horses, refused the food prepared for them, and threw the government's gifts into the street. Soon they indicated a desire to speak with the Governor, and he invited the chieftains into the Palace.

There they complained in disgust that they had been given little of what they asked for, and the Governor subsequently related on September 8:

> For this reason, I consented to concede to them some additional things they asked for but still not contented they insisted that they should be given more. They made much evidence of their excitement in vehement terms, such as when the Chieftain Panasiyave explair. d that he had said before that he did not understand our language. At this stage seeing that they would not conform to my wishes, I ordered them to retire until they reached a decision about what more they should want and then return. I hoped in this way that they would calm themselves. This method produced worse excitement among the six chieftains with whom I talked, because all at once they broke into the most intolerable, inhuman insults for a long while until they all stood up and Panasiyave approached me with the same insults and beat me on the chest for which reason I

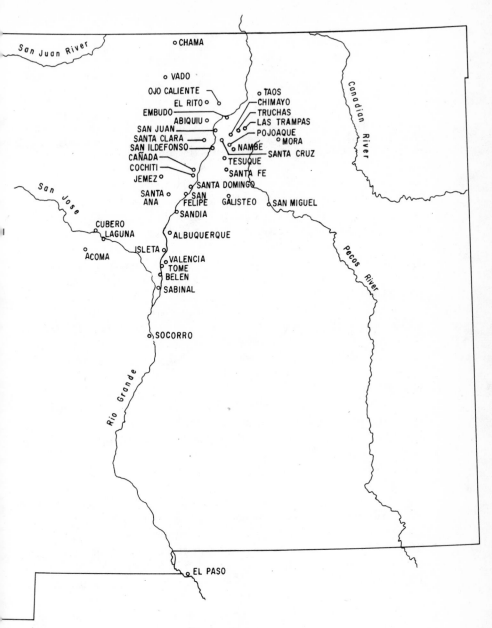

Locales in Northern New Mexico

111

gave him a push toward the door. In these moments, I saw myself attacked by all the chieftains, taking up their weapons as had the said Panasiyave, who turned on me with an axe in his hand; fortunately, I was able to hit him with the chair in which I had been seated and with which I knocked him to the floor, at the same time two of my orderlies and other officials, who had arrived by accident, restrained not only the remaining five Indians but also other large numbers who started through the window of the room. Under these circumstances, the guard of honor and various citizens, seeing the resistance and effrontery of the enemy and his hostile action, commenced a fight ending in eight deaths, in spite of everything I could do to stop this tragedy. (Author's Trans.)

After wounding three Mexicans, the remaining Utes escaped but were pursued through the streets. The Indians fired and destroyed everything in their camp as they passed through into the hills, although they were followed closely by 50 troops dragging an artillery piece. The Governor immediately sent word to the Prefect Archuleta advising him to attend to the defense of Abiquiu and any other village which Utes might attack. He also alerted citizens of the whole Department to prepare for war.12

In spite of all this excitement, the Patriotic Council held its regular session on September 8 when the members argued about the masses and religious ceremonies to be contributed by the Vicar. At length that worthy consented to hold services on the 16th and 17th, although he complained about the shortage of wax and the expense of having the religious perform on both days. Felipe Sena reported that Francisco Nava had contracted to furnish music for the principal dance. The meeting closed with the decision to send José Antonio Chávez a special invitation to contribute to the glorious celebration of Independence.14

At the juncture, over 3,000 Ute warriors were estimated on the warpath in the First District. Abiquiu was particularly harassed, and the Governor ordered Colonel Archuleta to defend that place with 100 well-armed men.15 Meanwhile, he dispatched Lieutenant Tomás Armijo, a nephew of ex-governor Manuel Armijo, with 60 troops and three artillery pieces from the capital. The largest gun was for Abiquiu and the other two for Ojo Caliente and El Rito. The Lieutenant also carried 120 muskets with orders to issue 40 in each of the three villages.16

By separate letter, the Governor advised that despite the arrangements of the Patriotic Council the Pueblo Indians would omit their dances from the celebrations, because the defense of the First District might suffer.17 On Tuesday, September 10, the Governor

112

shipped 15 guns, 15 carbines, and 50 packs of cartridges to Taos.[18] On the following day, he sent to Chihuahua for 200 muskets.[19]

At the same time, the Patriotic Council pursued its charge and met on September 12, at which date everything seemed to be in readiness. However, José Antonio Chávez responded to the special invitation with a contribution of only five *pesos*.[20] The members proceeded with a discussion about food and lodging for those Indians who would appear for the dances, since they were not involved in the Ute fracas. After deciding that the Indians would most likely bring some things for themselves, the Council purchased 30 sheep at nine *reales* each from Justo Pino and furnished these along with wood, bread, and salt. Agents had gone to San Miguel del Vado, Cubero, and Galisteo for the bulls, but the eighth committee reported its failure to secure rope for use in the Plaza de Toros. An account of the expenses anticipated for the religious ceremonies included 100 wax candles at two reales each and 30 pesos for the priests assisting the Vicar. Finally the seventh committee reported its decision to spend ten pesos on a platform for the musicians at the main dance and submitted an invoice to cover all expenses for the dances. There had been nails and 180 tallow candles to buy, servants to hire at three pesos each, invitations to print, as well as the decorations and refreshments.

The committee planned to offer cakes, cookies, and candy, along with 43 bottles of wine and 25 bottles of aguardiente. The menu included *marquesotes* made of sugar, almond, and eggs; *puches* of sugar, eggs, flour, anis, and *aguardiente; coronas* made of flour, sugar, *aguardiente,* red, blue, and gold coloring; *soletas* of eggs, sugar, and almond; *encaladillos* of flour, sugar, and wine; *dulces* made with sugar and eggs; and *biscochos de regalo* made with flour, sugar, lard, and butter. The wine and *aguardiente* were combined with sugar and cinnamon, coffee and spices for punch and *mistelas.* For the preparation of refreshments the council paid 40 *pesos*.[21]

Simultaneously, the Assembly met and discussed items related to the coming celebration. They blamed the Town Council for its lack of cooperation, particularly in policing the city and cleaning the streets and markets. Without restraint, citizens tethered animals along the portals or allowed them to graze in the plazas. Worst of all the Council allowed the bodies of the dead Utes to lie unburied and that fetidness, mingled with the stench of dead dogs and garbage, had begun to infest the city. The Assembly adjourned after discussing a pavilion of their own construction where they planned

113

to meet on the 16th and 17th at nine o'clock each morning.²²

Meanwhile, the attack upon Abiquiu subsided, but word of impending attacks spread along the northern borders as far east as Las Vegas.²³ From the west Colonel Francisco Sarracino sent word that the Navajo Chieftain Narbona had offered to help hold off the Utes along the frontier at Abiquiu. Governor Martinez, undoubtedly concerned about an attempt made by Navajos and Utes to unite during July in an all-out campaign against the Mexicans, advised the Colonel only to guard Jémez against possible attack.²⁴

Although Las Vegas was sufficiently warned, the citizens lacked enough arms. The Governor could only promise a shipment when those expected from Rio Abajo or Chihuahua arrived.²⁵ At this point, on September 26, residents of Taos suggested that the Governor send protection to the haciendas along the northern borders. If the Utes were checked along that line, they could be starved into submission as it was too late for buffalo hunting. Otherwise, the area from Taos to Lo de Mora and Las Vegas was open to pillaging. They thought that a guard of 100 men at Ocaté could block the passage into the Lo de Mora–Las Vegas region.²⁶

On the first of October, detachments were in place at Abiquiu, El Rito, and Ojo Caliente, with the greater concentration of troops and auxiliaries at Abiquiu. The latter volunteers alternated every 15 days to help at home with the corn harvest. A cannon was at Abiquiu, but the firearms were mostly useless requiring the constant attention of a gunsmith.²⁷

In the meantime the Independence Day fiesta took place and was enjoyed by all not preoccupied with matters of defense. The 13th and final session of the Patriotic Council convened on October 13, primarily to settle its accounts. Strangely enough, they had bottles of wine and *aguardiente* left over, and forty wax candles had not been burned in the church ceremonies. Three bulls proved useless in the *corridas* and remained to be sold. The Vicar decided to retain the extra money for independence celebrations in 1845. Jesús Maria Porras then explained that the Independence Day temple cost more than the 125 pesos originally planned and that the Governor provided the extra money to complete construction. Some of the unusual expenses included eight pesos for paper and printing tickets, three pesos to Captain Francisco Baca for putting up the decorations, and three pesos, four reales, to Ramón Sandoval and Teófilo (no last name given) to pay for two lost benches and three broken ones. There had been only two dances, the principal one and another for the people and troops. Vicar Ortiz closed the session with congratulations and thanks to all the Council and a written report to Governor Martínez.[28]

During the first week in October, the greatest concentration of Utes moved down to San Ysidro below Jémez in the Second District. From Jémez on October 6, the Governor heard that the Navajo Chieftains Narbona and Cayetano had withdrawn their allegiance to join the Utes in a possible attack on that point. He immediately warned the Pueblos to ready their defenses for surprise attacks. He offered no aid, because the troops were deployed on the northern borders.[30] At the same time the Governor again called on all the districts to prepare themselves so as not to be taken unawares by the enemy.[31]

On October 10, Navajos and Utes together attacked along the old Spanish Trail, and the Governor ordered Colonel Sarracino to gather 100 men, probably *rurales,* to retrieve what was stolen and to punish the Indians.[32] Galisteo also suffered raids, but the troops out of San Miguel del Vado chased off the Indians.[33]

The fall and winter of 1844-1845 must have been a bitter experience for Governor Martínez. Early in December, he found it necessary to dispense over 1,000 pesos worth of food to various groups of allied Navajos, Jicarillas, Comanches, and Utes as they appeared in Santa Fe.[34] To the north, the Chihuahua pickets complained of the cold and lacked shoes and clothing.[35] The Governor promised to help when he received goods and supplies for that purpose.[36] Other resources were scarce; and at least on one occasion, when the Departmental Treasury ran out of funds, it was replenished by a personal loan from the Governor himself.[37]

Ute raids continued sporadically throughout the winter. On the morning of January 21, 1845, some 60 warriors launched a severe attack at Ojo Caliente, leaving four Mexicans dead and five badly wounded.[38] A few days later, they threatened Taos again; and during these latest outbreaks, the Governor began receiving word that Utes freely traded for munitions and supplies at the forts located outside the Department.[39] He also entertained a petition from foreigners to lead an expedition against the Utes. A few days later, he was both relieved and "honored" when Charles Beaubien furnished arms and provisions for the war against the Utes.[40] At this point, the Utes sued for peace; and Governor Martínez assured them that the old treaties were still valid.[41] He then instructed Colonel Archuleta that citizens residing along the borders should not be permitted to abandon the area "because of the enemy." In the face of danger, their presence was required as always to guard and to secure the frontier. Those who changed residence left at the cost of the "land granted [to] them because they were residents of the frontier."42

Despite peace overtures, still another Ute raid occurred at Abiquiu with 16 animals stolen. On April 20, Martínez instructed Colonel Archuleta that any incident caused by Utes would be cause to chase and to punish them if caught.43

The political affiliation of the Department within the Republic posed a big question early in 1845. During the first two weeks of January, Governor Martínez had received an invitation to declare for the Mexican General Mariano Paredes y Arrillaga, who led an apparently successful revolution against President Santa Anna.44 Martínez' immediate response was filled with displeasure that Santa Anna's government should be challenged, and he expressed his sentiments accordingly to the northern departments of Mexico.45 Locally, Governor Martínez immediately sought the loyalty of the troops and government officials. "I send you the declaration which the troops of this Department raised today," he wrote ex-governor Manuel Armijo, "and if your sentiments are the same as theirs, I ask that you place your signature beside mine."46 General Armijo was reluctant to sign the document. He predicted that such a gesture on the part of the troops might result in bloodshed throughout New Mexico and proposed such a declaration would put the Department in a bad light.47

Kaleidoscopic changes on the national scene meanwhile resulted in the successful revolution of General José Joaquín de Herrera. On January 21, barely a week after his efforts to support Santa Anna, General Martínez gathered military officials at the Palace in Santa Fe pledging New Mexico to the new President. During this meeting, all disavowed Santa Anna.48

During these critical days, the Departmental Treasury was empty again, and the Governor badly needed funds to pay the troops. On January 19, he sent to Chihuahua for "any amount of money" as soon as possible.49 At the end of the month, he approached the Assembly for 12,000 *pesos*. For collateral, he pledged the income anticipated from foreign trade during the coming year.50 In Taos, Charles Bent predicted: "I doubt whether the governor will get any money from this place, they appear not to be disposed to pay."51

Although the Assembly assessed the citizens for the necessary funds, Martínez failed to force the loan. From this time on, the activities of the Governor appeared completely curbed. Routine matters were handled as before, but it became clear that his days in office were soon to end. During February, he received orders for his subsequent relief as Commandant General.[52]

Various matters continued to claim the Governor's attention. In February, Ute war parties were reported in the vicinity of Las Vegas. Unidentified bandits also attacked a foreign wagon near the same place, and Martínez tried to improve the defense of that area.[53] Early in April, a foreigner by the name of Skolkin was investigated for retailing merchandise in the Department.[54] Two weeks later, the Governor arbitrated a dispute between the Jicarilla Chieftain Gipalle and citizens of Lo de Mora. The chief laid claim to a "large Navajo woman," in the possession of the justice, as well as to some swapping debts which certain citizens there failed to settle. Apparently both claims were satisfied at the wishes of the Governor.[55]

Finally on May 1, 1845, command of the troops in the Department returned to General Armijo.[56] Two days later, General Mariano Martínez was furnished an escort for the long march toward Mexico, and the office of governor devolved upon José Chávez.[57] At this moment, Ute Indians attacked the northern frontier once more, and the new Commandant General badly needed 5,000 pesos from the treasury to support the troops.[58]

Temporarily disassembled during the winter months, the Utes began to rally in force by May 1845. In alliance with Navajos, they threatened to commence a campaign against the Department, and General Armijo warned other officials early that month.[59] Until at least 1839 and 1840, New Mexican officials considered the Utes harmless, if not entirely friendly. But now simultaneously a series of attacks against Ojo Caliente and the surrounding region marked the center of Ute operations.[60] Thus, the unhappy tribe joined the growing number of Indians raiding the North Mexican frontier in the 1840's. Their problems passed to the United States by the Treaty of Guadalupe Hidalgo in 1848.

NOTES

1. The author is indebted to Lloyd H. Cornett, Jr., for reading the manuscript. He is a specialist in Plains Indian history and is currently serving as Chief Historian for Aerospace Defense Command in Colorado Springs, Colorado.

2. Secretariat to the Gentlemen listed in the Margin, Santa Fe, July 26, 1844, in Letter Book of the Secretariat, 1844; *Acta de la instalación de la Patriótica para la celebridad del anniversario de la Independencia Mejicana en la Ciudad de Santa Fe* Capital del Departamento de Nuevo Mejico el dia 16 de Setiembro de 1844, reunida en 28 de Julio de Dicho Año, Santa Fe, July 28,1844, New Mexico State Records Center (SRC). The following citizens were named to serve on the Council, specifically invited because of the "good qualities with which they have adorned their persons."

Cura Vicario Juan Felipe Ortiz
Colonel Pedro Muñoz
   (died two days later)
Felipe Sena
Antonio Sena
Jesus Maria Porras
Francisco Ortiz
Donaciano Vigil
Juan Bautista Vigil
Francisco Ortiz y Delgado
Tomas Ortiz
Benito Larrogoito
Juan Escolley (John Scolly)
Justo Pino

Santiago Armijo
Serafin Ramirez

Antonio Sena Rivera
Antonjo Jose Rivera
Agustin Duran
Antonio Matias Ortiz
Felix Zubia
Nicolas Pino
Bernardo Vázquez Franco
Jose Abreu
Francisco Martínez
Francisco Leiba
Ygnacio María Flores

3. *Acta de la instalación de la Patriótica, etc.*

4. *Acta de la instalación de la Patriótica, etc.*; Secretariat to Vicar Ortiz, Santa Fe, August 3, 1844, in Letter Book of the Secretariat, 1844.

5. *Acta de la instalación de la Patriótica, etc.*, sessions of the Patriotic Council for August 4 and 16, 1844, SRC.

6. Vicar Ortiz to the Governadorcillos of Tesuque, Nambe, San Ildefonso, Taos, Santo Domingo, San Felipe, and Cochiti, Santa Fe, August 23, 1844, SRC.

7. Minutes of the Seventh Session of the Patriotic Council, Santa Fe, August 25, 1844, SRC.

8. Minutes of the Eighth and Ninth Sessions of the Patriotic Council, Santa Fe, August 29 and September 1, 1844, SRC.

9. The First District in 1837 included the Alcaldías of Vado, Santa Fe, San Ildefonso, Cañada, Abiquiu, Ojo Caliente, San Juan, Chama, Trampas, and Taos. In 1844, a governmental reorganization by Martínez placed these towns in the District of the North which, in turn, was subdivided into two parts called Rio Arriba and Taos. The first included Santa Cruz de la Cañada, Chimayo, Quemada, Truchas, Santa Clara, Vega, Chama, Cuchillo, Abiquiu, Rito Colorado, Ojo Caliente, Ranchitos, Chamita, San Juan, Rio Arriba, Joya, and Embudo. The chief center was Los Luceros, and the population was 15,500.

10. Colonel Archuleta to the Secretariat Zubia, Rio Arriba, September 1, 1844, SRC.

11. Vicente Martínez, Justice at Abiquiu, to Martínez, September 4, 1844, in *Diario del Gobierno,* Federally sponsored newspaper published in Mexico City, December 22, 1844; Secretariat to the Justice at Abiquiu, Santa Fe, September 4, 1844, in Letter Book of the Secretariat, 1844.

12. Manifesto que el Gobernador del Departamento de Nuevo Mexico Hace á sus Habitantes, Santa Fe, September 8, 1844, NMRCAA, Prince Collection. This is the Governor's own version of his meeting with the Ute Chiefs on September 6, 1844. His recital is fortified by a letter, Donaciano Vigil to Jose Ramon Vigil, Santa Fe, September 6, 1844, NMRCAA, which describes the events of the same day. There are other accounts which are probably not quite as authentic. See Lansing B. Bloom, New Mexico Under Mexican Administration, *Old Santa Fe* (1915) 2:225; Benjamin Read, *Illustrated History of New Mexico* (New Mexican Printing Co., Santa Fe; 1912):410-411; and the account of Demetrio Perez, transcribed from testimony taken on June 22, 1903, in Manuel Alvarez Papers, 1833-1862, SRC. See also Archuleta to Felix Zubia, Rio Arriba, September 4, 1844, in *Diario del Gobierno.* December 28. 1844.

13. Secretariat to the Prefect Archuleta, Santa Fe, September 6, 1844, in Letter Book of the Secretariat, 1844; Commandant General to Inspector Archuleta, Santa Fe, September 7, 1844, in Record Book of the Commandant General, 1844; Notice of Attempted Assassination, in *Diario del Gobierno,* October 14, 1844.

14. Record of the Tenth Session of the Patriotic Council, September 8, 1844, SRC.

15. Secretariat to Justice at Abiquiu, Santa Fe, September 9, 1844, in Letter Book of the Secretariat, 1844; Commandant General to Archuleta, Santa Fe, September 9, 1844, and to Commander of the 5th Company of Auxiliaries Tomas Salazar, Santa Fe, September 9, 1844, both in Record Book of the Commandant General, 1844.

16. Commandant General to Colonel Archuleta, Santa Fe, September 9, 1844, in Record Book of the Commandant General, 1844.

17. Secretariat to Prefect Archuleta, Santa Fe, September 9, 1844, in Letter Book of the Secretariat, 1844.

18. Secretariat to Prefect Archuleta, Santa Fe, September 10, 1844, in Letter Book of the Secretariat, 1844.

19. Commandant General to Commandant General of the Department of Chihuahua, Santa Fe, September 11, 1844, in Letter Book of the Commandant General, 1844. These were probably the same 200 guns Martínez had originally requested early in June; at any rate, by September 30, General Monterde was making plans to send them on. Monterde to Martínez, Chihuahua, September 30, 1844, SRC.

20. Individuals who contributed to the patriotic function of the 16th of September 1844 averaged 11 pesos each. John Scolly gave 55 pesos, and other foreigners as well as the military participated.

21. Records of the Eleventh Session of the Patriotic Council, Santa Fe, September 12, 1844, SRC.

22. Record Book of the Assembly of the Department of New Mexico, Session of September 12, 1844, SRC.

23. Commandant to Lieutenant Tomás Armijo, Santa Fe, September 13, 1844; Commandant to Military Commander at the Port of Las Vegas, Santa Fe, September 13, 1844, both in Record Book of the Commandant General, 1844.

24. Commandant General to Prefect of the First District Archuleta, Santa Fe, July 11 and September 18, 1844; Commandant General to Colonel Sarracino, Santa Fe, September 18, 1844, all in Record Book of the Commandant General, 1844.

25. Commandant General to Lieutenant Antonio Ulibarri at Las Vegas, Santa Fe, September 19, 1844, Commandant General to Colonel Archuleta, Santa Fe, September 19, 1844, both in Record Book of the Commandant General, 1844; and Secretariat to Justice at Las Vegas, Santa Fe, September 25, 1844, in Letter Book of the Secretariat, 1844.

26. Citizens of Taos supplication to the Prefect and Inspector of Arms, Juan Andrés Archuleta, Taos, September 25, 1844, SRC. Such a plan probably was not carried out because of the general shortage of arms and troops and because the Utes still could trade at the foreign forts for provisions.

27. Felix Lerma, Piqueta de Caballería de Presidiales de Chihuahua, to Martínez, Santa Fe, October 1, 1844; Archuleta to Martínez, Rio Arriba, October 4, 1844, both in SRC.

28. Unfortunately, the records of the 12th session held on September 15, 1844, are missing. Distribution for Expenses of a Temple built for the 16th of September of the Current Year. Records of the Thirteenth Session of the Patriotic Council, Santa Fe, October 13, 1844.

29. Colonel Sarracino to Secretariat Zubia, October 4, 1844, SRC. The Second District in 1837, consisted of the Alcaldías of Cochití, Jemez, Sandia, Albuquerque, Isleta, Tome, Valencia, Belen, Sabinal, Socorro, and Laguna, together with the Pueblos of Acoma and Zuni. Part of these entered the Southwest District (such as Isleta), some the Central (Cochití), and others the final district, the North during the reorganization of 1844. Often, however, in the documents the writers do not worry themselves with the niceties of governmental organization and continue to use subdivisions.

30. Secretariat to Justice at Jémez, Santa Fe, October 6, 1844, in Letter Book of the Secretariat, 1844.

31. Circular to the Prefects, Santa Fe, October 6, 1844, in Letter Book of the Secretariat, 1844.

32. Martínez to Colonel Sarracino, Santa Fe, October 10, 1844, in Record Book of the Commandant General, 1844.

33. José Francisco Ortiz, Official of the Party, to Martínez, October 11, 1844, SRC; Martínez to Ortiz, Santa Fe, October 12, 1844, in Record Book of the Commandant General, 1844; Secretariat to Lieutenant of Police at the Hacienda of Galisteo, Santa Fe, October 12, 1844; and Secretariat to Military Commander of San Miguel del Vado, Santa Fe, October 25, 1844, both in Letter Book of the Secretariat, 1844.

34. Record Book of the Departmental Treasury, 1844, entries for December.

35. Felix Lerma, Commander of the Presidial Pickets of Chihuahua, to Martínez, October 21, 1844, SRC.

36. Martínez to Lerma, Santa Fe, October 22, 1844, in Record Book of the Commandant General, 1844.

37. Record Book of the Departmental Treasury, 1844, entry for December 28, 1844.

38. Secretariat to Colonel Archuleta, Santa Fe, January 23, 1845, in Letter Book of the Secretariat, 1844.

39. Secretariat to Colonel Archuleta, Santa Fe, January 27 and 28, 1845, in Letter Book of the Secretariat, 1844.

40. Martínez to Colonel Archuleta, Santa Fe, February 5, 1845, in Record Book of the Commandant General, 1844; Martínez to Minister for Foreign Affairs, Government, and Public Order, Santa Fe, February 15, 1845, both in Letter Book to the Minister of Foreign Affairs. The request to lead an expedition came from a Sr. Magombre (Montgomery?).

41. Secretariat to the Justice at Jémez, Santa Fe, February 10, 1845, in Letter Book of the Secretariat, 1844.

42. Secretariat to Colonel Archuleta, Santa Fe, February 14, 1845, in Letter Book of the Secretariat, 1844.

43. Martínez to Colonel Archuleta, Santa Fe, April 1 and 20, 1845, both in Record Book of the Commandant General, 1844. Six months after the Ute attack on the Governor in Santa Fe, the permanent and auxiliary troops were still alerted along the northern border. Martínez to Colonel Archuleta, Santa Fe, March 18, 1845, in Record Book of the Commandant General, 1844.

44. Martínez to General Mariano Parades y Arrillaga, Santa Fe, January 14, 1845, in Letter Book of the Governor, 1844. It is doubtful that the Department knew much about this revolution at this time. Possibly Governor Martínez had a better concept of it than anyone else in Santa Fe because of his familiarity with the Mexican scene.

45. Martínez to General Paredes y Arrillaga, January 14, 1845, Martínez to General Hernando Franco, Jalisco, Santa Fe, January 14, 1845; Martínez to Departmental Assembly of Jalisco, Santa Fe, January 14, 1845; and passim, in Record Book of the Commandant General, 1844. The insurgents had captured 39 field-pieces in November. These had been directed to the Governors of Durango, Chihuahua, Sonora, and New Mexico. See Martínez to Commandant General of Durango, Santa Fe, January 15, 1845, in Record Book of the Commandant General, 1844.

46. Martínez to Armijo, Albuquerque, Santa Fe, January 13, 1845, in Record Book of the Commandant General, 1844. The declaration (*acto*) was found in Act of all the Chiefs, Officials, and Governor and Commandant General Pledging Allegiance to Santa Anna, X1/481.3/2047, Archivo Historico Militar Mexicano (AHMM), Mexico City.

47. Martínez to General Franco, Santa Fe, January 14, 1845, X/481.3/2047, AHMM; Martínez to Minister of War and Navy, Santa Fe, January 15, 1845, in X/481.3/2047, AHMM. These letters were acknowledged from Zacatecas and Durango where Santa Anna's government was then located. Martínez to Armijo, Santa Fe, January 17, 1845, in Record Book of the Commandant General, 1844.

48. Act of the Chiefs, Officials of the Garrison, The Governors, and Commandant General, Santa Fe, January 21, 1845, in X1/481.3/2047, AHMM; Martínez to General Paredes y Arrillaga, Santa Fe, January 31, 1845, in Record Book of the Commandant General, 1844. Until Feburary 15, Governor Martínez was not aware that the Government of Santa Anna had fled Mexico City on January 1.

49. Martínez to Commandant General of the Department of Chihuahua, Santa Fe, January 19, 1845, in Record Book of the Commandant General, 1844. The urgency for the money was laid to reports of approaching Texans. Martínez to Prefect Archuleta, Santa Fe, January 22, 1845, in Letter Book of the Secretariat, 1844.

50. Martínez to President of the Departmental Assembly, Santa Fe, January 31, 1845, in Letter Book of the Governor, 1844.

51. Charles Bent to Manuel Alvarez, Taos, February 23, 1845, Manuel Alvarez Papers, SRC.

52.   Bloom 1915,2:234, 234n. Bloom stated that notice of the pending change of command arrived in New Mexico on February 14, 1845. This writer has not been able to locate any documentation which either supports this statement or reveals anything about the circumstances surrounding the change of command. Bloom's source remains the sole evidence in the matter: it is a letter which acknowledged receipt of the orders from Chihuahua. However, the copy lacks both address and signatures; see Commandant General to _____ , Santa Fe, February 15, 1845, in Record Book of the Commandant General, 1844. One may speculate first of all that the political climate in Mexico no longer favored Martínez. Beyond that it seems reasonable to assume that the chronic problems of New Mexico might well discourage an ambitious man such as Martínez, particularly since his efforts were resented by the citizenry.

53.   Secretariat to Prefect Archuleta, Santa Fe, February 6 and 21, 1845, in Letter Book of the Secretariat, 1844; Bent to Alvarez, Taos, February 23, 1845, in Manuel Alvarez Papers. Due to the scant population of Lo de Mora, the governor ordered Captain Juan Antonio García not to conscript citizens there for service with the detachment at Abiquiu. On March 30, some Comanches brought five runaway Negroes into Taos. Whatever happened to them the records do not reveal; however, Bent believed that the United States should demand their return under an article in "our treaty with this country in which prisoners taken by allies of either nation are to be sent to their respective nations..." Bent to Alvarez, Taos, March 30, 1845, in Manuel Alvarez Papers.

54.   Secretariat to First Justice of this Capital, Francisco Ortiz, Santa Fe, April 3, 1845, in Letter Book of the Secretariat, 1844.

55.   Secretariat to Justice at Lo de Mora, Santa Fe, April 18, 1845; Secretariat to First Justice of the Second District, Santa Fe, April 18, 1845, both in Letter Book of the Secretariat, 1844.

56.   Commandant General to President of the Assembly; Commandant General to President of the Ayuntamiento; Commandant General to the Treasurer of the Department, Jose Serafin Ramirez; Commandant General to the Prefects of the three districts; all dated May 1, 1845, and all in Record Book of the Commandant General, 1844.

57.   Commandant General to Inspector of Arms of the Third District. Colonel Francisco Sarracino, Santa Fe, May 3, 1845, in Record Book of the Commandant General, 1844; Bloom, 1915, 2:235.

58.   Commandant General to Inspector of Arms of the Second District, Santa Fe, May 2, 1845; Commandant General to Departmental Treasurer Jose Serafin Ramirez, Santa Fe, May 3, 1845, in Record Book of the Commandant General, 1844.

59.   Commandant General to Inspector of Arms of the Second District, Rio Arriba, Santa Fe, May 3, 1845; Commandant General to Military Commandant at Jemez, Santa Fe, May 3, 1845, both in Record Book of the Commandant General, 1844.

60.   Commandant General to the Inspector of Arms of the Second District, May 3, 5, and 6, 1845, all in Record Book of the Commandant General, 1844. The Record Book continues with entries for 1845.

Ward Alan Minge currently serves as Air Force historian for Air Force Systems Command (Kirtland Air Force Base, New Mexico), is Chairman, New Mexico Public Records and Archives Commission, and a member of the Acoma Economic Development Committee, of the Architectural Review Board for Albuquerque City Commission, and of the Board of Directors for the Albuquerque Historical Society. He has served as research historian for New Mexico Pueblo Indians (Acoma, Jemez, Laguna, Santa Ana, and Zia) and for land claims and for water rights (Nambe, Pojoaque, San Ildefonso, and Tesuque), and was the instigator and author of the New Mexico Public Records Act. In addition to his publications on historical subjects relating to the Southwest and the Indians, Dr. Minge has produced various historical studies on Air Force projects. He has received the New Mexico Distinguished Public Service Award for 1969, The Greater Albuquerque Chamber of Commerce Award for Distinguished Public Service in 1969, and was nominated for the Rockerfeller Public Service Award by the Secretary of Air Force.

THE MESCALERO
APACHES AT
FORT STANTON

Andrew Wallace

On the evening of October 16, 1869, the lieutenant colonel of the 15th United States Infantry arrived with two mule-drawn wagons and an escort at Fort Stanton in the Capitan Mountains of southeastern New Mexico Territory. The stocky, black-bearded officer who dismounted by the adjutant's office was grimed by five days travel over the alkali desert west of Tularosa. Brevet Maj. Gen. August V. Kautz[1] had commanded Fort Craig, 90 miles to the west on the Rio Grande, for the past three months. Now he was ordered to take charge of the most important military post in the country of the Mescalero Apache Indians. He would govern its affairs for two and a half years and in that time inaugurate a new reservation for the Mescaleros.

Fort Stanton was only a two-company post, but it was important in the scheme of frontier defense against the Apaches. The fort has been initially established in 1855, but abandoned and partially destroyed on the outbreak of the Civil War. Since October of 1862, it had been continuously occupied, first by volunteers, then by regulars. After the Civil War, it was thought that raids to the east by New Mexican Apaches could be prevented by a cordon of forts ranged in an eastward arc, 400 miles long, from the Navajo country in northwestern New Mexico to the Pecos River, thence southwestward to Fort Bayard near the Arizona line. On the southern sector of this arc sat Fort Stanton, 15 miles southwest of Capitan Mountain on Bonito Creek. The surrounding country was sparsely settled by a few Anglo and Mexican families who sought a living in stockraising and mining. The mountains were well timbered, the woods full of game, and the creeks teeming with trout. An official description of the post noted that "the region is known as the Apache country, which tribe is in open hostility."[2]

The Mescaleros[3] mainly avoided the white man's way. They numbered only about 750 people and during winter dwelt in the desert mountains, especially the Guadalupe range of extreme southern New Mexico. In the summer, they would go into the Sacramento, Sierra Blanca, and Pajarito Mountains near Fort Stanton. Hunting and raiding took them far to the east and south. In 1855, Governor David Meriwether had given them a reservation on the Rio Ruidoso,

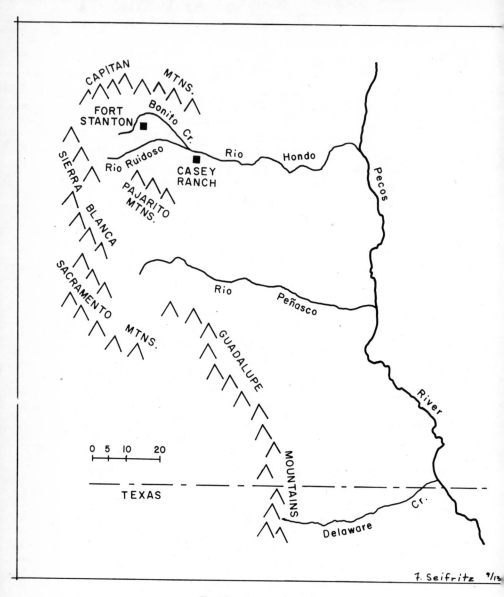

Fort Stanton and Vicinity

F. Seifritz 9/13

126

and the army had established the fort to watch over them.

The various tribes of Apaches in southern New Mexico were to offer resistance for many more years. They had been subjected to several campaigns since the American annexation of 1848, but the war seemed to grow in space and in numbers involved as the white settlement advanced. In 1861, when federal troops were withdrawn to oppose the Confederates, the Chiricahua Apaches of Arizona virtually declared war on all whites, and the Warm Springs and Southern Apaches of New Mexico occasionally joined with them. Their cousins the Mescaleros increased their activities, but in 1863 more than 400 surrendered with their chief, Cadete, and were confined to the Bosque Redondo reservation with the Navajos. The two tribes proved incompatible, and the Mescaleros drifted from the Bosque Redondo in 1864 and 1865 as much from antagonism with the Navajos as from the poverty of the land. During the three years that followed, while the volunteers were sent home or discharged, the impoverished Apache bands kept up continual depredations. The garrison at Fort Stanton was maintained to curb their incursions.

By 1865, all the tribe had escaped to their former haunts. Their depredations in southeastern New Mexico and western Texas could not have been considered too serious, in view of the number of Indians and the thin settlement of the country, but it was the Army's mission to protect the frontier. Real peace would come only when the Indians were settled on a definite reservation, a task of the Office of Indian Affairs in the Department of the Interior. But the Indian Office was moving slowly in 1869; few reservations had been selected and fewer organized. The Mescaleros wandered without restraint.

Mounted scouting expeditions were an indispensable means of obtaining timely information about Indians, as the forts were isolated and there were not enough soldiers to man a line of picket posts. Fort Stanton was over 200 miles from Fort Selden, which lay to the southwest, and it was 250 miles from Fort Davis, Texas. There was no telegraph line to either point. Only alert, inquisitive patrols could keep a post commander informed of the disposition and activity of the Indians.

To accomplish its purpose, Fort Stanton was garrisoned by Company I, 15th Infantry, and Comany F, 3rd Cavalry. The mean strength, month-to-month, was only 111 officers and men; but due to the healthy climate, most of them could be counted as effective at any time.[4] The cavalry troop was the principal force for scout-

127

ing, but the infantrymen might be included in an expedition if riding mules were available or if replacements for horse soldiers were required.

The officers of Colonel Kautz' little command were an assorted lot. Company I was led by Lt. Casper H. Conrad, who had served as an enlisted man in a volunteer infantry regiment during the war.[5] Kautz described him as "intensely opinionated and self-confident." He held command of the company temporarily until the return of Capt. Chambers McKibbin, absent on leave. Company I had another officer present, 2nd Lt. Charles E. Slade, who was the post adjutant and the acting assistant quartermaster. He had served as an enlisted man in a volunteer infantry regiment and obtained a commission in 1868.[6]

Company F of the 3rd Cavalry was commanded by a first lieutenant, Howard B. Cushing, a member of an illustrious military family. "He was about five feet seven in height," as John G. Bourke described him; "spare, sinewy, active as a cat; slightly stoop-shouldered, sandy complexioned, keen gray or bluish-gray eyes, which looked you through when he spoke and gave a slight hint of the determination, coolness, and energy which had made his name famous all over the southwestern border."[7] Second Lieutenant Franklin Yeaton of Company F was the only West Point officer at Fort Stanton other than Kautz, and Yeaton had just graduated without any prior service.[8]

The non-commissioned officers at Fort Stanton must remain regrettably unknown and nearly anonymous. However, there must have been several capable leaders in their ranks, such as Company F's first sergeant, John Mott, and the post sergeant-major, J.C.A. Warfield. They formed the muscle and sinew of the fighting troops, yet today they are mostly names on muster rolls.

One of Kautz' closest friends at the Fort was Dr. Joseph R. Gibson, the post physician, or "assistant surgeon" with captain's grade as he was carried on returns. The society at Stanton was more male than usual at an army post, for none of the officers had wives except Lieutenant Slade. He had married in Texas the previous spring,

> on an acquaintance of twenty-four hours, and a month after [he] started with his regiment for this territory. He is but a Second Lieut. and consequently short of means and liable to be greatly inconvenienced on account of his wife. He will probably discover that matrimony is not one of the wisest things a 2nd Lieut. can do.[9]

Brevet Major General A.V. Kautz

In mid-November he was granted a leave to fetch her.

Nor were there any towns of importance near the fort where civilian society might flourish. La Placita was a poor Mexican village of about 100 souls, ten miles east of Stanton. It was destined for immortality of a sort a decade later after it was called Lincoln and attracted Billy the Kid.

The center of social life was the post sutler's store operated in partnership by Col. Emil Fritz, a veteran of the war,[10] and Judge Lawrence G. Murphy, an ambitious merchant. Kautz soon observed that they were "very liberal." Their "mess is not expensive and they will make no charge for billiards or beer." Fritz, like Kautz a native German, had come to New Mexico from California with the 1st California Volunteer Cavalry in 1862 and had taken his discharge in the territory. His personality was in marked contrast to Judge Murphy who was an unscrupulous and volatile Irishman addicted to drink.[11]

The usual recreations for the officers were billiards, hunting and fishing, and drinking. The last Kautz generally eschewed, but champagne and the locally brewed beer, made by an immigrant from Baden, were too easily obtainable for Kautz to neglect them entirely. The art of the billiard table he assiduously pursued; and when in December he visited Fort Craig, he found that he could beat the gentlemen at Mr. Wardwell's store. The greatest pleasure for Kautz, however, was trout fishing in Bonito Creek. Several days of that first November were spent angling amid the beautiful, autumn-tinted mountains with Dr. Gibson and other officers. It was not unusual to catch 40 or 50 trout in an afternoon.

Colonel Kautz had less than a month to adjust to the spartan life at Fort Stanton before there were Indian troubles. He had discussed the Mescalero problem with Lt. Argalus G. Hennisee who was sent there as an agent for the Mescalero Apaches, a tribe he had never seen as he confessed in his first annual report to the Office of Indian Affairs.[12] But Kautz had made no detailed study of the situation nor planned any scouting expeditions. On November 14, Robert Casey, a rancher who lived below the junction of Bonito Creek and the Ruidoso River, came to the fort to report the theft of 115 cattle. Casey said that he had followed a clear trail for a mile down the Rio Hondo (as the two streams are called after they join) and that he had determined the thieves were Indians, presumably Mescaleros.[13]

Without delay, and ramrodded by Lt. Cushing, Company F hit

Personnel of the Firm L.G. Murphy & Co.

the Ruidoso trail before sunset. Four days later, 200 miles southeast in the Guadalupe Mountains, they struck a Mescalero rancheria which held the stolen stock. The troops recovered most of the cattle as well as some mules and horses. On the 23rd, the expedition returned, having marched altogether 370 miles.14

In December, Kautz was called to Fort Craig to preside over a court-martial. While there, he likely discussed the Mescalero problem with 2nd Lt. John G. Bourke of the 3rd Cavalry. Bourke obtained permission to return to Fort Stanton with Kautz who noted in his diary that the young officer was "anxious to familiarize himself with the country." Kautz made the journey back to Stanton and resumed command on December 10. Bourke, however, could not stay to accompany the next expedition with Cushing; he departed on the 12th.15

Although Kautz laid much of Cushing's first success to blind luck, he accepted his lieutenant's proposal to go out again and find the Mescaleros. This time, many local citizens were determined to accompany him. A proclamation of the Territorial Governor, William A. Pile, had urged citizen action against the Indians, and Kautz was authorized to ration, but not to arm, as many civilians as his discretion allowed.16 Plans were carefully laid from the time Kautz returned until the 19th. .That Sunday evening he recorded in his diary:

> It threatened snow this morning, but the day improved materially, and we were all interested in the preparations for the scout which took up the entire day. About thirty citizens collected to accompany Mr. Cushing...There was a great deal of delay but before night set in the post was clear of the crowd that had collected. There was a good deal of whiskey drinking, and some of the party were scarcely able to leave the post.

With a pack train carrying 20 days' rations and extra ammunition, Cushing and Yeaton marched over the trail to the Ruidoso and camped after dark. That night snow fell.

Christmas 1869 was very merry at Fort Stanton. Kautz had a little champagne the night before, spent the morning reading in his quarters, and then went up to the sutler's store for lunch and billiards. Fritz and Murphy served fresh oysters "brought out from the States in cans. They were quite an improvement on the partially cooked canned oysters." At four o'clock, the officers from the post, together with the traders, a brother of Fritz, and Paul Dowlin,

132

owner of the sawmill near the post, sat down to a dinner of wild turkey. Kautz and Dowlin afterward retired to Dr. Gibson's quarters and played cribbage. They returned to the store late in the evening to gossip and to enjoy one more convivial round before sleep.[17]

Christmas for Lt. Cushing and his command was far from cheerful.[18] They already had marched over rough trails into the Guadalupe Mountains, through and across deep canyons, in search of the elusive Apaches. After entering the north end of the Guadalupes, they camped late on December 23. On Christmas Eve, Cushing surveyed the scene of his November 18 combat, but he was unable to find any fresh signs of Indians. On Christmas Day, the soldiers pursued some fairly fresh signs and camped near the summit of the mountain range.

The following morning, Cushing came to the remains of a recently abandoned rancheria on the west side of the mountains, "but, although many quite fresh trails led in, no trail was found heading out." Very soon they picked up an occasional track of an Indian pony among the rocks, apparently headed south. "I struck out southeast," reported Cushing, "and soon struck a cross trail leading southwest with one pony-track. This I followed, and after marching ten miles, my one pony-track had become twenty." The trail seemed about four days old, but Cushing pushed his men on rapidly until, about noon, the sign became fresh. At 1:30 p.m., Cushing pushed out a dismounted skirmish line and rapidly ascended a steep ridge on which a few Indian ponies were seen grazing. Then the mounted troops rushed forward.

Although the Mescaleros stood their ground, their fire was ineffective. When it ceased, the troops charged. The Indians suddenly cut loose "one good round volley from guns and bows; and Lieut. Yeaton while gallantly pushing up the left of the line was struck by a ball and seriously wounded in two places." The soldiers and citizens were now full on the Indians among the rocks; they charged with a yell. "The Indians broke and fled for the neighboring hills." Pursuit, however, proved difficult in the broken country with tired horses, and the men were called back.

Cushing had attacked a village of nearly 50 Mescalero lodges in Sanguinara Canyon of the Guadalupe Mountains, a point just over the Texas line. From the long list of goods captured and from the long time required for their destruction, the attack must have dispersed the principal band of the Mescaleros.

133

On the evening of the attack, Cushing's command camped by the light of the burning Indian village. The next day, a litter was improvised for the wounded Yeaton, and they marched north and east. The route, after traversing Dark Canyon, must have approximated the modern federal highway U.S. 62-180. On the morning of December 30, Cushing took 40 men with the best horses and four days' rations to back track and attempt another surprise attack. The pack train, the captured stock, Lt. Yeaton, and an escort under First Sergeant Mott proceeded toward the Pecos River, while Cushing swiftly re-crossed into Texas. He swung over the southern end of the Guadalupes and later that afternoon found another, smaller Mescalero rancheria.

In the second attack, on Delaware Creek in Texas, 20 head of cattle were recovered and another 25 lodges were burned. At this second village, the great number of families in proportion to the number of lodges convinced Cushing that he had struck the refugees from the attack of December 26. After a brief rest, the flying column marched all night, and early on New Year's Eve they reached the place they had left the previous morning.

Cushing spent New Year's Day in the saddle. The weary troopers of Company F covered 35 miles and the next day reached the mouth of the Rio Peñasco on the Pecos. Four days later, they were back at Fort Stanton. Cushing estimated the total distance marched in 19 days to have been 530 miles. "This scout was made," he observed, "in very severe weather and the men frequently suffered greatly from cold, but they bore all that and the hard marching extremely well and in the two actions they behaved very bravely." They returned to the post with about 50 captured horses and mules as well as the captured cattle.

Cushing's report of his scout was received at District Headquarters on January 18. Along with it was a lengthy endorsement by Kautz who recommended a brevet promotion of one grade for "each of these gallant young officers." We may suspect, however, that Kautz had missed the significance of the work done by Cushing. The colonel failed to observe that many Mescaleros in New Mexico had in all probability been driven south among their kin in Texas or were badly broken in strength. On the contrary, Kautz was convinced that "with two more companies of cavalry at this post, the Mescalero Apaches could in a few months be brought to sue for peace." Finding them would prove the most difficult job of all.

It developed that Department Headquarters thought cavalry was

134

more useful elsewhere. On January 29, Fritz and Cushing returned from a visit to Fort Selden with news that the 3rd Cavalry was being transferred to Arizona. Kautz immediately penned a letter in which he outlined a plan to send out another expedition in cooperation with troops from Selden.[19] When that request was denied, Company F was ordered to change station and march to the Mimbres River.[20]

Indian depredations in the vicinity of Fort Stanton continued through May, but there were no deaths and there was even some doubt that Mescaleros were responsible On May 7, in fact, Emil Fritz had learned through a Mexican that the Mescaleros were camped in the Comanche country of southwest Texas and that they were near starvation and wished to surrender. When on the 7th of June a Mexican herder was killed, Indian "sign" suggested to some that the culprits were renegade Navajos.[21]

On April 13, 1870, Cap. (Brevet Lieutenant Colonel) William McCleave arrived at Stanton with 2nd Lt. Oresmus B. Boyd and Company B of the 8th Cavalry. Colonel McCleave was an Irishman of about Kautz' age, 42, and had spent ten years as a non-commissioned officer of dragoons on the Western frontier before accepting a commission in the California Volunteers in 1861. He had come to New Mexico with General James H. Carleton and had been fighting Indians, especially Mescaleros, since 1863. Kautz thought him "jovial and kind but illiterate and he lacks manners...and is too old to improve."[22]

Slade and Boyd had brought their wives to Fort Stanton, the former returning from Texas with Mrs. Slade in January. Kautz was thankful that both women were resourceful and adaptable ladies. "Mrs. S.," he noted, "is quite a pretty woman and much smarter than Mr. Slade." Mrs. Boyd had also brought a baby daughter who was the delight of the entire garrison.[23]

Through the spring of 1870, there were frequent Indian alarms, and the soldiers at Stanton viewed the incidents as welcome breaks in the boring drills and construction work. Although the post had been reoccupied for seven years by 1869, it was rebuilt only with the advent of Kautz. Occasionally an escort had to be provided for travelers, and such details also were welcomed as a break in routine by the few men who might be spared.

On May 13, 1870, Kautz mailed a letter through channels requesting a leave of absence for 60 days. In his diary Kautz expressed a determination to go East and secure either a better army

135

assignment or else a lucrative civilian job, and maybe a wife to boot. On June 15, the mail brought approval of his request. Kautz was obliged to turn the post over to Capt. McKibbin of his own regiment, still absent on leave; and he had considerable official business to conclude before he could depart. McKibbin and his family at last returned on July 2, and four days later Kautz left for the States.

Neither goal was realized. Kautz put aside his dissatisfaction with the Army and shrugged off the disappointments of an overextended leave. By the time he had completed a leisurely journey back to Fort Stanton on November 18,1870, he was determined to face the military problem anew and to accept the best that the situation might offer.

After Kautz had left in July, McKibbin convinced himself that the Mescaleros were again in their old haunts in the Guadalupe and Pajarito Mountains. He thought they could be found where Cushing had fought them. McCleave's troop of cavalry accordingly was sent on "several scouts from this Post each of ten days duration," as McKibbin reported, "but McCleave has been unable to accomplish anything as he had neither the force nor the rations to justify him in going to and scouting the country where the Indians are supposed to be." McKibbin, therefore, proposed to conduct a larger scout from Stanton on or about the 1st of September, and he asked for the attachment to the fort of 40 men and one or two commissioned officers from Forts Selden and Craig. His plan to divide the command, once in the field, into two flying columns and leave the trains with a small guard was approved on August 19, and the 8th Cavalry was ordered to send 20 men and one officer from each of the other two posts to Fort Stanton in the first week of September.[24]

Some Mescaleros, however, got to work sooner. Late in the day on September 3, a war party attacked a train bringing wood to the post. By the time Capt. McCleave and Company B could find the trail, it was dark. On the following morning, McCleave and all available mounted troops with a few citizens went in pursuit. The trail seemed to lead toward the Guadalupes, but it was cold and after 225 miles they gave up, returning September 18.[25]

The detachment from Fort Craig arrived September 5: 2nd Lt. Pendleton Hunter and 12 men, all that could be supplied from Company A, 8th Cavalry. On the 6th, 20 men drawn from Companies I and G arrived from Fort Selden.[26] McKibbin thought he might mount some infantrymen on mules but dispaired of going out at all when McCleave's exhausted troop reined in on the 18th. Fortuitously, Lt. Boyd returned from Fort Union just three days later with 27 recruits for the 8th Cavalry and 9 for the 15th Infantry. On October 6, McKibbin at last mounted his expedition.[27]

As planned, they marched into the Guadalupes guided by Robert Casey and there divided into two columns under McCleave and McKibbin. Hunter was left with the trains. McCleave penetrated a Mescalero hide-out, surprised a rancheria, and captured three women and five children. The expedition returned to Fort Stanton on October 27. It had been a wasteful chase.[28]

McKibbin had been back at Stanton only three days when a Mexican teamster rode in to report that Indians had attacked a large government supply train only 18 miles below and had driven off 59 mules. The next morning, McCleave was again in the saddle at the head of 67 troopers. Hunter went with him as well as Lt. Slade on his first scout. They tracked the Mescaleros about 200 miles, but the command was poorly mounted and fatigued as result of the recent expedition. The Indians, moreover, used their newly acquired mules to ride in relays. The troops returned without making contact November 14.[29] When Kautz returned from leave four days later, the bully boys of the 8th Cavalry were leaving Fort Stanton somewhat the worse for wear.

For some time previous to McKibbin's expedition, Colonel Fritz and his partner Murphy had been trying to attract the Mescaleros into Fort Stanton and settle them on a reservation.[30] Kautz concurred in their plan and now decided that the captured women might serve a purpose. On November 23, he had McKibbin escort one of the women to the Pajarito Mountains to contact her people. She returned three weeks later with the information that she had found a rancheria willing to come in, but the great majority of Mescaleros were widely scattered and it would require much more time to communicate with them.[31]

Kautz learned that one of the captured Indian women was a wife of a prominent sub-chief of the Mescaleros called José La Paz, "Peaceful Joe." In January 1871, McKibbin took her to the mountains, but she soon returned without finding the Indians. Kautz himself then persuaded the third woman, "Timber Head," to try to communicate with the Mescaleros.[32] On January 14, he sent her off on her own. It was she who found the main body of the tribe encamped on the Pecos River. On February 6, the Indians were reported on the Ruidoso, and Fritz volunteered to meet them with presents and escort them in. Within 24 hours he was back with José La Paz, another man, Timber Head, four other women, and several children, the rest to follow.

On February 8, Kautz interviewed José La Paz and promised nothing except protection from citizens and that he would arrange for Fritz and Murphy to feed them. It was apparent that the Apaches were quite destitute. José said the entire tribe wanted peace and that they were mostly camped on the Llano Estacado where they had taken refuge with the Comanches. He agreed to try and persuade the other Mescaleros to surrender.

Shortly after meeting with Kautz, José travelled to southern Texas, located his kinsmen in the Comanche country, then returned to Stanton for rations. Revictualled, he left again on March 6.

Settlement of the Mescaleros was now a matter of time. On April 12, Jose returned with assurances that his people were coming but that they waited for better grass to subsist their horses. An employee of Fritz' returned three days later with word that he had seen 300 lodges moving west. Kautz was at Sante Fe and Fort Union most of May; when he returned he found small groups of Apaches arriving. He organized a camp for them south of the fort near the dam on Bonito Creek. On June 10, another sub-chief, Pablo, came in. The next day, the regular agent of the Indian Bureau, A.J. Curtis, arrived to take charge. At this time Curtis arranged with Fritz and Murphy to supply the Apaches temporarily with beef and corn at the contract rates, pending selection of a permanent reservation.[33]

In mid-July 1871, the principal chief and acknowledged leader of the Mescaleros appeared at Fort Stanton with about 70 members of his personal band. This was Cadete. Agent Curtis called a council in which Cadete "said they wished to live at peace, and had come in for that purpose; that this was the land of their fathers and also their land, and here they wished to live and die, and calling upon heaven and earth to witness, said they wanted to make a peace not to be broken, but one that would be firm and lasting." Curtis then made a "treaty" with them, promising protection, a school, and land to cultivate. He allowed them to keep their livestock and all of their property. Cadete agreed and swore they were at peace.[34]

Nearly 700 Mescaleros, however, were still out. Perhaps 50 were still at the Cañada Alamosa agency west of the Rio Grande.[35] The rest were en route from the Pecos. They continued to dribble into Fort Stanton so that by September 18, when Curtis wrote his annual report, there were 325 accounted for.[36] A year later, virtually the whole tribe was present. On September 2, 1872, all but 16 square miles of the Fort Stanton Military Reservation was transferred to the Interior Department for use as an Indian reservation.[37]

By and large, the Mescaleros of New Mexico kept their word. The government of the United States did not. Possibly a sympathetic, experienced military officer in command at Fort Stanton might have prevented the worst white depredations to come. Certainly the later record of August Kautz as commanding general of the Arizona military department suggests such a possibility. Yet Kautz left to go on temporary duty in the East on April 16, 1872. Although he returned to the District of New Mexico next year, he never saw a Mescalero again.[38]

Probably no military or civilian agent could have saved the Mescaleros from the ill treatment received in the next eight years at the hands of insensitive soldiers and lawless civilians.[39] To start with, Agent Curtis and his successors were powerless to provide the promised school or to have the reservation surveyed and the white squatters removed from Indian land. Nor could the agents prevent the Fort Stanton post trader from selling whiskey to the Indians. Murphy, who had assumed control of the tradership from his ailing partner, had been evicted from the reservation by Kautz' successor for selling whiskey to soldiers. Murphy's successor was Paul Dowlin who continued to sell it to Indians and soldiers alike. In desperation, Agent Crothers removed the Indian agency from the fort in 1874, eventually establishing it near Blazer's Mill, forty miles south. This marked the beginning of the present-day Mescalero reservation which no longer includes the old military domain.

In 1873, Major W.R. Price invaded the Mescalero reservation with troops bent on recovering "stolen" livestock. Price was poorly informed as to either the boundaries of the reservation, which made many of the animals legally Indian property, or the flimsiness of white claims. The Indians did not fight but fled, and those who remained suffered even more from murdering, thieving white desperadoes as well as from other raiding Indians. In 1875, still more Mescaleros slipped away to Old Mexico, and next year many died of a smallpox epidemic.

Still the Mescaleros of New Mexico did not wage war. All military engagements reported with Mescaleros in 1877 and 1878 were confined to Texas. In 1879, a few warriors did join the renegade Chiricahuas led by Victorio and Nana.

Nevertheless, the army succumbed to civilian pleas that the Mescaleros be disarmed. In mid-April of 1880, nearly a thousand troops concentrated on the agency at Blazer's Mill. Their approach was a well-kept secret, and almost 400 Apaches were rounded up. The soldiers were told to regard as hostile any Indian who failed to come to the agency. The army took the Mescaleros' horses and firearms and indiscriminately killed an untold number of "hostile" Indians who didn't know they were supposed to assemble at the agency or fled to the hills when menaced by the troops. Still the Mescaleros refused to begin a general war, even with the primitive weapons that remained to them. Not until the deaths of Victorio and Nana did peace come to New Mexico in 1882, and with it a new hope for the sorely persecuted Mescaleros.

NOTES

1. Kautz, though born in Germany in 1828, was reared in Ohio. After service in the Mexican War, he graduated from West Point in 1852 and was sent to the Pacific Northwest where he served until 1861. His Civil War experience included pursuit of the Confederate raider John Hunt Morgan and command of the cavalry division in the Army of the James. He was a member of the commission that tried the conspirators in the Lincoln assassination and he performed Reconstruction duties in Louisiana and Mississippi. Subsequently he was assigned to the 15th Infantry en route to New Mexico. George W. Cullum, *Biographical Register of the Officers and Graduates of the U.S. Military Academy*, 3 vols., rev. ed. with supplement (James, Miller, New York, 1879) 1:504-506. See also the article in *Dictionary of American Biography*, 11 vols. (Charles Scribner's Sons, New York, 1936-58) 5 (1):263f.

2. U.S. War Department, Office of the Surgeon General, *Report on Barracks* (Washington, 1870):250. H.H. Bancroft, *History of Arizona and New Mexico* (History Company, San Francisco, 1889):670; Ralph H. Ogle, *Federal Control of the Western Apaches* (University of New Mexico Press, Albuquerque, 1940):82. Gen. John Pope, who would take command of the Department of the Missouri in 1870, thought the idea impractical and would seek to abandon several posts, including Stanton. U.S. War Department, *Annual Report of the Secretary of War for the Year 1870* (Washington, 1871):15f; see also Robert M. Utley, Captain John Pope's Plan of 1853 for the Frontier Defense of New Mexico, *Arizona and the West* (1963)5:149-163.

3. Besides the purely ethnographic literature, the only general history of these Indians is by C.L. Sonnichsen, *The Mescalero Apaches* (University of Oklahoma Press, Norman, 1958), to whom I am indebted for most of this information.

4. National Archives, Record Group 94, Post Returns, Fort Stanton, 1869-1870, cited hereafter as *Post Returns.*

5. William H. Powell (comp.), *Records of Living Officers of the United States Army* (L.R. Hamersly, Philadelphia, 1890):140.

6. Francis B. Heitman, *Historical Register and Dictionary of the United States Army*, rev. ed. (2 vols., Washington, 1903)1:890.

7. *On the Border with Crook* (Scribner's Sons, New York, 1891):30.

8. Cullum 1879, 3:394-400.

9. Diary of A.V. Kautz for 1869, Kautz Papers, Library of Congress; cited hereafter as *Diary* with the year.

10. Fritz File in the Hayden Biographical Files, Arizona Historical Society Library, Tucson.

11. *Diary*, 1869, 1870. Philip J. Rasch, "The Rise of the House of Murphy," *Brand Book* of the Denver Westerners (Denver, 1956):57-84; William A. Keleher, *Violence in Lincoln County* (University of New Mexico Press, Albuquerque, 1957):32f, 51-53.

12. U.S. Interior Department, *Annual Report of the Commissioner of Indian Affairs for the Year 1869* (Washington, 1870):245-247. Hennissee, a regular army officer, was appointed Mescalero agent on July 23, pending appointment of a civilian agent by the Board of Indian Commissioners.

13. *Diary,* 1869. For background on Casey, see James D. Shinkle, *Robert Casey and the Ranch on the Rio Hondo* (Hall-Poorbaugh Press, Roswell, N.M., 1970).

14. Gen. George W. Getty, commanding District of New Mexico, to Assistant Adjutant General, Department of the Missouri, Dec. 3, 1869, in National Archives, Record Group 98, Letters Sent, District of New Mexico. See *Diary,* 1869; and Shinkle, 1970:75-78. Shinkle's account is based on testimony taken in 1898 for a claim against the government for Indian depredations and confuses this scout by Cushing with the later one next described.

15. *Diary,* 1869.

16. *Ibid.;* and Acting Assistant Adjutant General, District of New Mexico, to Kautz, Dec. 5, 1869, in National Archives, Record Group 98, Letters Sent, District of New Mexico. See Calvin Horn, *New Mexico's Troubled Years* (Horn & Wallace, Albuquerque, 1963):143f.

17. *Diary,* 1869.

18. For extended treatment of Cushing's career see John P. Wilson, Lt. H.B. Cushing: Indian Fighter Extraordinary, *El Palacio* (1969) 76 (1):40-46. The account of Cushing's scout which follows is drawn from his report transmitted with endorsement of Kautz to the Adjutant General, District of New Mexico, Jan. 8, 1870, in National Archives, Record Group 98, Letters Received, District of New Mexico. References to this letter file are cited hereafter as *New Mexico Letters.*

19. Kautz to Acting Assistant Adjutant General, Feb. 1, 1870, in *New Mexico Letters;* and *Diary,* 1870.

20. *Post Returns.*

21. *Diary,* 1870.

22. *Ibid.;* McCleave File in the Hayden Biographical Files, Arizona Historical Society Library, Tucson; Powell 1890:376f.

23. *Diary,* 1870. Mrs. Boyd in *Cavalry Life in Tent and Field* (J.S. Tait & Sons, New York, 1894) gives a good account of life at Fort Stanton.

24. McKibbin to Assistant Adjutant General, Aug. 11, 1870, in *New Mexico Letters.*

25. *Ibid.,* Sept. 5, 1870. *Post returns.*

26. *Ibid.* The 8th Cavalry had a reputation of being rather disorderly. It was first recruited in 1866 from drifters, penniless emigrants, and discouraged miners on the Pacific Coast; some officers such as Hunter had no training or experience. Nevertheless, it performed creditably in a hard campaign in Arizona despite a desertion rate of 42 per cent. In 1870, it was sent to New Mexico. T.F. Rodenbough and W.L. Haskin (eds.), *The Army of the United States* (Maynard, Merrill, New York, 1896):268-279.

27. *Post Returns.*

28. McKibbin to Assistant Adjutant General, Nov. 3, 1870, in *New Mexico Letters.* One of the children captured was a Mexican, Timeo Ansura, about 17 years old, whose life Casey saved and who thereafter lived at his ranch. Shinkle 1970:60, 79-83.

29. *Post Returns.*

30. *Diary,* 1870. U.S. Interior Department, *Annual Report of the Commissioner of Indian Affairs for the Year 1871* (Washington, 1872):401; cited hereafter as *Indian Affairs Report, 1871.* Rasch 1956:65f.

31. This account of events leading to the surrender of the Mescalero Apaches and the establishment of the Fort Stanton reserve is based primarily on Kautz' *Diary*, but some details of the next six paragraphs are also found in letters of Kautz to the Assistant Adjutant General, District of New Mexico, Feb. 1, March 9, and April 13, 1871, in *New Mexico Letters*. Kautz' involvement has been overlooked by all previous writers.

32. The woman's name was probably translated by Kautz from a Spanish appelation which might have been "Tarugo," meaning a blockhead. Perhaps the interpreter said blockhead and Kautz rendered it Timber Head in his *Diary* without realizing the disparagement implied.

33. *Indian Affairs Report,* 1871:371.

34. *Ibid.:*401f.

35. As reported in 1870; see *Annual Report* for that year (Washington, 1871):624. At any rate, Kautz noted in his *Diary* on Jan. 20, 1872, that "more Indians are coming, about thirty came in from the Cañada Alamosa, a day or two since."

36. *Indian Affairs Report, 1871:*402.

37. This is the date of the order from District Headquarters. Formal application for the land had been made in August 1871 by Vincent Colyer, a special Indian commissioner traveling about the Southwest to select reservations.

38. In June 1874, Kautz became colonel of the 8th Infantry and moved with his regiment to Arizona Territory. On his brevet rank of major general, he succeeded his old friend George Crook in command of the Military Department of Arizona. For three years he sought to continue Crook's policy of justice and firmness with the Indians. At one time, for instance, he seconded an application for U.S. citizenship from Alchesay, chief of the White Mountain Apaches, in consonance with the 14th Amendment. Quarrels with other military and territorial officials led to his relief in March 1878. See Andrew Wallace, "Soldier in the Southwest," Unpub. Ph.D. thesis (University of Arizona, 1968).

39. Sonnichsen 1958:140-197.

Andrew Wallace is an assistant professor of history at Northern Arizona University in Flagstaff. He was previously in charge of the research library of the Arizona Historical Society at Tucson and edited the society's quarterly journal. He has been a member of the Tucson Corral of Westerners, which in 1963 published his study of the Mexican Punitive Expedition. He also has published two books about his adopted state: *Pumpelly's Arizona* (The Palo Verde Press, Tucson, 1965) and *The Image of Arizona* (University of New Mexico Press, Albuquerque, 1971).

Born in Springfield, Illinois, Wallace came with his parents to Tucson in 1946 where he graduated from the University of Arizona. As an officer in the army, he served four years in the 6th Armored Cavalry. He returned to the University in 1960 for doctoral graduate study specializing in the military history of the American West and the Civil War.

THE LONG MARCH:
1863-1867

Frank McNitt

Point-to-point distances by wagon road 100 years ago were often a matter of guesswork. This especially was true when routes of travel were new or little used. Asa Bacon Carey may be excused, therefore, for erring in his testimony before the James R. Doolittle U.S. House-Senate joint committee meeting in June 1865 at Fort Union, New Mexico. In the aftermath of Kit Carson's Navajo campaign, Captain Carey told the committee that about 500 Navajos were taken in small groups, by force, to the reservation at Bosque Redondo. Others went voluntarily, but a great deal of talk was required "to convince them that the Bosque was the best place for them. The distance was about three hundred and fifty miles."[1]

Captain Carey was mistaken; the Long March from Navajo country to confinement on the Pecos River was accomplished over several major routes after the captive columns reached Albuquerque, rather than by one as Carey's statement implied. By the shortest and most infrequently used route, the distance was 375 miles. By the favored Mountain Route, a weary 424 miles stretched between Fort Canby and the Bosque. Alternate routes by way of Santa Fe and Fort Union extended the journey to 436 and 498 miles, respectively.

Comparable in agonizing hardship to the 1838-39 Cherokee removal from the southern Atlantic seaboard states to what is now eastern Oklahoma, the Navajo removal uprooted fewer families but spanned a longer period of time. Between the summer of 1863 and December 1866, a total of 11,468 Navajos were reportedly started on their way toward confinement at the Bosque Redondo. How many actually reached their destination and how many died or otherwise were lost on the way are points less certain. Late November 1864 saw the highest count of captives held on the reservation: 8,570 men, women, and children.

A mass desertion of about 1,000 Navajos from the reservation in June 1865 makes it impossible to determine how many Indians were moved from their homeland to the Pecos in this period. Even the number who left the reservation is uncertain; of the 1,338 officially reported missing, an indeterminate number were said to have died. Some of those who escaped soon returned voluntarily to the

145

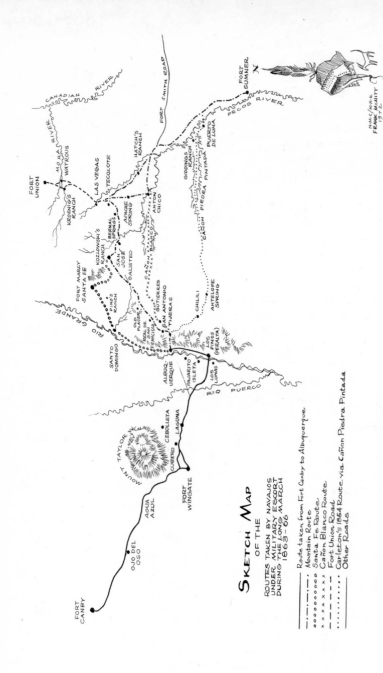

Sketch Map of the Routes Taken by Navajos Under Military Escort

Bosque. A great many more apparently succeeded in reaching their former homes. It is conceivable that a large proportion of the Navajos sent to the Bosque in 1866 had escaped in 1865 and so were going back a second time.

Trains of Indian prisoners were often started toward the Pecos under conditions of chaotic confusion. Intensely involved in the operation but far removed from the scene, Brevet Brig. Gen. James H. Carleton issued no orders from his department headquarters in Santa Fe that required officers in command of escorts to report fully on losses sustained by their trains while en route. Only occasionally, then, were such reports made.

Carson's summer 1863 campaign was in its opening phase when the first small contingent of captives was sent to the Bosque Redondo. It included eight Navajos gathered at Fort Canby, among them five women and children captured by Capt. Albert H. Pfeiffer on or about August 6, below Calites Canyon. At Fort Wingate, they were joined by 43 other Navajos who later were identified as friendly *Diné Ana'aii* (Enemy Navajos) of the late headman Sandoval. Some of these were brought in from a scout by Lt. D.B. Haskell; the others either had been living near the fort or were found between the post and nearby Cubero. Nothing in the attitude of the 51 prisoners could be termed defiant or hostile, but when they left Wingate for the river on August 27, their military escort was under Carleton's Draconian orders to bring the men in irons, if necessary– "and in case any attempt to escape is made by them they will be shot down."[2]

To his credit, young Lt. Thomas Holmes, commanding an escorting troop of the 1st Cavalry, New Mexico Volunteers, found no cause to put chains on his charges or to shoot them. He accomplished his task swiftly and with slight incident. Although future trains of captives would be taken to a military depot on the Rio Grande at Los Pinos, Holmes was ordered to take the customary wagon road directly to Albuquerque, thereby saving some 24 miles.[3]

Passage of the captives through Santa Fe on September 2 was noted casually by the *Weekly Gazette* which observed: "We presume they will be transferred to some military post to the East of this, and there retained separated from...the balance of the tribe to the end of the war." Soon to become General Carleton's virtual mouthpiece, the *Gazette* for once was indifferently informed. Carleton was firmly determined, since the previous April, that Navajos captured in the then-forthcoming campaign would be sent to the reservation on the Pecos he had created earlier for captive Mescalero Apaches.[4]

Five days later, in the evening of September 7, Navajos arrived at Fort Union. Here one of the children in their train died, the first of hundreds of such deaths. Three wagons were furnished to the Indians by the fort's commander when the journey resumed September 10. Although no reference to other means of transportation has been found, the fact that the train averaged about 20 miles a day suggests that the Navajos had horses. A second death, that of a woman, occurred soon afterward of causes unstated. Then, in an elapsed time of 24 days (two of which were spent in rest at Fort Union), the first contingent of Navajos reached Fort Sumner, headquarters of the Bosque Redondo reservation, on September 19. The distance traveled from Fort Wingate was somewhat more than 370 miles, with an additional 100 miles for those sent from Fort Canby.

The same route to Santa Fe and Fort Union was followed two months later when a train that included headman Delgadito and about 200 other captives left Fort Wingate with an escort commanded by Capt. Rafael Chacon. Upon reaching the capital, the Navajos were turned over to Lt. V.B. Wardwell. At noon of November 22, as temperatures dropped below freezing, the column set out once more, proceeding into the head of a winter storm that covered the mountain road with eight inches of snow. Wardwell later gave a detailed account of his progress, the first of a number of such reports that serve now as the basis for reconstructing the routes by which Navajos were removed to Bosque Redondo.

Wardwell's train encamped the first night in hills eight miles east of Santa Fe, and thereafter made overnight stops at Kozlowski's Ranch, San José, Tecolote, Las Vegas, and William Kroenig's Ranch on Sapello Creek, about 2.5 miles southwest of Watrous.[5] At Fort Union, the Navajos were placed under a new escort of troops commanded by Capt. William P. Calloway, 1st Infantry, California Volunteers. Upon their arrival at Fort Sumner on December 10, Delgadito's party, some 15 of their number missing and unaccounted for, received an emotional welcome from kinsmen and friends already there. Observing the scene, Maj. Henry D. Wallen, the post commander, later noted that the meeting was "truly affecting—many tears were shed on both sides."

Fort Sumner at this time was a miserable assemblage of tents and small adobe huts situated approximately 100 yards southwest of the later, permanent fort site. As temporary accommodation for the new arrivals, Major Wallen remarked that "I have encamped them adjoining those [Navajos] already at the Post, and only about seventy five yards from the extreme right of my Camp; they are comfortably quartered in old Sibley tents..."[6]

A third train of captives was conducted to the Bosque by way of Fort Union in January 1864, and other escorts may have taken the same road without leaving any record of it. However, this route is known to have been used at least twice again, in May and August of 1866. (In the last instance the escort was returning to garrison at Fort Union.) Because the Fort Union route served no apparent purpose, but only prolonged an already arduous journey by some 70 miles, one naturally casts about for an explanation. Up to this point none has been found.

Carleton initially intended that captives taken in the Carson campaign "be sent to Santa Fe by every practicable opportunity" and from there moved on to the Bosque.[7] His orders to this effect were hastily modified early in 1864, when the numbers of captives surrendering after the successful sweep through Canyon de Chelly reached flood tide. As the size of prisoner trains increased from a few score to 1,000, and then to 2,000, Carleton was compelled to divert the great straggling columns away from the capital and its narrow winding streets. Santa Fe occasionally was a stopping point for small groups of prisoners, thereafter, but from early in 1864 until either the following year or 1866, a majority of Navajo captives traveled to the Bosque by what became known as the Mountain Route.

Several natural advantages favored this road. Water, and wood for campfires, were to be found at convenient intervals and in good supply. Against winter's harsh elements, never inescapable, some protection was offered for much of the distance by sheltering arroyos, narrow valleys, and the canyons between mountains and mesas. For the greater part of its length, the Mountain Route was within reach of emergency supplies and also within range of military surveillance by the garrisons at Albuquerque, Fort Marcy, Fort Union, and Fort Bascom. Closely skirting General Carleton's best checkpoints, the route bypassed the center of Santa Fe by half a day or less.

An early test of the new road was made in February 1864 when nearly 1,500 Navajo women, children, and men were escorted to confinement on the Pecos by Capt. Joseph Berney. He soon was

149

followed by Capt. John Thompson with a column of 2,500 prisoners and by Capt. Francis McCabe with almost 1,000 more.
Citizens from Peralta to Anton Chico, and in all of the river and mountain villages lying between, became sharply aware of ill-clad and often sick Navajos following the course of the Mountain Route; not by any printed words in newspapers, but from close personal observation. While the territorial press generally turned its back on the grim drama, the people of the settlements had no choice but to become involved witnesses. The sight and sound of the swelling caravans as they passed the doorways of the settlements were vivid realities then, realities that may only be imagined in pallid outline now. Some few of the citizens, as will be seen, were not content to be passive witnesses but became scavenging participants, preying on and plundering the passing columns.

Before considering the Mountain Route in more detail, it would be helpful to mention briefly the rather well-known wagon road over which the Indian prisoners were conducted to the Rio Grande. From Navajo country to Los Pinos, a single route of no appreciable deviation was established by early fall in 1863. The route continued in use without change until Fort Canby was abandoned October 20, 1864; thereafter, and until the removal of captives finally ended in June 1867, Fort Wingate served as the western staging point. Distances from Fort Canby (Carson's headquarters, renamed from the earlier Fort Defiance) to Cubero are quoted here in part from a survey conducted in 1853 by Lt. Armistead L. Long, 2d Artillery, of the Fort Defiance garrison.[8]

Fort Canby		0.
Ojo del Oso (site of New Fort Wingate)	38.5	38.5
Agua Azul (Bluewater)	36.5	75.
Upper crossing of Rio Gallo	23.5	98.5
Lower crossing of Rio Gallo	9.	107.5
Cubero	6.	113.5

Distances by wagon road between Fort Wingate and Ojo del Oso (Bear Spring) and Cubero were 60 and 25 miles, respectively.[9] From Cubero, which some of the trains bypassed to the south, the road as far as Laguna pueblo closely approximated the route followed and measured in 1849 by Lt. James H. Simpson. Some 16 miles east of Laguna, the trains of captives left the Albuquerque road and traveled southeasterly toward Los Lunas. Near that village but north of it, a crossing of the Rio Grande was made to the northern limits of Peralta and the depot at Los Pinos. (Distances between Laguna and Los Pinos are computed from modern road maps and so may be in error by as much as ten miles.)

Laguna pueblo	8.7	122.2
Suwanee (formerly San Jose)	19.	141.2
Vicinity of Los Lunas	30.	171.2
Los Pinos	4.	175.2
Ranchitos de Isleta	2.	177.2
Upper Pajarito crossing	13.1	190.3
Albuquerque	3.8	194.1

From Los Pinos, the escorted trains traveled northward, usually on the east bank of the river, to Albuquerque, a distance measured as slightly less than 20 miles by the 1874-76 topographical surveys conducted by Lt. George M. Wheeler. Upon arriving at Albuquerque, the trains had reached the western terminus and starting point of the Mountain Route.

Stopping places on the Mountain Route were first mentioned by Captain Thompson, following his arrival with captives at the Bosque in April 1864. Similar reports by other officers confirm the increasing acceptance of the road regardless of season or condition of weather.[10] Winding north over the eastern slopes of the Sandia and Placer mountains to Galisteo, the road joined the old Santa Fe Trail east of Santa Fe at Koslowski's Ranch. A few miles northeast of Tecolote and in the vicinity of present Romeroville, the road abruptly turned south, dividing into two alternate branches of almost equal length; both were familiar to all persons of the time whose business took them south from Fort Union into the Pecos Valley.

The more westerly of the roads, once taken on a survey of the Pecos by Carleton in 1852, passed Apache Springs before skirting the settlements of Tecolotito and Anton Chico. When this route was followed by Captain Berney in March 1864, citizens of these two villages succeeded in stealing three Navajo boys from his train; others stole four Navajo horses while his column was encamped at Apache Springs.[11]

The alternate road, slanting off eastward of the rapacious settlements, roughly followed the course of the Rio Gallinas to the vicinity of Alexander Hatch's ranch, three miles south of Chaparito. The two roads merged once more near the crossing of the Gallinas with the old Fort Smith road, and from this point onward the Navajo columns moved down the east bank of the Pecos until thickets of mesquite and groves of cottonwood, in an otherwise barren prairie, made it clear they had arrived at Bosque Redondo.

Distances from Albuquerque, at 194.1 miles from Fort Canby, have been correlated from the reports of escorting military detachments, maps, and other contemporary sources.[12] Those places specifically mentioned as way-stops on the route are marked below with an asterisk.

Tijeras*	17.8	211.9
San Antonio*	2.	213.9
San Antonito*	3.2	217.1
San Pedro*	4.5	221.6
Real de San Francisco (on Tuerto Creek)*	8.	229.6
Galisteo*	21.3	250.9
Kozlowski's Ranch*	21.6	272.5
San José*	18.6	291.1
Bernal Springs*	9.	300.1
Tecolote*	5.	305.1
Vicinity of Romeroville	5.	310.1
Via Anton Chico:		
Anton Chico*	23.	333.1
Rio Gallinas junction*	17.6	350.7
Fort Sumner	73.4	424.1
Via Hatch's Ranch:		
Vicinity of Hatch's Ranch*	30.	340.1+
Fort Sumner	84.5	424.6+

Other references offer further evidence of frequent use of this route to Bosque Redondo. Lt. Col. J. Francisco Chaves in September 1864 went to Galisteo, expecting to intercept a column of Navajo captives. Finding no trace of the train, Colonel Chaves was about to proceed to Anton Chico when he learned the Navajos had indeed "been in the vicinity of the Placer," near Galisteo. Accordingly, he proceeded to San José and there met the train on September 15. The next day he accompanied the Navajos and their escort as far as Tecolote.[13]

Early in April 1865, General Carleton had occasion to visit Fort Sumner. Leaving Santa Fe, he went first to Tecolote. Two days later, he was at "Cedar Bluffs near Alamo Gordo," confident of reaching the Bosque that night. On April 20, he was back at Hatch's Ranch and on April 22 at Tecolote. In July 1866, Superintendent of Indian Affairs A. Baldwin Norton noted his departure from Santa Fe: "I leave here this morning for Ft. Sumner. I will be at Tucalote tomorrow night & go by Hatches Ranch." In the summer of 1864, Maj. Henry D. Wallen measured the distance between Santa Fe and Fort Sumner, via Tecolote, as 180.76 miles.[14]

In addition to the major Mountain Route and lesser alternate routes by way of Santa Fe and Fort Union, reference was made in 1866 by General Carleton to a fourth road used in escorting Navajos to the Bosque. No other mention of this route, of the four, the most direct and shortest, has been found. Such evidence as there is, and it is all negative, suggests that the road was not used at all until 1865 or 1866, and then only rarely and by small trains. Running nearly parallel to, but north of, present Highway 66, the route connected Albuquerque with Anton Chico by way of Tijeras, the village of Gutierres, and Cañon Blanco. From Albuquerque to the Bosque the distance by this road was 180 miles.

The last large contingent of captives taken to the Pecos was a group of 417 Navajos who left Fort Wingate December 13, 1866. Advised of their approach to the river, Carleton issued instructions to Maj. David H. Brotherton, commanding the military post of Albuquerque. "I am afraid that the parties of Navajoes who come in, and are sent by you from Albuquerque *via* Cañon Blanco to the Bosque Redondo, will, at this season of the year, suffer for want of fuel and of shelter of bluffs and groves by that routing..."Carleton directed, therefore, that all future parties of captives be taken by way of Tijeras, Placer del Tuerto, Eaton's Ranch (4.6 miles east of Galisteo, on Arroyo San Cristóbal) to Kozlowski's Ranch--in other words, the Mountain Route.

A reduced garrison made it impossible for Major Brotherton to supply an adequate escort; in addition to the large number of their train, the Navajos were bringing some 300 horses and about as many sheep and goats. With the few men he could spare, Brotherton sent the train upriver to Pino's Ranch, 15 miles southwest of Santa Fe, there to await a larger escort furnished from Fort Marcy.[15]

Navajo confinement at the Bosque was nearing its end in 1868 when Barboncito, addressing Gen. William T. Sherman and a council of headmen, declared,"...I would like to go back [home] the same road we came by, by way of Tecalote, Bernal, Tijeras and

Paralto." A few days later, informing Sherman of his plans for returning the Navajos to their former country, the new District commander, Brevet Maj. Gen. George W. Getty, said, "The route marked out is via San Jose, Tijeras Canon, Albuquerque and [New] Ft. Wingate."[16]

To this point, attention has focused on military routes to the Bosque with no reference to a more direct trail well known to the Navajos from past forays into eastern New Mexico. Explored by Carleton (then a brevet major) in 1854, this route turned south at Tijeras into the Manzano Mountains. After some 40 miles and near the village of Chilili, the trail took a course nearly due east by way of Antelope Spring, Cerro Pedernal, and the pink and white sandstone cliffs of Piedra Pintada Cañon, emerging near the James M. Giddings ranch at the junction of the Pecos and Agua Negra. Here, about three miles north of Puerto de Luna, the trail climbed to the high prairie and joined the commonly used wagon road down the east bank of the Pecos. The distance from Albuquerque to Bosque Redondo by this route was 167 miles as compared with 230 miles by the Mountain Route or 292 miles by way of Fort Union.[17]

A small train of 70 Navajos escorted to the river from Fort Wingate in August 1866 narrowly missed being sent by this route. At Albuquerque, where they awaited a change of escort, the Navajos "expressed a wish to go direct to Fort Sumner by way of Pintado and Giddings Ranche" Maj. Emil Fritz, commanding the post, later explained that he would have much preferred to send the Indians by that direct route, "but I had to avail myself of the train that came here with troops from below" who were returning to Fort Union.[18]

This instance is the only occasion when the Piedra Pintada Cañon route was mentioned during Navajo removal, but it is likely that the trail was used frequently during the Fort Sumner era by Navajos escaping from the reservation or returning to it voluntarily.

Only occasional mention is made by military officers, and then obliquely, of the outfitting of a train conveying Navajo prisoners to the Bosque. Navajos usually came to the gathering centers at Canby or Wingate with little more than they could carry in their hands. Many were nearly naked, more were dressed in rags. Rags became ribbons before the prisoners reached Los Pinos where, on a few occasions, a young junior officer in a mixture of horror, revulsion, and compassion, somehow provided blankets for those most desperately in need. There were, of course, exceptions. A few *ricos* among them rode into captivity in comparative comfort: warmly dressed, well mounted, and driving their herds of livestock before them. True, there were not many of these, but enough to account for a January 1865 count made on the reservation of 3,038 Navajo horses, 6,962 sheep, and 2,757 goats.[19]

It was customary for Navajos to gather in groups at the forts and wait, often for several weeks, for the arrival of the wagons that, in addition to supplies, were supposed to carry the aged, women, and children, and those too weak or sick to walk. Sometimes there was another long wait at Los Pinos where new trains and new relays of escorts were formed. The size of the military escort might be determined as much by the number of troops available as by the number of Indians forming a train. For the first contingent of 51 Navajos sent to the Bosque, Lt. Thomas Holmes commanded an escort of two non-commissioned officers and 20 privates. When Captain Berney left Fort Canby in January 1864, entrusted with an ultimate total of 1,473 captives, his detachment numbered 50 men. But when Sergeant Herrera was placed in charge of 147 captives on their way to Los Pinos, his escort numbered only 16 privates.

Oxen were used with some of the trains but mules were preferred. When Captain Thompson's escort left Fort Canby with 2,170 Navajos in March 1864, his train included eight ten-mule wagons and 20 six-mule wagons. When Captain McCabe followed Thompson from Fort Canby in the same month, his train of 836 Navajos was furnished 23 wagons. But at Los Pinos, when a new train was formed with more than 100 Navajos added to his command, he started for the Bosque with 21 wagons.

Most of the wagons and their teams were military property, but some were owned and operated by citizen contractors like William H. Moore who came to the territory in 1846 and soon was identified with both Tecolote and Fort Union as freighter, supplier of beef to military posts, and post sutler at Union.

The distance a train traveled each day could be governed by the pace of teams hauling the wagons or the pace that unmounted and often starving Navajos could walk. Other determining factors would be the size of the train, whether it was accompanied by herds of livestock, and the harsh or favoring condition of the weather. By way of comparison, a wagon train of military supplies moving from Fort Union to Navajo country normally averaged from 15 to 20 miles a day. The military escorts convoying Navajo prisoners to the

Bosque were consistently slower, averaging 12 to 13 miles a day.

Kit Carson's campaign of systematic crop destruction left the Navajos little choice: they could starve or freeze to death or they could surrender. They surrendered, therefore, in such numbers that military transportation lines collapsed. One thousand Indians were gathered at Fort Canby by the middle of February 1864, and more continued to arrive each day. Commanding the Navajo Expedition in Carson's absence, Capt. Asa B. Carey was helpless. Until more wagons arrived, his prisoners must wait.

Never had such a mass of humanity choked the narrow limits of Cañoncito Bonito. "Many of the Navajo Indians arriving are almost unable to Travel, resulting from hunger and destitution," Carey observed.[20] Ten days later, the number of captives had swelled to 2,500, engulfing the garrison of 335 officers and troops. Between February 20 and March 6, waiting for the wagons to come, 126 prisoners died.

Figures in the accompanying table of Navajos sent to the Bosque Rodondo may be regarded as being close to, if not entirely, accurate. Errors of arithmetic as well as errors of omission are found in a few reports by post commanders and officers conducting escorts. A major discrepancy is discernible in reported Navajo losses. More than 2,000 Navajos who reportedly were sent to the Bosque remain unaccounted for. It is certain that some of them did reach the reservation (how many is purely conjectural), but their arrival went unreported. What happened to the others will never be known.

Not included in the tabulation are the numbers killed or captured and sold into peonage or slavery by New Mexican raiders when Navajos began coming to Canby and Wingate to surrender. Post commanders usually received only spotty information of these raids and such information, if not unreliable, often was lacking in necessary detail. Two incidents, among scores, may illustrate the point.

In February 1864, as hundreds of Delgadito's people were coming to Fort Wingate to surrender, Maj. Ethan W. Eaton, the post commander, was informed by Delgadito that "a party of Mexicans... killed some of his men and took some women and children prisoners, and drove off some of their stock, and [Delgadito] feared that they might again attack the rear of his people before they could get in." (Delgadito had been permitted temporary leave from the reservation in order to induce his followers to surrender.) Similar episodes near Fort Canby caused Kit Carson to complain of the "audacity" of citizen raiders. Lt. Charles M. Hubbell was sent out with his company to "capture whatever band of citizen marauders" as he found preying on the surrendering Indians.[21]

Capt. Edmund Butler, commanding Fort Wingate in May 1867, remarked that a Navajo girl, 13 or 14 years of age, had appealed to him for protection. "She states," Butler reported, "that she was stolen from a party of Navajos who were on their way to this Post to surrender last Fall, but who were attacked by citizens, the males killed, and the women & children captured and sold into peonage. She was held as a peon...in the Rio Arriba and north of the Pueblo of Jemez. She effected her escape...taking nine days, she says, to accomplish the journey."[22]

General Carleton's miscalculation of the size of the Navajo nation and his consternation, which amounted to near-panic when he realized that there were insufficient food stores on hand to feed the swelling thousands pouring into Fort Sumner, may account in part for the sharp decline in the number of Navajos sent to the Bosque in 1865. As late as April 24, 1864, disregarding Colonel Carson's better information, Carleton brashly advised Adj. Gen. Lorenzo Thomas that "the whole number of the [Navajos] to be eight thousand." Carson's conservative estimate indicated a Navajo population of 12,000.

By the end of October 1864, with 7,381 Navajos already drawing rations on the reservation and with untold hundreds more forming in new trains for the Long March, Carleton conceded his error. Transportation problems coupled with an alarming shortage of supplies at Fort Sumner threatened captive Navajos with starvation unless he acted quickly. Carleton accordingly issued directions to halt all further movement of Navajos beyond the Los Pinos depot, which in effect halted movement everywhere, until further orders. At the same time he cut the Indians' daily ration in half, to 12 ounces of grain meal and eight ounces of meat. This in itself bordered the limits of a starvation allowance.[23]

A second factor of importance, unquestionably influenced by Carleton's damming of the Los Pinos dike, was almost complete cessation of military operations into Navajo country in the spring and summer of 1865 by the garrison at Fort Wingate. Carleton then virtually assured Navajo withdrawal into the most remote recesses of their land when, in July, he gave his sanction to supplying citizen raiders with ammunition in order that they might campaign more freely against their old enemy.[24]

"If you can *safely* spare any ammunition you can issue some to

157

the parties of citizens who are to make *bonafide* expeditions against the Navajoes," he advised Fort Wingate's commander."...The old Navajo Country must be made too hot to hold Navajoes. Tell the Zuñis they shall have all [the booty] they can get from the Navajoes. That we are determined to kill all Navajo *men* who run away from the Bosque, or who will not go there."

Some perspective on the overall removal of the Navajo nation is provided through the experiences of four of the larger trains. The perspective, of course, is a reflection of the prevailing military viewpoint. One of the early trains to move out, before the avalanche of surrendering Indians descended, was that of Captain Berney who left Fort Canby January 25, 1864 with 165 Navajo men, women, and children. To feed his hungry charges, Berney carried supplies enough to issue rations of one pound of beef and one pound of flour until he reached Fort Wingate. There, the beef ration was replaced with bacon.

> The bacon was nearly all wasted as the Indians evidently did not like it [Berney reported]; its place was supplied as far as practicable, by game, which their hunting parties had killed on the route. During the march [to the river] the Indians suffered intensely from want of Clothing, four were entirely frozen to death.25

After a layover of 16 days at Los Pinos, Berney's train, increased now to a total of 1,445 captives, started upriver with accompanying herds of about 200 horses and between 300 and 400 sheep and goats. Another variety of meat had been substituted for the unwanted bacon, but the flour, equally foreign and abhorrent to the Indians, caused trouble. Treating it as they did their favored corn meal, the Navajos consumed it half-cooked, as a mush. In consequence, many of them became sick. Closely observant, Berney neglected to mention this but did recommend that corn, instead of flour, be issued in the future. This in time was done. His report continued:

> In my first Camp [out of Los Pinos] I had them divided into parties each under a Chief, for the purpose of issuing them their rations. I then had the beef killed and gave a portion to each Chief, and instructed them to divide it equally among their people: the flour was divided in the same manner. After the second day I had no difficulty in dividing their rations...

Invariably when the Indians would receive their rations, they would go to their fires, and cook and eat their entire ration of beef at once. The flour they made into dough, using their sheepskins for this purpose - and cooked it in hot ashes, or on flat stones, picked up for this purpose: in this way a large amount of flour is wasted. I would here respectfully suggest that a proportion of corn in lieu of flour, would be far preferable to the Indians. I remarked in many instances that they would give a ration [one pound] of flour for a single ear of corn.

All the hides and sheepskins were carefully cut up and divided, by the Chiefs; the hides were worked into Moc[c]asins, and the sheepskins were dried and used to sleep on, and in some cases made into garments for protection against the cold.

When he arrived at Fort Sumner March 13, Captain Berney reported losing only 19 prisoners. Three were stolen by citizens, and two captives escaped while the train was encamped on the Pecos. Fourteen others froze to death.

Greater suffering was experienced by Navajos who made the journey with Captain Thompson. Old Herrero, a headman of much influence, was among the prisoners whose march of 41 days was made in snow of late winter. The train was the largest ever sent to the Bosque, numbering 2,170 when Thompson left Fort Canby March 4, 1864, and gaining 427 more captives along the way. "It was a great sight," one witness, doubtless a soldier, later remarked. "We stretched from Fort Defiance to the Window Rock haystacks," a distance of about seven miles.[26]

Outmarching his supply wagons, Thompson stopped in the mountains above Tijeras to wait for them to catch up. From his camp near Real de San Francisco, he advised General Carleton that "There has been a heavy fall of snow...making it very difficult to travel, the snow on the road averaging about 10 inches." He made no allusion beyond this to the hardships that were decimating his column. Only when he reached Fort Sumner was it learned that 197 Navajos had died during the march, nearly one-tenth of the Navajos in his column. At various points, the prisoners were harassed by civilians who managed to steal 50 animals from the herds of horses and mules. General Carleton in a few lines attempted to describe the Navajos' ordeal: "The weather was very inclement, with terrible gales of wind and heavy falls of snow; the Indians were nearly naked; and, besides, many died from dysentery, occasioned by eating too heartily of half-cooked bread, made of our flour, to which they were not accustomed..."[27] Herrero Viejo, Old Blacksmith, was one of those who survived.

159

THE LONG MARCH: 1863-67

A tabulation based on reports of the New Mexico Military Department, Indian Superintendency, & Santa Fe Gazette

	CAPTIVES SENT				REPORTED LOSSES				ARRIVALS AT BOSQUE	
Year	From Fort Canby	From Fort Wingate	From Other Points	Total Sent	Reported Escaped	Reported Died	Reported Stolen	Lost & Unaccounted for	Arrival at BR Reported	Reported Sent but Arrival Unreported
1863	9	305	21	335	31	4		15	275	60
1864	5,631	2,985	1,592	10,208	189	332	3	143	7,856	2,352
1865		50	17	67					39	28
1866		992	4	996			17		660	336
1867		6		6					16	
TOTALS	5,640	4,338	1,634	11,612	220	336	20	158	8,846	2,776

Revised Tabulation: Deductions for Captives Known Sent for a Second Time

	From Fort Canby	From Fort Wingate	From Other Points	Total Sent	Reported Escaped	Reported Died	Reported Stolen	Lost & Unaccounted for	Arrival at BR Reported	Reported Sent but Arrival Unreported
1864		1	1						(Delgadito & Pino Baca)	
1866		51 / 91							(Caballo Blanco & followers) (Barboncito & followers)	
Final Revised Totals	5,640	4,195	1,633	11,468	220	336	16	158	8,850	2,772

4 (who escaped & reached BR in 1867)

160

Not far in Thompson's rear, another train of 836 Navajos left Fort Canby March 20, escorted by Captain McCabe. At several points on the way, more prisoners were added to the column until their numbers totalled 982. At the head of the line of Navajos, a lieutenant was posted with a guard of 15 privates.

> I placed as many of the women and children and old people as possible in the wagons [McCabe reported], and had one empty wagon placed every morning under the control of the officer of the day for the purpose of travelling with the Guard to receive such sick and aged Indians as might have given out...On the Second days [sic] march a very severe snow storm set in which lasted for four days with unusual severity and occasioned great suffering amongst the Indians, many of whom were nearly naked and of course unable to withstand such a Storm.[28]

In marches not exceeding ten miles a day, McCabe's train turned south at Ojo del Gallo and reached Fort Wingate March 29. Although at Fort Canby they had been furnished with rations for eight days, the Navajos had been on the road for ten. Captain McCabe had cause for anxiety, therefore, when the Fort Wingate commissary was unable to issue more than half rations for the journey to Los Pinos. Hoping to forestall mutiny or mass desertion by his charges, McCabe called the principal headmen and warriors together and explained "that I believed they would receive their full amount of rations at Los Pinos...that the present diminution was but a temporary arrangement...This seemed to satisfy them."

At Los Pinos, where his train was delayed for nearly three weeks, McCabe received additional prisoners, among them the notorious Pino Baca, a *Diné Ana'aii* of the late Sandoval's band. For a long time, the captain observed, Pino Baca had lived at the mountain village of Cebolleta "where his habits (naturally bad) had been still more depraved by the class of associates he lived amongst." Baca lost no time in proving to McCabe that his odorous reputation was deserved. Complaint was made by certain of the Navajo headmen that two captive children of the column had been kidnaped and sold to Puebloans of Isleta. Lt. Donaciano Montoya was detailed with a small squad to investigate the matter and, if possible, recover the children and return them to their parents. The children were found in the pueblo without great trouble and Lieutenant Montoya quickly traced the deed directly to Pino Baca.

Captain McCabe ordered Baca seized and confined under close guard, pending possible disciplinary action on his arrival at Fort

Sumner. But this was not to be. Three days after the train resumed its journey, in the vicinity of Tijeras Canyon, Pino Baca escaped. Twenty-five women and children deserted from the column at about the same time.

A week later and now safely out of reach of McCabe's escort, Pino Baca turned up at military headquarters in Albuquerque. His story sounded convincing to Captain Brotherton, the commanding officer.[29] What he told Brotherton, in effect, was that he was a fortunate survivor of the last train that passed through town. When a number of Navajo captives became sick and unable to travel, Captain McCabe detached them from the column near Tijeras and left them in Pino Baca's care. Baca was told to administer medicine to them, bury any who died, and conduct any survivors back to Los Pinos. Unfortunately, however, they had encountered six New Mexicans from the village of San Antonita. These people, who were armed with rifles and bows and arrows, wrested from Pino Baca a safe conduct pass given to him by Captain McCabe and seized as captives eight women and five children who they took back to their village. Captain Brotherton presently learned that at least part of Pino Baca's story was true: a number of the women and children had indeed been seized by a citizen band. Too late, however, did he learn that Baca was an escaped prisoner and himself a kidnaper now at large again and hiding out near his home at Cebolleta.

After he arrived at the Bosque on May 10, McCabe remarked that he had the Navajos of his column "marched into the Fort and Seated in lines to be counted, and the Officer of the day counted 786 Indians." In this and other details (McCabe said he arrived at Fort Sumner May 11), he appears to have been in slight error.[30] If the report of the fort's commander is correct, McCabe lost 205 Navajos during the march. According to McCabe, about 110 of these died. His losses, in any case, moved Colonel Carson, again in command at Fort Canby, to advise Carleton

> I have unofficially learned that Captain McCabe lost while *en route* by Desertion one hundred (100) Indians, headed by a son of the late Chief "Juanico"; Cause, want of a sufficiency to eat. I would respectfully suggest to you the propriety, and good feeling of giving to the Indians while at Forts Canby and Wingate, and while en route to the Bosque Redondo, a sufficiency to eat.[31]

The most disastrous recorded escort of Navajo captives was made in October 1864 by Lt. Charles M. Hubbell. In some small measure,

162

the fault may not have been entirely his. Shortly before the abandonment of Fort Canby and dispersal of its garrison, Hubbell was directed to "proceed with the Utmost dispatch" with his Company H, 1st Cavalry, New Mexico Volunteers, to Fort Union. Before his precipitous departure, 414 Navajos were entrusted to his care as far as Fort Wingate where he was instructed to leave them.

Unless he received verbal orders as well, of which there is no record, it would appear that Lieutenant Hubbell recklessly interpreted the sense of "Utmost dispatch" as meaning "and damn the consequences." He drove the train at a killing pace: 18 miles the first day, 27 miles the second, 24 miles the third, 23 on the fourth, and 18 miles into Fort Wingate on the fifth. His explanation leaves much unanswered: "I turned over to the Commanding Officer p[e]r to Instructions 250 Indians 10 having died and the remainder Strayed off in Small parties owing to the Cold weather and the Quickness of the march. Weather cold rains and wind...Agreeable to my Orders I could not prevent the Indians from scattering off in small parties not with standing I used every exertion in my power to prevent them doing so."[32] In short, over a distance of 110 miles (as he measured it), Hubbell lost 164--more than one-third--of his captives.

On his approach to Albuquerque, Hubbell received word that his orders had been changed; instead of reporting to Fort Union, he would proceed with Company H to Los Pinos and there await a forming train which he would conduct to Bosque Redondo. When he left Los Pinos with this new consignment, Hubbell commanded a column of 1,073 Navajos. Among them, and now in chains, was a truculent Pino Baca who had been recaptured some days previously. Hubbell's progress now was moderate; he was a month in reaching the Bosque. He submitted no report upon his arrival, but on this second stage of his march he lost 53 more Navajos by death, theft, or desertion. Thus, his total loss was 217 prisoners.

Navajo memory of the Long March is of misery, hunger, frequent mistreatment, and death. In the testimony of those who recalled the stories told by their parents, the impersonal detachment that characterizes so much of the military record is conspicuously absent. Dates, and numbers, and many of the names of persons and places are absent as well. What is present is a sense of continuing involvement, a deep and emotional concern for what happened to a small nation of people more than 100 years ago. The accounts, admittedly second-hand, each share a certain repetitive detail; in

163

each may be detected a ring of truth.33

The surrender of Manuelito in late summer 1866 signaled the end of armed resistance to Carleton's troops and precipitated the final phase of Navajo removal to Bosque Redondo. By his refusal until now to come in, Manuelito had encouraged some 800 Navajos to follow his example. His surrender at Fort Wingate with a small residue of his band on September 1, a capitulation planned in concert with Barboncito, Ganado Blanco, and Caballo Blanco, no doubt exerted a decisive influence. Before the end of the year, six more groups of Navajos, numbering in all 784, surrendered and were sent to the Bosque from Fort Wingate. Beyond reach of Manuelito's influence were possibly 200 other Navajos who never surrendered; these people remained in hiding, many in the vicinity of Navajo Mountain, a few others in or near the Grand Canyon. Their number is entirely conjectural.

A man of huge stature and normally grave or downcast in expression, Manuelito had surrendered once before, in April 1864, but was allowed to remain for weeks in camp in Calites Canyon. At the last moment, he had changed his mind and, with a large number of followers, escaped before he could be sent to Fort Sumner. At nearly the same time, the commander of the post on the Pecos had mistakenly reported his arrival there with Captain Berney's large train.34 Since then, conflicting stories of his whereabouts and his activities had increased the already considerable aura of legend that surrounded him.

The first reliable word of him in months was received in June 1866 when three women of his band, arriving with their children and other captives at Fort Sumner, said Manuelito had been badly wounded in the left forearm and left side in a fight with Hopis. When they saw him last, some 60 nights ago, he and about 40 of his people indicated that they intended to give themselves up and come to the Bosque. Nothing more was heard of them until late in July when a Navajo warrior, a man of some importance, judging from the silver head-stall of his horse and his other fine equipage, surrendered at Fort Wingate. He identified himself as the son of Yusu-ni Nez and a member of Manuelito's band. He came from the Sierra Escudilla where he had left the war leader with Caballo Blanco, Barboncito, and Ganado Blanco at their mountain camp some distance to the south and across the dry plains from Zuñi Salt Lake. (With Barboncito, the other two headmen had been leaders of the mass departure of Navajos from the reservation in June 1865.) They all spoke of their desire to surrender. The fire of defiance in Manuelito was gone; he was destitute now, weak and suffering from the wound that stiffened his left arm.[35]

With their headman, 50 members of Caballo Blanco's band came in voluntarily to Fort Wingate a few days later, but Manuelito and Barboncito, suspicious and fearful of the treatment they would receive, remained in the mountains. Ganado Blanco, unlike the others, firmly opposed the idea of surrendering at Wingate; instead, he planned to return to Bosque Redondo by himself on a southern route, presumably through Mescalero Apache country.

Meanwhile, at Fort Sumner, a son of Manuelito appeared with a companion early in August. They came from the Sierra Escudilla, they said, to see with their own eyes the conditions that prevailed on the reservation. Manuelito had asked them to do this and told them to come back and tell him if it would be safe to go there. After a long talk with the two young emissaries, Brevet Lt. Col. William McCleave told them "to go out amongst the Navajoes...and see for themselves." They did so, McCleave advised General Carleton, "and two days afterwards reported in readiness to go back and tell their people all they had seen and ask them to come in."[36]

Word that the last war leader of the Navajo nation was coming from the direction of Agua Fria to give himself up reached Fort Wingate by messenger. Capt. Edmund Butler, the post commander who personally had directed and led the closing troop operations of the Navajo War, rode out to meet him. This courteous gesture was one that Manuelito was well able to appreciate. His followers, who two years before numbered 500, now were reduced to 23. Despite recent reports of their poverty, the Navajos were well mounted, their horses and mules all in good condition.

"Manuelito comes from the head waters of the Colorado Chiquito," Captain Butler informed General Carleton the next day. "He met the messenger I sent out to him about ten days since. His wound is healed, but has almost entirely lost the use of his left arm from its effects. His son, son-in-law, nephew &c. are with him."[37]

Captain Montoya commanded the escort when Manuelito's party left Fort Wingate for the river on September 9. Instead of sending him by the Mountain Route, General Carleton thought it would be well to parade the fallen war leader before the people of Santa Fe. Ignored by the Santa Fe *New Mexican,* rabid in its opposition to Carleton and all of his policies, the event received only three bland

165

sentences in the *Gazette:*

> Manuelito, the Navajo Chief and quite a large party of his band were brought to Santa Fe last week. They are to be taken to the Bosque Redondo Reservation and furnished a new home where they will have less of the cares of State on their minds and more bread and meat to eat. Manuelito was the most stubborn of all the Navajo Chiefs and was the most difficult to be brought to terms.38

Three weeks later, on October 5, when Manuelito's arrival at Fort Sumner was greeted quietly, almost in official silence, there were few, if any, who realized how important this moment was in bringing the Long March to an end.

NOTES

1. Senate Exec. Doc., 39 Cong., 2 sess., Report No. 156, "Condition of the Indian Tribes...," 1867, Appendix, p. 345. Three members of the joint congressional investigating committee headed by Senator Doolittle took Carey's testimony June 20, before proceeding to Santa Fe for further hearings in July. Doolittle was accompanied to New Mexico by Vice President L.F. Foster and Rep. Lewis W. Ross.

2. *Ibid*, p. 127: Aide-de-Camp Cyrus H. Deforrest, Dept. HQ, to Capt. Rafael Chacon, cmdg. Ft. Wingate, August 15, 1863; Capt. Julius C. Shaw, Ft. Wingate, to Capt. Ben C. Cutler, AAG, Dept. HQ, August 27, 1863, National Archives (NA), Record Group (RG) 393, Ft. Wingate correspondence combined with Fort Defiance Letter Book, Letters Sent (LS), 1861-64.

3. Twenty miles south of Albuquerque, Los Pinos depot occupied unplanted land at Peralta owned by Gov. Henry Connelly. Leased May 10, 1862 for $5,500 per year by Capt. Herbert M. Enos, assistant quartermaster, its garrison in early 1863 included Companies E and I, 5th U.S. Infantry. Among its adobe buildings were company quarters, guard house, commissary and quartermaster's offices, "a very large and expensive" storehouse, and a hospital. In an 1863 inspection report, Maj. Henry D. Wallen observed that most prevalent of hospital cases were gonorrhea and syphilis, relevant here in view of the quick spread of these diseases among Navajos removed to Bosque Redondo. Los Pinos was abandoned in late September or early October 1866. (Enos to Col. E.R.S. Canby, May 10, 1862, NA, Records of Army Commands (RAC), RG 393, E-31-1862, LR; Wallen to Capt. Samuel Archer, cmdg. Los Pinos, February 11, 1863, NA, RG 393, W-58-1863, LR.)

4. *Santa Fe Gazette,* September 5, 1863. When Carleton visited Fort Wingate in April, he apparently was undecided where to send Navajo captives, wavering between Fort Sumner (a creation that satisifed no need but that of his own vanity) and a proposal made by his predecessor, Colonel Canby, for a Navajo reservation on the Little Colorado. Remarking on this indecision, Wingate's commander, Col. J. Francisco Chaves, noted that Carleton "appeared anxious to glean all the information he could about the Colorado Chiquito...he was not entirely satisfied about the location that would be most suitable for the Indians." (Chaves to Supt. James L. Collins, May 4, 1863, NA, New Mexico Superintendency of Indian Affairs, microcopy 234, roll 551.) A few days later, when Carleton met with the headmen Barboncito and Delgadito at Cubero, his mind was made up. He told them that Navajos who wished to be regarded as friendly must go to Bosque Redondo. Those who refused to do so would be considered hostile and treated accordingly. "Condition of the Indian Tribes...," Appendix, p. 116.

5. Wardwell to Cutler, December 8, 1863, NA, RG 393, W-412-1863, LR.

6. Wallen to Carleton, December 11, 1863, NA, RG 393, no file mark, unentered miscellaneous papers. Lateral channel cutting of the Pecos has obliterated all trace of the original fort site.

7. DeForrest to Chacon, August 15, 1863, cited above.

8. Long to Col. D.T. Chandler, April 10, 1853, enclosures #3 & #4 with Maj. H.L. Kendrick, cmdg. Ft. Defiance, to Col. Samuel Cooper, May 15, 1853, AG, U.S.A. NA, RG 393, K-8-1853, LR.

9. Old Fort Wingate Post Returns, October 1862; New Fort Wingate Post Returns, July 1868, NA, RG 94.

10. Thompson to Carleton, March 29, 1864. NA, RG 393, 437-T-12-1864, LR; Thompson to Cutler, April 15, 1864, 514-T-17-1864, LR; McCabe to AAG, May 12, 1864, 312-M-137-1864, LR; Lt. George K. Withers to Carleton, memorandum enclosed with June 12, 1864; 575-W-177-1864, LR; Lt. Joseph Felmer to AAG, July 2, 1864, 168-F-23-1864, LR; Lt. William Nelson to Cutler, September 10, 1864, 347-N-19-1864, LR.

11. Berney to Cutler, March 14, 1864, NA, RG 393, 615-B-58-1864, LR.

12. Principal sources include Wheeler Survey maps of 1877, Part of Central New Mexico, Atlas Sheets #77, #77A, #78A, Office of the Chief of Engineers, NA, RG 77; 1859 map of the Territory and Military Department of New Mexico compiled in the Bureau of Topogl. Engrs. of the War Dept..., NA, RG 77, W55 (1), Office of the Chief of Engineers; 1864 map of the Military Department of New Mexico...[drawn] by Capt. Allen L. Anderson...NA, RG 77, W83 (2); undated Sketch Map of that Part of the Interior of New Mexico embraced by the Rivers Rio Grande del Norte & Pecos drawn by...Lt. I[saiah] N. Moore, NA, RG 77, W34; Carleton to Sumner, February 25, 1852, NA, RG 393, #16, LR; "Journal of an Expedition to the Bosque Redondo" by Lt. Henry B. Davidson, enclosed with Carelton to Bvt Maj. W. A. Nichols, December 22, 1864, AAG (NA, RG 393, Unregistered Letters Received, 1854); M. Bloomfield to Enos, August 11, 1864 (NA, RG 393, 361-B-449-1864, LR).

13. Chaves to DeForrest, September 28, 1864, NA, RG 393, 391-C-280-1864, LR.

14. *Santa Fe Gazette,* August 27, 1864.

15. Carleton to Brotherton, December 21, 1866, NA, RG 93, Dept. of N.M., Miscellaneous Documents, Box 35; Brotherton to DeForrest, December 28, 1866, NA, RG 393, B-271-1866, LR.

16. Proceedings of a council of May 29, 1868 at Ft. Sumner, NA, RG 75, Office of the Secretary of the Interior, Indian Division: correspondence re Indian Treaty Commission, 1867-68; Getty to Sherman, June 7, 1868, NA, RG 94, Dept. of N.M., Adjutant General's Office (AGO), LR.

17. Lieutenant Davidson's "Journal of an Expedition to the Bosque Redondo," cited in note 12.

18. Fritz to DeForrest, August 29, 1866, NA, RG 393, F-60-1866, LR.

19. Census of the Navajoe Indians, enclosure with Brig. Gen. Marcellus M. Crocker, cmdg. Ft. Sumner, to Cutler, January 7, 1865, NA, RG 393, 58-C-1865, LR.

20. Carey to Cutler, February 14, 1864, NA, RG 393, Old Book 124, Vol. 76, Correspondence of the Navajo Expedition.

21. Eaton to Cutler, February 2, 1864, NA, RG 393, Fort Defiance Letter Book, LS, 1861-64; Carson to AAG, April 13, 1864, NA, RG 393, Old Book 124, Vol. 76; Correspondence of the Navajo Expedition.

22. Butler to DeForrest, May 5, 1867, NA, RG 393, W-38-1867, LR.

23. Carleton to Butler, cmdg. Los Pinos, October 28, 1864, "Condition of the Indian Tribes..." p. 170.

24. Carleton's endorsement with Lt. Col. Shaw, cmdg. Ft. Wingate, to Cutler, July 10, 1865, NA, RG 393, S-180-1864, LR.

25. Berney to Cutler, April 7, 1864, NA, RG 393, 620-B-98-1864, LR.

26. Eleanor Friend Sleight, Fort Defiance, *El Palacio* (1953)/60(1):8.

27. Thompson to Carleton, March 29, 1864, and Thompson to Cutler, April 15, 1864, NA, RG 393, 437-T-12,1864, LR, 514-T-17-1864, LR; Carleton to Brig. Gen. Lorenzo Thomas, April 24, 1864, in "Condition of the Indian Tribes... p. 179.

28. McCabe to AAG, May 12, 1864, NA, RG 393, 312-M-137-1864, LR.

29. Brotherton to AAG, May 2, 1864, NA, RG 393, no file mark.

30. Capt. Henry B. Bristol, cmdg. Ft. Sumner, noted that: "There has been 777 arrivals among the Navajoes--186 men--266 women and 325 children, who arrived on the 10th of this month, under charge of Capt. Francis McCabe..." (Bristol to AAG, May 13, 1864, NA, RG 393, 49-B-178, LR). Fort Sumner Post Returns for May 1864 report that McCabe arrived May 9 with 777 Navajo captives.

31. Carson to Carleton, April 10, 1864, NA, RG 393, Old Book 124, Vol. 76, Correspondence of the Navajo Expedition.

32. Hubbell to Lt. E. Butler, cmdg. Los Pinos, October 19, 1864, enclosure with Butler to Cutler (same date), NA, RG 393, 548-B-583-1864, LR.

33. Howard Gorman of the Navajo Tribe acted as interpreter when four men testified January 16-17, 1951 at Window Rock, Arizona before Louis J. O'Marr, associate commissioner of the U.S. Indian Claims Commission. Atty. Charles J. Alexander represented the Navajo Tribe and Atty. Ralph A. Barney represented the United States (Indian Claims Commission, The Navajo Tribe vs. The United States, Docket 229, Washington, D.C.)

34. Maj. H.D. Wallen, reporting Berney's arrival March 13, 1864, noted that in his train were "Manuelito and fourteen hundred and thirty Navajoes" (Wallen to AAG, April 26, 1864, NA, Military Dept. of N.M., LR by the AGO, microcopy 619, roll 284). Wallen's report, a detailed survey of conditions at Fort Sumner, has been published by J. Lee Correll in *The Navajo Times,* December 8, 1966, and by John P. Wilson, Prisoners without Walls, *El Palacio* (1967) 74(1). Major Wallen was in error: it was Delgadito, not Manuelito, who came with Berney's train.

35. Bristol, cmdg. Ft. Sumner, to Post Adjt. W.R. Savage, June 23, 1866, NA, RG 393, B-132-1866, LR; Butler, cmdg. Ft. Wingate, to DeForrest, July 28, 1866, published in the *Santa Fe Gazette,* August 4, 1866.

36. McCleve to DeForrest, August 11, 1866, NA, RG 393, Mc-98-1866, LR.

37. *Santa Fe Gazette,* September 15, 1866. Barboncito, with 90 followers, started from Ft. Wingate to the Bosque on November 15.

38. *Santa Fe Gazette,* September 29, 1866.

Frank McNitt, 1912-1972

On December 10, 1972, Frank McNitt died peacefully in his sleep, even as the first copy of his latest book was on its way to him. Whether as journalist, historian, colleague, or generous friend, all who knew him are immensely saddened by his passing.

Frank was born December 5, 1912 in Cleveland, Ohio. After attending the Yale School of Fine Arts and the Art Students League in New York City he worked for the family newspaper, the *Southbridge* (Mass.) *Evening News,* and for cartoonist John Streisbel. For twelve years, 1941-1953, he was employed at the Westwood Hills Press in West Los Angeles. He then settled in New Mexico and for the next seven years lived in Farmington, Albuquerque, and - while writing his second book - at Burnham's Trading Post. The move to New Mexico marked his expansion from journalist to author, and his first book, *Richard Wetherill: Anasazi,* appeared during his employment at the University of New Mexico Press. In 1960 he returned east to North Woodstock, Connecticut and resumed association with the *Southbridge Evening News,* where he was both owner and publisher from 1964 until he sold the paper to devote full time to research and writing.

His interest in the Navajo people, their history and the prominent early traders in Navajoland carries through all of his works, and his already enormous research files were continually expanding. For any new bit of information, however minor, Frank never failed to express his gratitude and to somehow leave you feeling that your own research was so very important. As his own knowledge and resources expanded, he willingly shared these with others, and often subordinated his own research inclinations for awhile to pursue topics in which his friends expressed interest, however remotely these might relate to his own. For this alone, no measure of gratitude is sufficient, and many key Southwestern historical sources would yet lie undiscovered but for his persistence.

Navajo Wars, his latest and now his last book, was the product of some eight years of research and writing. This was to be followed by a history of the Navajo incarceration at the Bosque Redondo, which he had begun to draft, and by a biography of the trader Lorenzo Hubbell, for which he was still interviewing Hubbell associates and assembling other records. For both projects, his experience and scholarship made him eminently qualified. Hopefully someone will write these books, perhaps incorporating the large body of information which he had already assembled.

A mutual friend expresses feelings not limited to himself when he writes that "I regret his passing exceedingly for his worth was not measured by his work alone; he was one of the most gracious gentlemen that I have ever known".

THE NAVAJO "LONG WALK": RECOLLECTIONS BY NAVAJOS

Crawford R. Buell

The time was June of 1868. Some 7,500 Navajos were walking the 300 miles of plains country from captivity at Fort Sumner, New Mexico, to freedom at Fort Wingate, New Mexico. Most of them had been held in the Fort Sumner internment camp for four years. Now all were going home. This was the end of a forced migration - under military control - of families and groups of families.

Among the groups was a father with his wife and baby. The mother had not been able to nurse the baby adequately because of the poor diet, so the little child was very weak and seemed to be growing weaker.

The mother kept lagging behind the group, trying to do something for the child; and the father grew impatient, wanting her to hurry and keep up, else they would be left behind. Suddenly the baby gave a little cry and seemed to die. The mother stopped to grieve over it, but the father insisted that she place the cradleboard in a tree and go on. This she did, but at every few steps she turned around, loath to leave her child. Finally she heard it give another little cry, and this was too much for her mother heart. She ran back to the baby.

The father grew angry. "All right, stay there if you like," he growled, "but I'm going on. The baby is going to die anyway. Why don't you leave it?"

Of course she would not.

As the father hurried to catch up with the group ahead, he noticed where they had broken some stalks of cactus in passing. A thick, pearly-looking juice oozed from the broken stems. He noticed that it looked like milk; and he wondered if it would be anythink like milk in effect.

He broke off some stems and ran back to his wife and baby. Carefully, he squeezed some of the juice into the baby's mouth; the baby seemed to retain it well. Another few drops - more - the baby began to look brighter!

Gathering a supply of the life-giving cactus stalks, the father and

171

mother hurried back to their group with the baby. They were able to make the rest of the Long Walk home without incident. "That baby," Kayah David concluded, "was my grandfather!"1

The Navajos, along with their linguistic cousins, the Apaches, had seen their homelands occupied, first by Spaniards and later by Anglos, when American forces under Brig. Gen. Stephen Watts Kearny occupied Santa Fe in 1846. Among General Kearny's first concerns was marauding by Apaches and Navajos.

Sixteen years later, when Brig. Gen. Henry H. Sibley's Confederate forces invaded New Mexico, Union troops became fully occupied with the Civil War, and the Apaches and Navajos became more aggressive. However, later in 1862, Brig. Gen. James H. Carleton, commander of the Department of New Mexico, ordered Col. Christopher (Kit) Carson to contain the Mescalero Apaches. By early 1863, Carson had subdued the Mescaleros and sent about 400 men, women, and children "from their fastnesses around Fort Stanton" to internment on the 1,600 square mile Bosque Redondo reservation at Fort Sumner on the Pecos River.2 Persons of Spanish descent had called this area Bosque Redondo or Round Grove of Trees. The Navajos called it Hwelte, from the Spanish *fuerte, fort,* but pronounced colloquially as though the Spanish spelled it *juerte.*3

Following the subjugation of the Mescalero Apaches, Carleton turned his attention to the Navajos. He issued General Orders No. 15 on June 15, 1863.4 Carleton's letter to Lt. Col. J. Francisco Chavez of June 23 gave the Navajos "until the twentieth day of July of this year to come in - they and all those who belong to what they call the peace party; *that after that day every Navajo that is seen will be considered as hostile and treated accordingly."*5 Carleton's typical instructions to commanders was to "kill every male Navajo or Apache Indian who is large enough to bear arms."6

Carson, who was essentially a humane man, sought to use personal persuasion instead of following the orders of Carleton literally. He aggressively sought the Navajos in their home lands; and he enlisted the support of several Navajo headmen. Military action was his last resort. He used the "scorched earth" policy of burning cornfields, storage areas, and hogans; and he destroyed their orchards. These actions starved hundreds of Navajos into surrendering. They were taken as prisoners under military guard to Bosque Redondo.7 On June 27, 1865, the official count of Navajos in captivity was 8,474 but many others were out hunting and were not counted.[8] Probably an equal number remained free in the vast recesses of the Navajo land.

After the Navajos had been in captivity for more than four years, two Peace Commissioners, Lt. Gen. W. T. Sherman and Colonel S. F. Tappan, signed the last treaty of peace with the Navajos on June 1, 1868 at Fort Sumner. Signing for the Navajos were head Chief Barboncito and 28 other Navajo chiefs and headmen.[9]

The terms of the peace treaty were first translated from English into Spanish by J. C. Sutherland. Jesus Arviso then translated the Spanish into Navajo.[10] Arviso was a Mexican captive of the Apaches who traded him to Navajos for a horse. He is said to have learned English while at Fort Sumner. In December of 1874, he was the interpreter for a delegation of Navajo headmen who visited Washington to discuss land problems with President Grant.[11]

Supply wagons and equipment were assembled promptly after the treaty was signed. On June 18, the return walk commenced. On July 23, 7,304 Navajos arrived at Fort Wingate. They were led by their Indian agent, Thomas H. Dodd,[12] and escorted by a military force under Maj. Charles J. Whiting, 3d U. S. Cavalry. Not the least useful of the official party was Jesus Arviso, the interpreter.

Interpreters were vital to the administration of the Bosque Redondo in the 1860s; and they were still necessary to translate into English the recollections of the Navajos as given in this present account, even into the second quarter of the 20th century. Julian Sandoval, Navajo, was the interpreter for the Crown Point Agency during the four interviews obtained in 1933. Howard Gorman, Navajo, was the interpreter for the Indian Claims Commission 1951 hearing at Window Rock, Arizona, during the four interviews cited here. Gorman had been vice-chairman of the first Navajo Tribal Council when it passed a loyalty resolution of June 3, 1940 when "war clouds were seen around the world." A granddaughter and grandniece of Peshlakai Etsedi interpreted for him. The interpreter for No-mah's grandmother is not known.

Interpreting from a language such as Navajo into English cannot be exact. In order to convey the meaning of a Navajo statement, the interpreter's choice of words and phrases will depend to a considerable extent upon his command of the English language as well as his knowledge of the intricate nuances of Navajo. On the Navajo Historical Calendar, the observation is made that "Probably due to this dual interpretation [English to Spanish to Navajo at the signing of the peace treaty], it is doubtful that the Navajos fully understood the terms of the peace treaty."13

Most of the recollections below are of stories told by parents or grandparents concerning aspects of the journey to Fort Sumner, the stay there, and the return journey. The Navajos from time immemorial have communicated the detailed accounts of tribal, family, and religious history to the next generation by word of mouth. In a non-literate society such as the Navajo Tribe of the 1860s was, it is likely that young folks then remembered the stories of the Long Walk more accurately than they would in a similar situation today.

Peshlakai Etsedi, one member of that generation, was one of the grand old men of the Navajo people when he told his story to Sallie Pierce Brewer about 1927. She reports that the Navajos said of him, "It will be bad when he dies; he is a good man."14

Etsedi was a boy about six years of age when his family, with its flocks, moved over a wide expanse of the rugged Navajo land seeking security from ever advancing American troops. Finally the family decided to leave the Grand Canyon area and to surrender to Kit Carson.

In the 1860s, a great many Navajos had never seen a white man. Etsedi said that near Zuni, on the way to surrender, his family's group was about to be attacked by Zunis but "was saved by the first white man he had ever seen." Blue-clothed soldiers rode up the next morning and took charge. The following day they arrived at Toseto (old Fort Wingate near Grants, N. M.) where there were many soldiers. Here he saw his first wagon.

As they left Fort Wingate, the soldiers put the old women and children in five mule-drawn wagons. Travel was slow. "The next day I did not ride in the wagons," Etsedi recalled, "they went too slowly, so I walked. The mules could not keep up with the sheep and goats."15

Another six-year old, Jake Segundo of the Shiprock, N. M. area, had a similar experience with supply wagons drawn by mules and oxen: "if the people got sick or old people got too tired they were allowed to ride awhile." Little Segundo "would ride awhile and then walk again until tired."16

Asozaa Ts'osi (Slim Woman) from the same area was about 14 when she and her 22-year old sister were taken from Fort Defiance to Fort Sumner in the last band of prisoners. They drove

174

their sheep there and brought them back to their home country in 1868. The journey to Fort Sumner was in the spring, and the native grasses did not yet supply enough feed for the sheep. The weaker ones died or were killed for food. Asozaa Ts'osi traded sheep and goats to the Spanish people for corn. The sisters were not rich but were well to do. Asozaa married Jesus Arviso, the Mexican interpreter, after she had been at Bosque Redondo for two years. Arviso was already married to Asozaa's sister.[17]

Kinnepa (Margie), coming from the Canyon de Chelly area, was 15 when she returned from Fort Sumner. She said that on the eastward journey many people walked but she rode all the way.[18]

In a different vein, John Daw (born about 1868, and later a Navajo scout for the U. S. Army during Apache campaigns) testified before the Indian Claims Commission that his parents told him that when a man would complain about getting sorefooted or tired, "the soldiers rebuffed him and said, 'he is just shamming... He wants to go back home.' The soldiers immediately took the liberty to shoot him. Many of them died that way."[19]

Before the same commission, Dougal Chee Bikis testified that the women and children "had to keep up the same pace as the march was making and the women and children, girls and boys, and even old people - some were even on crutches - when they could not go any more they disposed of them like that. They did not know where they were going or why they were going."[20]

Mrs. Walter K. Marmon of Laguna Pueblo tells a story related to her by her mother. When Lagunans learned that American troops were rounding up Navajos to send to Bosque Redondo, the Lagunas rendered aid to Navajos where they could. Mrs. Marmon's grandparents hid Navajos in the corn and wheat storage bins in the family home at Paguate. These Navajos were not captured by the troops. Today in Laguna there are descendants of these Navajo refugees.[21]

John Bowman, born about 1864 in the Shiprock, N. M. area, gave testimony similar to that of Bikis, saying, "The children would get exhausted from the day's walk and want to ride on these wagons...and if the children were a little bit too large or a little older and able to walk, the soldiers would just cast them aside and make them walk until the time came when they would dispose of them by other says."[22]

The military, on the many trips to Fort Sumner, was not consistent in the manner of disposal of the dead. When Etsedi's mother's uncle died, the soldiers buried him;[23] but Daw was told that

175

Delegation to Washington, 1874

Indian Scout Jake Segundo

Indian Scout John Daw

176

"Some were killed on the way for disobedience" and that when relatives of a man shot and killed on the march would ask for permission to bury him, they were refused. The bodies "were left to lay right on the spot where they were killed. Left to be devoured by coyotes and other animals..." The military, Daw explained, wanted to keep the Navajos in a group and could not hold the march up because of one Navajo who died.[24]

Bikis, mentioned earlier, was born west of Fort Wingate a day or so after his family returned from Hwelte. He came before the Indian Claims Commission and testified that "they were told when they lost a child or somebody died, and groups wanted to bury them...the soldiers poked guns at them and poked them ahead with guns and said, 'You will be left behind if you do not hurry' and they left the dead lay just where they died without being buried."[25]

Asozaa Ts'osi commented on what the military did with people who died on the way, "They just put them away and left them."[26]

Jeff King, born about 1868 south of Mt. Taylor, N. M., when questioned concerning general conditions on the march, replied that "The first story that came out was there was a group of Navajos found dead right on the other side of Tse Bonito in that pass near the Divide."[27]

Daw, in his testimony, repeated what he had heard about the treatment of the women: "The womenfolk on the long march were molested...to the extent that the soldiers, after nightfall, came around and forced some of the men to go away and had sexual intercourse with these women on the long march."[28]

King's testimony supported Daw's account: "These soldiers did not have any regard for the women folks. They took unto themselves for wives somebody else's wife, and many times the Navajo man whose wife was being taken tried to ward off the soldiers, but immediately he was shot and killed and they took his wife. They did not treat the women like they should have."[29]

No-mah's grandmother, from the Shiprock area, remembered the long march. She said, "We walked for many, many days. Some of the old poeple fell down and died on the way. When we got to Hwelte, we were very tired and so hungry."[30]

Segundo told that on the march to Fort Sumner people stole from their camps (the interpreter said "probably Mexicans"). "They would also steal babies and children," Segundo added, and, "there were people in charge but they did not keep close watch at night."[31]

177

In contrast to reports of Mexicans stealing from the camps, other Mexicans gave to the Navajos. Etsedi mentioned that at Bay Il Deel Dah Si Neel (Albuquerque) "We camped inside the corral; it was full of Navajos. The Mexicans gave us corn and the soldiers gave us hard pieces of bread and some meat in skins; a few of our people had brought their metates so we ground the bread and corn on them with the meat in it."[32]

Food issued on the eastward journey was not the same for the different wagon trains that followed the several routes at different times of the year. Flour, beans, and pork were commonly issued without instructions as to how to prepare them. Sometimes flour was eaten raw or as uncooked mush or as dough. Bacon was cooked over coals like the Navajos cook mutton today. When instructions were given on food preparation, the Navajos "couldn't understand, remember or follow them," Segundo said. So many of Segundo's party got sick that a halt was called near the Albuquerque crossing of the Rio Grande for about eight days. Several Navajos died.[33]

Asozaa Ts'osi told her interviewer that most of the Navajos didn't know how to cook. Some learned to bake bread in ashes, and some made cooking utensils out of clay. Asozaa Ts'osi traded sheep and goats for corn from Spanish people.[34]

There was just enough food issued for the prisoners to survive, according to King's information. Most of the food, such as flour, was issued raw; the coffee was not roasted, and the small pieces of meat were not fit for human consumption.[35]

The testimony of Bikis was in much the same vein. He added, however, that the Navajos also lived off raw foods such as yucca plants, berries, and the grain of different plants.[36] Bowman told the Commission that "many of the Navajos say they did not have enough to eat. They had to substitute grasses with grain. They had to pluck them out by the roots and carry them along. They ate grass to keep alive."[37]

Hardships were not wholly physical. The morale and psychological aspects of the Long Walk were emphasized by some of the Navajos interviewed. When King was questioned as to whether the Navajos asked the soldiers why they were not given medical attention, he replied, "Yes, they pleaded with the commanding officer: 'Why do you do this to us? We do not know why we are here. Why don't you do a good job if you don't want us to go back to our land? Kill us all off here.' They asked the commanding officer to do that."[38]

Bikis told of the Navajos being threatened with guns by the soldiers when they wanted to bury a dead man or woman. They had to leave him unburied. He went on to say that "They were terribly frightened to the extent that they were moaning, and so on. They were not riding horses. They were talking to themselves saying, 'My country. My land. I will probably die somewhere between here and the destination.' They were terribly frightened." Bikis also testified that the military never told the Navajos where they were going, but they were to "go ahead - keep on going."[39]

Bowman related the quality of food to the psychological aspects mentioned earlier when he stated, "The meat, for instance, was not fit to eat, and every time somebody died from the food they would say, 'Perhaps they are trying to poison us.' Rather than die they got along without it and naturally many died of starvation."[46]

Bowman's testimony provided another statement given to the Indians as to why they were being moved to Fort Sumner. He said that "they did not know where they were going. They were just being forced out of the area, out of the Navajo country, and the commanding officer told the group at Fort Defiance that they were going to protect the Navajos from other tribes. Up to this time the Navajos had taken care of themselves pretty good as far as other tribes were concerned but the commanding officer said they would protect them by taking them out of the country."[41]

"Out of the country" to Navajos meant being taken to Hwelte. Etsedi's group reached it after 34 days travel from the Grand Canyon area. "There," he said, "the soldiers took us to a corral and gave each of us a blue ticket and some food. Then they told us we could make our home in this corral."

Etsedi related that the first winter, 1867, everything went well. The next summer there was trouble when the Comanches captured a girl and a boy herder and a woman. The soldiers chased them and came back without any prisoners and very thirsty. The woman got away that night. The boy got back next winter, but the girl never came back.

In the same summer, a Navajo, Adin Lechlizhee, and his friends killed five soldiers they thought were going to steal his horses. They used arrows. The American captain "called all the Navajos together and explained that it was bad that the men were killed. But no one wanted trouble and everyone must forget about it." Later in the summer, Lechizhee moved farther down the river where the soldiers could not watch him. One night he and his fami-

179

ly left for their old country.[42]

Cuddy and Segundo during their interviews mentioned that while at Fort Sumner they had a boss "like Mr. Stacher," Indian agent at Crown Point in the 1930s. The older people asked him to let them go back to their home land. This agent, Theodore L. Dodd, said, "if they would promise to behave and not steal horses and sheep and cattle they would let them come back. In years to come they would have to let their children go to school and be educated, and not just roam as before. The headmen talked it over and promised."[43]

One time, Apaches came in a band and killed several Navajos. Jesus Arviso, called "the old man" by Cuddy and Segundo, got a band of Navajos and went to the Apache country. One Apache was killed but no Navajos. The Navajos fought afoot with bows and arrows."

Another incident occurred the third year when a band of Utes came on horseback. The Navajos were raided, but the soldiers fought off the Utes who had guns as well as bows and arrows. As Cuddy and Segundo expressed it, "there was no fight."[44]

During the interviews at Crown Point, Kinnepa was asked whether anybody at Fort Sumner was provided to take care of them when they were sick. She replied, "Yes. There used to be some Catholic people who lived in the town about the fort. They were Spanish people, priests. They were called 'long-coat missionaries.' Later when they saw Protestant missionaries they called them 'short-coat missionaries.' The priests came a lot to the camps to help out with medicine."[45]

King and Bowman separately discussed medical care at Fort Sumner. According to King's information, "The only mention of where the Navajos received medical attention was by their own medicine men. They had the necessary herb medicines to give their people but no mention was made where the soldiers attended to their sick."[46] Bowman testified that if there had been medical aid, many Navajos would not have died from diseases. Some contracted terrible cases of venereal diseases. "They knew they could get herbs to cure them in the Navajo country," and, added Bowman, "They stayed that way and had it under control until they got back here when they cleared these things up."[47]

Although the same medicinal herbs were not available at Bosque Redondo as in the Navajo country, the Indians did raise crops with nutritional value. They planted corn, watermelons, and cane sugar.

Indian Lodges at Fort Sumner

Indian Scout Jeff King

Indian Scout Jim Cuddy

181

They didn't know how to eat the cane but they would suck the juice out. The Navajos were issued flour, pork, beans, coffee, sugar, and salt. The green issue coffee was boiled and boiled - then the Navajos would decide that it wasn't any good and would throw it away. Later, they learned it had to be ground and roasted. At that time in their history, Navajos had not learned to use sugar. They were taught to fish in the Pecos with hook and line. Taboos, however, kept them from eating fish - so they fished only for the soldiers.48

The flour issuance served a dual purpose, firstly for food and secondly for clothing. Cuddy remembered wearing a flour sack - typical garb for the "little fellows." He gave additional information about clothing for men. "The men," he said, "wore blanket garments, too, no trousers. They did not have pockets so they carried a bag worn by a strap over the shoulders. They used to make these of cloth. Now they make them of leather. It was much later that they learned to use velvet in shirts and bodices - after the white men had settled here."49

At Fort Sumner, Navajos were issued leather for moccasins, calico for dresses and other clothes, and needles, thread, and scissors. The authorities tried to show them how to make clothes. Some women did learn to sew. In other cases, possibly in the earlier days at the fort, the Navajos "simply cut a hole in the cloth and put their heads through it," as Segundo described it.50

Asozaa Ts'osi and her sister, as children, were well to do. At Fort Sumner she didn't get the issue "stuff" given to Navajos to make their dresses. Most of the women wore the blanket dress and did their own weaving, using vegetable dyes from local plants.51

No-mah's grandmother told that those Navajos who had no sheep had no wool to weave. At the trading post at Hwelte, they saw Germantown yarn. "It was nice and smooth," she said, "but not as hard and tight as Navajo yarn."52

As time went on, the yearning to return to their homeland surged in the breasts of many Navajos. Some years ago, Mrs. Jensen related to Mrs. Marmon that her grandmother was a young girl on the Long Walk. She told of the desire of a group of Navajos to run away from Bosque Redondo. When sentinels were not looking or were not on duty, her family killed sheep and dried the meat under trees. Soldiers hunted and hunted and went near the meat, but it was so well concealed that they didn't find it. After the meat was dried, the pieces were tied in bundles and hidden in trees until the family made their get-away one night.[53]

Those who remained at Hwelte lived in a variety of shelters. Cuddy and Segundo, by words and gestures, indicated that many lived in a kind of hogan built of cottonwood logs with dirt on top. Other families dug cellars to live in.[54] Bikis related that Manuelito said "some of the people had no shelter so they would dig out a hallow space or bank and the people lived in there.[55]

Asozaa Ts'osi mentioned that for their houses there was at first plenty of cottonwood poles that they could cut up-river and float down; but that after several years wood was "pretty scarce and they had to go quite a ways to get it."[56]

Manuelito, badly wounded, surrendered in late fall of 1866 - finally bowing to superior military force.[57] He must have reflected the feeling of all adult Navajos when he said:

> The days and nights were long before it came time for us to go to our homes. The day before we were to start we went a little way toward home, because we were so anxious to start. We told the drivers to whip up the mules, we were in such a hurry. When we saw the top of the mountain from Albuquerque we wondered if it was our mountain, and we felt like talking to the ground, we loved it so, and some of the old men and women cried with joy when they reached their homes.[58]

There were fewer problems on the return march than on the eastward journey, but Etsedi related that on the way to Albuquerque they waited several days while the escort sent a wagon to Albuquerque for food. Each family had just half a sack of corn left. In four days some Mexicans came with more corn. At Albuquerque the river was so high that three days were spent in making about eight rafts. Then "We took the sheep across on the large raft and swam the stronger horses across; then the men put the weak horses on the large raft with the wagons; the women and children crossed on small rafts...In one day we were all on the west side of the river and the soldier leader told us we were near our own country but we must stay together a little while longer."[59]

Near Mt. Taylor, the Navajos "found many prairie dogs in their holes and had a feast." The escort commander told them to go straight to Charsh Bito (Fort Lyon, later Fort Wingate) while the soldiers and wagons took the road, and to meet there in two days. When the Navajos got there they saw five new log houses. The Navajos were told that they were to stay there for three to five months while headmen and the military decided what was to be Navajo country.[60]

Bowman told of the feeling of the Navajos, "Many of them said that they were happy to get back to their country, and as a matter of fact expressed their appreciation for the commanding officer to bring them back so they can again sleep stretched out without being under pressure but rather sleep and rest again as a free people."[61]

The Navajos were home again and free.

NOTES

1. Personal communication from Mrs. Editha L. Watson, Mentmore, N. M., August 1966, relating information obtained in conversation with Kayah David, ca. 1949-50.

2. Condition of the Indian Tribes, Report of the Joint Special Committee Appointed Under Joint Resolution of March 3, 1865, with an Appendix, 39th Congress, 2d Session, Senate, Rep. Com. No. 156 (G. P. O., Washington, 1867):106. Carleton to Brig. Gen. Lorenzo Thomas, Adj. Gen., U.S. Army.

3. Leon Wall and William Morgan, *Navajo-English Dictionary* (Navajo Agency, Window Rock, Phoenix Indian School Press, Phoenix, 1958):36.

4. Condition of the Indian Tribes, 1867:245-247.

5. *Ibid.:*116.

6. *Ibid.:*122. Carleton to Capt. William H. Lewis, U.S. Army, Commanding at Albuquerque, N.M. Somewhat similar instructions had previously been issued to Carson about the Mescalero Apaches, p. 100.

7. Robert W. Young (compiler and contributor), *The Navajo Yearbook:* Report No. viii, 1951-1961, A Decade of Progress (The Navajo Agency, Window Rock, 1961): 543.

8. Condition of the Indian Tribes, 1867:343. Deposition of Capt. Henry B. Bristol.

9. Martin A. Link (ed.), *Navajo: A Century of Progress, 1868-1968* (The Navajo Tribe, Window Rock, 1968):6-9.

10. David M. Brugge, Story of Interpreter for Treaty of 1868, in *Navajo Tourist Guide* (Window Rock, 1966):22B.

11. Smithsonian Institution, Bureau of American Ethnology Negative No. 2410-c, information on reverse side.

12. Hubert Howe Bancroft, *History of Arizona and New Mexico 1530-1888* (The History Company, San Francisco, 1889):733.

13. Historical Calendar of the Navajo People (The Navajo Tribe, Window Rock, 1968): June 1 date.

14. Sallie Pierce Brewer, The "Long Walk" to Bosque Redondo as told by Peshlakai Etsedi, *Museum of Northern Arizona Musuem Notes* (1937) 9(11):56.

15. *Ibid.:*59.

16. Hester Jones Report on Historical Investigation at Crown Point, N. M., August 1933, p.13 (typescript). Interviews with Asozaa Ts'osi ("Slim Woman"), with Kinnepa ("Margie"), and with Jake Segundo and Jim Cuddy at Crown Point. Both men were Navajo scouts for the army during Apache campaigns.

17. *Ibid.:*29-30.

18. *Ibid.:*37.

19. Indian Claims Commission hearing at Window Rock, Arizona, January 16 and 17, 1951, The Navajo Tribe of Indians,/ Petitioner, vs. The United States of America, Respondent, p. 4 (typescript). Witnesses quoted, John Daw, Jeff King, Dougal Chee Bikis, and John Bowman, had been scouts for the army during Apache campaigns.

20. *Ibid.:*54.

21. Mrs. Walter K. Marmon, tape-recorded interview in October 1966 and personal communication in June 1972.

22. Indian Claims Commission, 1951:71.

23. Brewer 1937:59.

24. Indian Claims Commission, 1951:4, 14.

25. *Ibid.:*53.

26. /Jones 1933:30.

27. Indian Claims Commission, 1951:31. King was about 96 years old when he was buried in Arlington National Cemetery in January 1964. He had been a member of L Troop, 2nd U.S. Cavalry, during the Apache campaigns and had served 29 years as a scout. The army corrected an oversight when, on July 6, 1960, Lt. General John H. Hinrichs, Chief of Ordnance, presented an Indian Campaign Medal to King, then said to be the army's oldest living Indian Scout.28

28. *Ibid.:*5.

29. *Ibid.:*31-32.

30. Mrs. Mary Keeler Smith, No-mah, The Navajo Weaver, *The Desert Magazine* (April 1941):16.

31. Jones 1933:13.

32. Brewer 1937:59.

33. Jones 1933:13-14.

34. *Ibid.:*30.

35. Indian Claims Commission, 1951:31.

36. *Ibid.:*53.

37. *Ibid.:*70.

38. *Ibid.:*34.

39. *Ibid.:*53-54.

40. *Ibid.:*71.

41. *Ibid.:*69-70.

42. Brewer 1937:60.

43. Jones 1933:16.

44. *Ibid.:*17.

45. *Ibid.:*38.

46. Indian Claims Commission, 1951:34.

47. *Ibid.:*73.

48. Jones 1933:18.

49. *Ibid.:*17-18.

50. *Ibid.:*14.

51. *Ibid.:*31-32.

52. Smith 1941:16.

53. Marmon 1966-1972.

54. Jones 1933:16.

55. Indian Claims Commission, 1951:55.

56. Jones 1933:32-33.

57. Robert W. Young, The Role of the Navajo in the Southwest Drama, *The Gallup Independent,* Gallup (1968):41.

58. William A. Keleher, *Turmoil in New Mexico, 1846-1868* (The Rydal Press, Santa Fe, 1952):277.

59. Brewer 1937:60.

60. *Ibid.:*60-61.

61. Indian Claims Commission, 1951:76-77.

This paper is dedicated to those Navajos who served as Navajo scouts for the U.S. Army during the Apache campaigns of the 1880s and to those who have served in the armed forces in subsequent wars. Special mention is made of the Navajos who served as code-talkers or combat communication specialists in the U.S. Marine Corps in Africa, Sicily, Italy, and the South Pacific during World War II.

Crawford R. Buell graduated from the University of Arizona in 1924, and following graduate work at the University of California, Berkeley, he entered the U.S. Forest Service as a professional forester. Later, while serving with various government agencies in Washington, D.C. he attended American University, receiving a master's degree in 1958. He published numerous articles in logging trade magazines and public administration journals. Subsequent to his retirement from federal service in 1964 he has been active in historical endeavors, having been "alguacil" (sheriff) of El Corral de Santa Fe Westerners and president of the Santa Fe Historical Society. The New Mexican, in 1970 published his article "New Mexico Revolt Raises Many Questions: What Really Did Happen in 1837?" The present paper is an outgrowth of his interest in the "Long Walk" and his research of a decade.

THE FERTILE GROUND: THE BEGINNINGS OF PROTESTANT MISSIONARY WORK WITH THE NAVAJOS, 1852-1890

Michael J. Warner

The role of the missionary on the frontier has not been adequately treated, so he remains largely a forgotten pioneer in contrast to the overly romanticized activities of the soldier, the trappers, the miners, and even in comparison to the prosaic farmers.[1] While historians have most certainly treated extensively the heroics of Fathers De Smet and Blanchet, Jason Lee, Marcus Whitman, and Sheldon Jackson, there is a whole legion of lesser known and equally heroic missionaries whose deeds have been neglected. Likewise, the role of religion on the frontier has been rashly ignored. Too often it is forgotten that ministers played a vital role in bringing stability and respectability to rowdy frontier settlements.

The settlement of the West was the sole phenomenon which summoned the home missionary movement into existence. John Wesley's injunction to his preachers, "You have nothing to do but save Souls," applied to all Christian missionaries as well as to the Methodists. It was the distressing knowledge that pioneers were deprived of spiritual instruction that prompted men and women to leave the comforts of the East and to make the difficult trek to the western territories, solely for the purpose of ministering to settlers starved for salvation. The migratory character of the pioneers posed tremendous problems for the missionaries, and, as a result, their task of ministering to the settlers was made more difficult. Bringing the gospel to these roaming pioneers was frequently a matter of just simply keeping pace with them, and, consequently, it required almost herculean strength just to find these isolated groups. In addition, the missionaries unanimously felt that their task was pressing and the need for the gospel in the West was urgent. Most of them sincerely believed that existence in the wilds had a demoralizing effect on people, and because of that missionaries were habitually lamenting about the "moral wastes," the "spiritual destitutions," and the vast "sea of iniquities," all of which were rampant in the western territories. The task the missionaries set before themselves was in their eyes a prodigious undertaking, but, despite their ubiquitous pessimism, they faced the challenge, "like Abraham of old," and succeeded in bringing Christian integrity to the American frontier.

Although it was the settlement of the West that prompted the home mission movement, the actual motivation was based on denominational rivalries and fear of imagined Roman Catholic intentions. In fact, dread of Papal designs was a persistent horror which haunted the minds of many Protestant missionaries. The future role of the West in the Union was also a key determinant in the missionaries' attitudes in regards to the need for evangelism in the West. A great many missionaries in the latter half of the 19th century and the first couple of decades in the 20th century were infected with the pervasive spirit of nationalistic expansion which then gripped Americans. Like some politicians, these missionaries saw the West as an area in great need of regeneration because it would one day become the dominant section of the country. For the evangelists, then, it was a question of what influences would control the West. Naturally, they wished that Christian influences would prevail, and, for that reason, they honestly believed that their activities constituted the highest form of patriotism. One Lutheran author, writing in 1913 about the importance of home missions in the West, went one step further by advocating that "the future of the country is in the West, and that Church which shall evangelize the West shall be the Church which in the future shall dominate the religious life of America, if not of the world."2

Aside from the challenges presented by the isolated pockets of settlers, and in other regions by rapidly burgeoning settlements, the missionary was confronted by other types of problems too. In logging and mining camps, it was not uncommon to see preachers driven out of town as no worthy logger or miner, conscious of his status among his companions, could tolerate a "bible-totin." preacher interfering with his immorality. As an example of this sort of unruly behavior, Charles Woodmason, an Anglican circuit rider on the Carolina frontier in the 18th century, was rudely told by some frontiersmen there that they did not want any "D–d Black Gown Sons of Bitches among them." As Woodmason explained, the Carolina settlers wanted no interference in their "Revelling Drinking Singing Dancing and Whoring."3

Generally, ministers were more welcome in settled agricultural areas where religion complemented an already comparatively stable society. To meet the growing needs of these settlements and to cope with the opening of many new Indian fields, many of the Protestant sects organized special boards to coordinate their various efforts. Their primary duties were to initiate religious programs, found new churches, gain converts, and establish missions among the Indians and Spanish-speaking people.

Missionary work among the Indians was both an outgrowth of the home mission movement and an independent development, which in the latter case dates back to the work of John Eliot and the Mayhew family in 17th century New England. Besides sometimes encountering Indian hostility and indifference, the missionary was always confronted with the virtually insurmountable language and cultural barriers. Despite these seemingly insuperable problems, the Protestant churches sent out hundreds of missionaries to work among the Indians, and, in the process, to aid in the desired goal of assimilating the Indians into the mainstream of American society.

Although the original purpose of many of the missionaries had been to evangelize among the Indians, a large number, like Jason Lee, soon became discouraged and turned to the easier job of ministering among the white population. Those who had the perseverance to continue working with the Indians often worked in close cooperation with government representatives on the reservations. Wherever possible, Indian Agents extended their assistance because both they and the missionaries generally adhered to a policy of assimilation, and both considered missionary work as one of the most expeditious ways to accomplish the goal. That the missionary was considered an auxiliary to government efforts is succinctly illustrated by Indian Commissioner Francis E. Leupp's statement in 1903. "The most valuable adjunct of the Government work of civilizing the Indian is the missionary and education work of the various bodies of Christians who maintain schools and churches in the Indian country."[4]

A major problem confronting missionaries to the Southwest was the immense, desolate terrain. Alzinia Read, the wife of Rev. Hiram W. Read, referred to the Southwest simply as the "wretched land." The vast areas of inhospitable land meant that the preachers would have to travel many arduous and dangerous miles just to sermonize among the few isolated settlements. While this enormous field may have dismayed lesser sorts, it merely reinforced the missionaries' sense of urgency and it prodded the undaunted ones to exert even

191

more energetic effort in behalf of Christ. Most of them, like Sheldon Jackson, viewed their area as a gigantic battlefield, with the Mormons and the Catholics as the enemy and the souls of the Indians and Mexicans as the fruits of conquest.[5]

In the Southwest, the Protestant missionaries were constantly confronted by an entrenched and inimical Catholic Church. Catholic priests working in the same regions as Protestant missionaries seldom helped their Christian colleagues, and usually, in fact, went out of their way to hinder the nurturing of Protestantism in their area. Mormons, likewise, opposed Protestant encroachments and very often openly competed with Protestants in evangelizing among the Indians. Indian reaction to Christian proselytism varied, often depending on the degree of assimilation or acculturation that had already occurred and which usually resulted in a breakdown of the Indian groups' cultural unity. A frequent consequence of the acculturative process was the lessening of Indian resistance to the missionaries' blandishments. Many of the Indian groups in the Southwest, on the other hand, were, and continue to be, remarkably successful in resisting the cajolery of the missionaries, insisting that their historic religion was relevant for them.

Though a number of Indians considered their religion sufficient for them, many missionaries, both Catholic and Protestant, felt differently. After arriving in Santa Fe in 1849, Mrs. Read, mentioned above, related later why she and her husband chose to stay in New Mexico rather than go on to California as they had originally planned.

> Simultaneously with California it became a part of our beloved United States, and while the attention of many was directed towards California and ministers of all denominations were inquiring their duty relative to that field, who O! who thus felt for New Mexico. Whose heart fired with love to God and immortal souls, exclaimed, "Here am I, send me" to preach the unsearchable riches of Christ to the 100,000 benighted, superstitious, and worse than pagans, in that wretched land?[6]

Her husband, the Rev. Read, deploringly noted that the Indians and Mexicans of New Mexico "...have scarcely any more knowledge of the laws of our government or of the laws of God, than the people of Afghanistan..."[7] Many years later, a Methodist missionary, Rev. F.A. Riggin, echoed the same sentiment when he observed on his arrival at the Navajo reservation. "No heathen country of which I read is more heathenish than these Navajo." Furthermore, he remarked, "their rites, ceremonies, and all their worship show them

192

to be entirely ignorant of God, and the light that comes from Christianity."8

From what has been said, it is readily apparent that the West, and the Southwest in particular, seemed completely devoid of the saving grace that comes from Christianity. In illustration of the spiritual destitution that existed in the Southwest, Frank D. Reeve related in a probably apocryphal story the plight of an eight year old girl from Pennsylvania. Each night this small girl was in the habit of saying her bedtime prayers, asking God to bless her mother, father, and the rest of the family. One night, after asking for God's blessing, she closed with the statement: "Goodbye God, we leave in the morning for Lordsburg, New Mexico."9

The Baptists were the first Protestants to provide ministers in New Mexico, Rev. Hiram W. Read and his wife reaching Santa Fe in July 1849. Partly because of a need for more missionaries and partly because of denominational rivalry, the Baptist Home Missionary Society sent out more missionaries in the following five years to join the Reads. Among these recent arrivals were Rev. Samuel Gorman and his wife Catharine who initiated Indian missionary work in New Mexico when they began missionizing at Laguna Pueblo in October 1852. That month, as Gorman later recalled, was "the most important of my live, for I am now on the ground of my future labor, among the people long enshrouded in the darkness of heathenism."10 To Rev. Gorman goes the distinction of having the first Protestant Indian convert in New Mexico, a Laguna named José Sanon.11 Though the challenge was great and there was much to do, life at Laguna was tedious and monotonous, particularly for Mrs. Gorman, and in part because of that the Home Mission Board ordered them to Santa Fe in February 1859.12

Also in 1852, another Baptist minister, Rev. John M. Shaw, was appointed chaplain at Fort Defiance. Mrs. Harriet Shaw remarked at that time that "we think now is the time to introduce the Gospel among the Navajo." Besides his chaplaincy, Rev. Shaw opened a day school for Navajo children and maintained an evening school for the soldiers. While attempting to learn the Navajo language, Mrs. Shaw also wrote to the Home Mission Board for more funds. Although the Shaws had made many friends among the Navajos, they made no converts and their work was discontinued in 1855.13

Before any other missionizing attempts were made with Navajos, they had become involved in a war with the United States and, as a result of their defeat, were incarcerated at Bosque Redondo in

193

eastern New Mexico. Removal of the Navajos from their traditional homeland, as myopic as it might seem, was at that time considered the most efficient and benign way to handle the Navajo problem. Special Agent J.K. Graves, for instance, praised the removal in 1866 as a "wise and laudable undertaking." It shifted, he said, "the scenes of their former barbarisms for the more elevating tendencies of their present home, surrounded as it is by all the arts of peace." Consequently, Graves continued, the conquest of the Navajos was to their benefit, because it "...placed these savages upon the broad road to civilization."[14] Removal of the Navajos was thus desirable as it eliminated the potential for bloody conflict between white settlers, who thirsted for the Indians' lands, and the Indians, who were prepared to sacrifice their lives to defend their land and preserve their culture. This was, of course, the period when Americans were innundating the western territories, and the Indian was an obstacle to the development of that "unused" land. Echoing those sentiments, Acting Commissioner Charles E. Mix summed up the feelings of many Americans in his 1867 Annual Report as follows: "The plea of 'manifest destiny' is paramount and the Indian must give way, though it be at the sacrifice of what may be as dear as life.[15]

While the views of Mix and Graves may have held sway with the majority of the American public, there was a considerable body of private citizens and a few public officials, including some in the Office of Indian Affairs, who actively sought to reform the government's misguided Indian policies. In regard to the Navajos' plight, Superintendent of Indian Affairs for New Mexico, A.B. Norton, issued an impassioned plea in 1867 on behalf of the Navajo.

> Do you expect an Indian to be satisfied and contented [while] deprived of the common comforts of life, without which a white man would not be contented anywhere? Would any sensible man select a spot for a reservation for 8,000 Indians where the muskite [mesquite] roots, 12 miles distant, are the only wood for the Indians to use...No matter how much these Indians may be taught the arts of peace, to cultivate the soil, and to manufacture; no matter how successful they may be in supporting and maintaining themselves; no matter how civilized and Christianized they may become, if they remain on this reservation they must always be held there by force, and not from choice. O! let them go back, or take them to where they can have good cool water to drink, wood plenty to keep them from freezing to death, and where the soil will produce independent and self-sustaining position, honor among men, and an honor to the government we live under, for having raised them from their present condition to one for better.[16]

In addition to all the above mentioned discomforts, the imprisoned Navajos had to endure the hostility of the former occupants of the region, the Mescalero Apaches, and they had worry about marauding Comanches. Even more serious, though, was the problem of disease, especially venereal disease which was widespread among the prisoners.[17] Finally, because of the strenuous efforts of men like Norton to redress the wrong done to the Navajos and because of the omnipresent threat of revolt, a treaty was signed with the Navajos in 1868 which permitted them to return to their homeland and created a reservation for them there.[18]

The first missionary to come to Navajos after their return from their internment at Bosque Redondo was Rev. James M. Roberts who had earlier worked at Taos Pueblo. He arrived at Fort Defiance in 1868, stayed there for several years, and then returned to Taos and established a church there in November 1874. While Roberts was still at Fort Defiance, he was joined by Miss Charity Ann Gaston in October 1869. Miss Gaston's coming to New Mexico Territory was due to the efforts of the Auburn Female Bible Society which had financed her trip and had hoped she would work with Rev. David F. McFarland in Santa Fe. For some reason, she left Santa Fe to work with the Navajos. She was ably qualified to work with the Indians since she had spent some time teaching among the Choctaws in Indian Territory. Rev. John Menaul joined Roberts and Miss Gaston in 1870, and while he was there he married Miss Gaston. Sometime, in either 1871 or 1872, the Menauls and Roberts left the Navajos; the Menauls going to Laguna and Roberts to Taos.[19] Earlier, in 1868, the Presbyterians established a mission at Jewett, New Mexico (now a ghost town) in the San Juan River valley. This mission led a tenuous existence throughout the last half of the 19th century, but it did not succumb until 1912 when it was transferred to the Presbyterian mission at Ganado, Arizona.[20]

The Presbyterian effort at Fort Defiance in the years 1868 to 1872 encountered various problems which stifled any serious missionizing attempt. As Rev. Dr. John C. Lowrie, Secretary of the Board of Foreign Missions of the Presbyterian Church, pointed out in his report to the Indian Commission in 1871, one continually annoying aspect the missionaires had to deal with was the lack of adequate facilities for their educational work. Furthermore, the roving nature of the Navajos posed special difficulties, but Lowrie noted optimistically that "we are making some progress in the civilization of the Indians."[21] What little progress being made was attributed to the small school organized by the Presbyterians under Miss Gaston's supervision. In its first year, the school's enrollment climbed from 35 to 40 with a concurrent rise in attendance of 16 to 24. Miss Gaston emphasized the teaching of the English alphabet and arithmetic, but also taught the more practical arts of sewing and knitting to Navajo girls. Usually, instructions were given in English, but occasionally Navajo was used. Miss Gaston praised the children, saying that "their capacity for numbers seems to be very good; and they acquire a knowledge of the English language readily." However, repeating Lowrie's complaint, Miss Gaston was convinced that the nomadic nature of the Navajos was a deterrent to the children's education, but, she added, "the desire for schools was growing."[22]

Agent James H. Miller, who was appointed in 1871 at the recommendation of the Board of Foreign Missions, observed in his first annual report that Roberts and Menaul were doing excellent work, but they were not accomplishing much in the way of converts. This was due, he felt, to "the prejudice of the Indians" and to "the great difficulty in getting the language." It was Miller's opinion that "the only hope of Christianizing these people is in the children, and that missionaries will be most successful, acting in the capacity of teachers in schools."[23] Though education may have been the best means for Christianizing the Indians, and synonymously, civilizing them, the Presybterian school was soon discontinued. Termination of the effort to educate the Navajos led Agent W.F.M. Arny to report in 1873 that no more than a dozen Navajos speak English. In despair, he complained, "all the effort for twenty-five years to civilize, Christianize, and make self-sustaining these Indians has been a failure, and the money expended a loss to the government and the Missionary Board."[24]

While the Presbyterians were abandoning the Navajo field in the 1870s, for a variety of reasons, government officials kept urging missionaries to continue working with Navajos, as this period was the height of President Grant's Peace Policy. L. Edwin Dudley, Superintendent of Indian Affairs for New Mexico, stated in 1873 that he knew of "no better missionary field." The time, he believed, was propitious, and the Navajos had reached a point where it is entirely feasible to begin the work of educating and christianizing them." In addition, he considered the Navajos "a people peculiarly adapted to receive religious instruction and to practice its teachings."[25] The Presbyterians during the Peace Policy were granted the responsibility for appointing the Indian Agent to the Navajos and held the contract to operate schools on the reservation, so their abandonment of the Navajos is perplexing, especially in view of the ominous warning issued by the Commissioner of Indian Affairs in 1876:

> The next twenty-five years are to determine the fate of a race. If they cannot be taught, and taught very soon, to accept the necessities of their situation and begin in earnest to provide for their own counts by labor in civilized pursuits, they are destined to speedy extinction.[26]

The Commissioner plainly underestimated the durability and resiliency of the American Indian, but his prophecy is not altogether untrue.

In the same year of the Commissioner's warning, Agent Alexander G. Irvine commented, "no missionary work has been done among the Navajoes." Although this was not entirely true, Irvine did accurately predict that "the Mormons will endeavor to enter the field, and are already making some advances."[27] The Mormons had indeed started moving into the area several years earlier. In the early 1870s, Jacob Hamblin had selected Moencopi as a possible mission post, and by 1875 the Mormons were firmly entrenched in that area. In gratitude for Mormon aid given to the Hopis, Chief Tuba of Oraibi donated a townsite to the Mormons. In recognition of Tuba's generous gift, the town was named Tuba City. Very shortly, Tuba City became the center for Mormon missionary efforts among both the Hopis and the Navajos.[28] The Mormon's Christian competitors were alarmed by the Mormon's apparent success, and they consequently became extremely suspicious of Mormon intentions. During the troubles with Navajos in the 1880s, when there was a constant threat of an uprising, the Mormons, along with Utes to the north of the Navajos, were usually accused of instigating the trouble; in fact, Sheldon Jackson put the blame on both groups, but he claimed that it was the Mormons "who without doubt... [have] been tampering with the Navajo."[29]

The 1880s witnessed very little in the way of Protestant missionary work among Navajos. In the first two years, there were some futile attempts. According to Agent Galen Eastman, Rev. A.H. Donaldson, a Presbyterian minister, had worked briefly with Navajos and then died in April 1880, and that two other missionaries, Mr. and Mrs. J.D. Perkins, had failed in their plans for setting up a boarding school. The latter couple apparently had some difficulty

197

in dealing with Eastman, and this may have been the primary cause of their failure. However, the Perkins did maintain a day school, for in 1883 Agent D.M. Riordan reported that a contract-school was in operation with an attendance of about 80 pupils. As Riordan noted, the school was intended to be an industrial boarding school, yet it appeared that "no system of teaching industrial occupations was in operation or could be under the conditions existing." He was of the opinion that this lamentable situation was not due to a failure of the missionary societies, but to "the usual failure of the United States to perform its agreements in connection with the Indian work."[30]

Protestant missionary effort in the period between 1850 to 1880 had never been vigorous, but by 1884 there had been a very definite and noticeable slackening of exertion and concern by the various missionary societies. In that year, Agent John H. Bowman reported that there were no missionaries among the Navajos and only one with the Hopis. Furthermore, he commented, "the agency school for the past two years has not been a success." By the end of the following year, even the Hopis had been abandoned, so that there were now no missionaries anywhere in the vicinity of the Navajos.[31] Two years later, Agent S.S. Patterson gloomily observed that "there are as yet no missionary posts established among these Indians, save what the Mormons have attempted to do in the north and west sides."[32] Though the 1880s represented the nadir of Protestant missionary attempts among Navajos, the period also contained the seeds of new efforts which promised to be much more vigorous. Patterson was able to cheerfully relate in 1888 that the Women's Home Missionary Society of the Methodist Episcopal Church had sent out representatives to select 80 acres for their use. They finally chose Pueblo Colorado, 30 miles west of the agency, for the location of their mission.[33] Their action was the harbinger of greater efforts in the 1890s and in the first decade of the 1900s.[34]

The general missionary neglect of the Navajos embittered many of their agents. like C.E. Vandever who in his 1889 report denounced the religious groups in general:

> Aside from the regular Sabbath exercises in the school by the superintendent, the Navajos are without religious instruction, and do not seem to be considered fit subjects for missionary work by any of the great religious denominations of the world. Still these Indians are religiously inclined, and all their ceremonies are religious in character, though not of the orthodox requirements. While remembering in a substantial way

the heathen of other lands and warmer climes, the Navajo of the United States should not be entirely blotted from memory.[35]

From the evidence available, Vandever's complaint was only too true; the Navajos had been erased from the American public's mind. For example, the Presbyterians in this same period had contract schools at Zuni, Laguna, Jemez, and Isleta, and an industrial boarding school in Albuquerque.[36]

Besides lacking schools on their reservation, except for the government boarding school at Fort Defiance, Navajo parents were exceedingly reluctant to send their children to any of the boarding schools distant from the reservation, and for good reason. Manuelito, the famous Navajo war chief, apparently had sent two of his sons to attend one of the special institutes, or training schools, set up for educating Indian and black children. Both sons, unfortunately, died while attending the eastern school. Since that time, no Navajo parent listened to any proposal to send their child to one of these schools. To Agent Vandever, a Navajo parent's dislike of boarding schools was a sign of his being "very superstitious, which will not allow him to send his children off the reservation."[37]

Missionary activity whether Protestant or Catholic, represented another and sometimes successful aspect of the United States government's program to introduce and assimilate the American Indian into the Anglo-American way of life. Generally, most of the missionaries to the Navajo agreed with the basic goal of assimilation, and the Indian Agents recognized the important role the missionary could play in achieving this goal. Agent Vandever, for instance, felt that "good missionary work would greatly assist the work of civilization which is being done by the Government."[38] In the agent's eyes, the missionaries' work was assisting in the incorporation of the Indians "into the great body of our nation" and was making them into "sober, religious men and women."[39]

Though it is obvious that a degree of reciprocity existed between the ideas of the mission boards and the Bureau of Indian Affairs, and that agents were especially solicitious about missionary activity on their reservations, it would be grossly unfair and manifestly false to unequivocally state that all missionaries supported governmental policies or worked too closely with Indian officials. There are too many exceptions to that generalization because there were a great many missionaries and other religious authorities who vainly tried to humanize the short-sighted policies of the government. Their activities in the formation of such reform groups as the Indian Rights Association and the Lake Mohonk Conferences are eloquent testimony of their concern for the welfare of the Indians.[40] The majority of the missionaries, however, adhered to ideas that closely coincided with official policy. This had the unfortunate result of blinding the missionaries to the real needs of the Indians (primarily medical and educational) and encouraged them to engage in proselytism. In spite of their mistakes, the missionaries avowed purpose, their only purpose, was to help the people whom they served.

As for the Navajos, missionary activity in the period between 1852 to 1890 had very little effect on them. Few Navajos were converted to Christianity as the majority preferred their ancient religion and traditions to that of the Anglo-Americans. Since the mission boards were not actively engaged in medical or educational work, few Navajos were educated (except for those who attended the government school) and their medical needs remained critical. In the next two decades, some missionary societies finally recognized the medical and educational needs of the Navajos and began to direct their efforts in those areas, but too many missionaries still failed to understand the intimate relationship between health, education, and social progress, and still engaged in proselytism.

NOTES

1. Gradually, the missionary is beginning to receive the attention he deserves. Within the last few years, several notable studies have come out, including R. Pierce Beaver's general work, *Church, State, and the American Indians: Two and a Half Centuries of Partnership in Missions Between Protestant Churches and Government* (Concordia Publishing House, St. Louis, 1966); Robert F. Berkhofer, *Salvation and the Savage: An Analysis of Protestant Missions and American Indian Response, 1787-1862* (University of Kentucky Press, Lexington, 1965); Howard L. Harrod, *Mission Among the Blackfeet* (University of Oklahoma Press, Norman, 1971).

2. Rev. J.R.E. Hunt, *Lutheran Home Missions: A Call to the Home Church* (Augustana Book Concern, Rock Island, 1913): 82-83.

3. Richard J. Hooker (ed.), *The Carolina Backcountry on the Eve of the Revolution: The Journal and Other Writings of Charles Woodmason, Anglican Itinerant* (University of North Carolina Press, Chapel Hill, 1953): 15-17.

4. *Report of the Commissioner of Indian Affairs,* 1903:22.

5. Colin B. Goodykoontz, *Home Missions on the American Frontier, with Particular Reference to the American Home Missionary Society* (The Caxton Printers, Caldwell, 1939):319-322. For more on the vigorous activities of the indefatigable Jackson, see Arthur J. Lazell, *Alaskan Apostle, the Life Story of Sheldon Jackson* (Harper & Brothers, New York, 1960).

6. Lansing B. Bloom, the Rev. Hiram Walter Read, Baptist Missionary, *New Mexico Historical Review* (1942) 17:39.

7. Frank D. Reeve, *The Church in Territorial New Mexico,* paper read at Minister's Continuing Education Conference on the Changing Southwest, University of New Mexico, Albuquerque, N.M., 1964:10.

8. Rev. Thomas Harwood, *History of New Mexico Spanish and English Missions of the Methodist Episcopal Church from 1850 to 1910,* 2 vols. (El Abogado Press, Albuquerque, 1910) a:267-268.

9. Reeve 1964:2.

10. Quoted in, Mrs. Samuel Gorman, Reverend Samuel Gorman—Memorial, *Old Santa Fe* (1914) 1:317.

11. Gorman has also been given credit for the first Protestant convert among the Spanish-speaking populace, a New Mexican named Blas Chaves. *Ibid.:*320.

12. *Ibid.:*321.

13. Reeve 1964:9-10. See also, Sytha Motto, *No Banners Waving* (Vantage Press, New York, 1966):43-44; Lewis Myers, *A History of New Mexico Baptists* (The Baptist Convention of New Mexico, n.p., 1965):466.

14. *Report of the Commissioner of Indian Affairs,* 1866:134.

15. *Ibid.,* 1867:1.

16. *Ibid.:*190-191.

17. See the report of Assistant Surgeon M. Hillary for details on the spread of venereal disease among the Navajos at Bosque Redondo. Hillary reported 235 cases of syphilis alone in 1866 *Ibid.,* 1866:150-151.

18. The 1868 treaty with the Navajo can be found in Charles J. Kappler (ed.), *Indian Affairs, Laws and Treaties,* 5 vols. (Government Printing Office, Washington, D.C., 1904) 2:1017.

19. Reeve 1964:20-21, 27; Motto 1966:104-107; Marcella Powers, The First Presbyterian's First 100 Years, *New Mexico* (1967)45:9, 11.

20. Motto 1966:107; Cora B. Salsbury (ed.), *Forty Years in the Desert: A History of Ganado Mission, 1901-1941* (n.p., n.d.):14-15.

21. *Report of the Commissioner of Indian Affairs,* 1871:177-179.

22. *Ibid.,* 1871:375-376;1872:688.

23. *Ibid.,* 1871:379;1872:441.

24. *Ibid.,* 1873:640.

25. *Ibid.:*634-635.

26. *Ibid.,* 1876:384.

27. *Ibid.:*513. See also, *Ibid.,* 1877:160.

28. Ira B. Judd, Tuba City, Mormon Settlement, *Journal of Arizona History* (1969) 10:37-42; James H. McClintock, *Mormon Settlement in Arizona: A Record of Peaceful Conquest of the Desert* (Phoenix, 1921):137, 157.

29. Quoted in Frank D. Reeve, The Government and the Navaho, 1878-1883, *New Mexico Historical Review* (1941) 16:301.

30. *Report of the Commissioner of Indian Affairs,* 1881:139; 1882:127-128. For more on Donaldson, see Salsbury, n.d.:14-15. For the Perkins' troubles with Eastman, see Reeve 1943 18:17-29.

31. *Report of the Commissioner of Indian Affairs,* 1884:133-136, 294-295; 1885: 363-364. Incidentally, during this period many of the Navajo agents doubled as Hopi, or "Moqui," agents.

32. *Ibid.,* 1887:176.

33. *Ibid.,* 1888:195.

34. For more on Protestant missionary activity among Navajos in the 1890s and the early 1900s, see Michael J. Warner, Protestant Missionary Activity among the Navajo, 1890-1912, *New Mexico Historical Review* (1970) 45:209-232.

35. *Report of the Commissioner of Indian Affairs,* 1889:261.

36. *Ibid.:*263. Further information on Presbyterian schools in New Mexico can be found in Lois E. Huebert, A History of Presbyterian Church Schools in New Mexico (Master's thesis, University of New Mexico, 1964).

37. *Report of the Commissioner of Indian Affairs,* 1889:259.

38. *Ibid.,* 1890:167.

39. *Ibid.,* 1903:22.

40.   For more information on Indian reform attempts in the second half of the 19th century, consult Loring H. Priest, *Uncle Sam's Stepchildren: The Reformation of United States Indian Policy, 1865-1887* (Rutgers University Press, New Brunswick, 1942); Henry E. Fritz, *The Movement for Indian Assimilation, 1860-1890* (University of Pennsylvania Press, Philadelphia, 1963); and, most recently, Robert W. Mardock, *The Reformers and the American Indian* (University of Missouri Press, Columbia, 1971).

Michael J. Warner received his undergraduate education at San Diego State College and Western Washington State College in Bellingham. At the latter school, he was awarded a B.A. in history and philosophy and a M.A. in history. He pursued doctoral work at the University of Washington and the University of New Mexico and expects to obtain his Ph.D. at the latter school sometime in 1973. His doctoral dissertation, of which this article is a part, is on Protestant missionary activity with the Navajos from 1852 to 1932. Mr. Warner has published other articles dealing with Protestant missionaries and Navajos and on the subject of historic preservation.

At present, Mr. Warner is the Coordinator of Education Programs and head of the Education Division at the Museum of New Mexico, having previously been the Curator of Collections in the History Division. He is a member of the Western History Association, the Historical Society of New Mexico, the Institute of Early American History and Culture, and the Sierra Club.

VINCENT COLYER AND
THE NEW MEXICO PRESS,
1871

Richard N. Ellis

In 1871, hostilities with the Apaches, which had for so long troubled the Southwest, reached a new plateau of intensity with the Camp Grant massacre in April. The murder by local citizens of possibly as many as 144 Indians, mostly women and children under the protection of the army at Camp Grant in southern Arizona Territory, shocked government officials and caused a wave of revulsion among eastern humanitarian groups interested in Indian affairs. President Ulysses S. Grant threatened to declare martial law in Arizona Territory if the guilty parties were not punished, and in the summer he authorized Vincent Colyer, secretary of the Board of Indian Commissioners, to visit the Southwest and make peace with the various Apache bands. Colyer's activities were scrutinized closely by residents of Arizona and New Mexico territories, while the local press questioned his every move and fired volleys of criticism ranging from mild questioning to outright hate at the intruder from the outside.

When Colyer arrived in the Southwest, he brought with him firm convictions regarding the causes of Indian hostilities and methods for restoring peace. He found that New Mexico and Arizona editors had equally strong opinions regarding Apaches and the value of peace commissioners. The conflicting viewpoints caused the explosion of verbal fireworks during 1871.

Vincent Colyer and the Board of Indian Commissioners were a group of unpaid philanthropists appointed to advise the government on Indian policy and to serve as an investigative and watchdog agency to eliminate graft and corruption in the Indian service. Colyer was representative of eastern humanitarians who had labored in the anit-slavery crusade and then turned their attention to Indians after the Civil War. A man of strong religious conviction, Colyer had worked with southern blacks during the war; in 1869, after he joined the Board of Indian Commissioners, he undertook a long journey throughout the nation to study the condition of Indian tribes and to search for solutions to Indian-white hostilities. Two years later, at the urging of the Board of Indian Commissioners,

Congress appropriated funds to collect the Apache bands of New Mexico and Arizona on reservations, and on July 13, President Grant summoned Colyer to Long Branch, New Jersey and gave him full powers to carry out this goal.[1]

Colyer was convinced that whites were largely responsible for Apache hostility, and indeed there was a long record of atrocities by scalp hunters and soldiers that indicated there was truth in his belief. The death of Mangas Coloradas and the treatment of Cochise by Lt. George Bascom in 1861 are but examples of this. Westerners, however, had different opinions and blamed the Indians, and they resented Colyer's attitude and that of eastern humanitarians in general. The Las Cruces *Borderer* expressed this view with the statement: "Let the tender-hearted philanthropists of the East howl and denounce us to their hearts' content."[2]

New Mexicans, generally opposed to eastern peace groups, charged that government Indian policies had failed. Democrat N.V. Bennett, editor of the *Borderer,* was close to the scene of hostilities and was among the most critical of government policies. Bennett had no faith in reservations and announced that the reservation system in New Mexico was a failure. "If the Government desires to continue this experiment," he proclaimed to the delight of his readers, "we beg of it to try it upon the Boston Common and Philadelphia where Boston philanthropy and Quaker fraternity may have full scope and effect upon the devilish 'Lo' Apaches."[3] A citizen from Silver City, writing under the pen name Legal Tender, chimed in with the statement, "It is this sickening sentimental twaddle that causes so much trouble."[4]

While Southwestern editors engaged in a newspaper war over federal Indian policy with the eastern press, the Camp Grant massacre occurred and Vincent Colyer was dispatched to the West. The *Borderer* announced his impending arrival by printing the statement that Southwesterners hoped Colyer would travel alone so that Cochise could treat him with proper respect. It would be in keeping with the custom of the friends of the administration in these parts, meaning the Apaches, to collect "*a lock of hair*" from him.[5] When the *Daily New Mexican* of Santa Fe learned of Colyer's visit, the editors announced the forthcoming event with the headline, "Humbug" and then launched into an attack upon the easterner. "We regret to learn that that old philanthropic humbug, Vincent Colyer, is about to inflict another visit upon our unfortunate Territory," editors W.H. Manderfield and Thomas Tucker announced. "We want no Vincent Colyer in our midst; we want no puritanical efforts to civilize wild beasts; we want no peace commissioner to travel with military escorts through the Indian country, and then return to Washington with the report that the Indians are peaceable and devoted to the constant observance of religious rites and ceremonies." Playing upon what would become a familiar theme, that of the ignorance of eastern humanitarians, the *New Mexican* announced, "We want no commissioner who does not know the difference between a war dance around a scalped victim, suspended over a slow fire, and a religious ceremony."[6]

When Colyer arrived in Santa Fe an August 12, the tone of the Santa Fe press became more moderate. Two days later, he left the territorial capital for the Cañada Alamosa agency southwest of Fort Craig. After inspecting the area, he created a new reservation for the Warm Springs Apaches in the Tularosa Valley near present day Reserve, New Mexico and then headed for Arizona with a military escort. With Colyer departing from the Territory, the *Daily New Mexican* became more bold and resumed the attack upon "this braying donkey." The paper suggested that Colyer should travel incognito through New Mexico and Arizona and "not let the brutal red scoundrels who infest that section of the country" know he is a peace commissioner. If he would only do that, the editors suggested, "we will wager all we possess that his scalp will prove the occasion of one of the finest religious demonstrations ever witnessed in the Apache nation. And at the risk of being called heathens, we will venture the remark that we would not much regret the occasion."[7]

This was the most violent statement made by the *Daily New Mexican*, but it was nevertheless pale in comparison to comments in Arizona newspapers. Colyer later complained in his report that the *Weekly Arizona Miner* of Prescott branded him a "cold-blooded scoundrel" and a "red-handed assassin" who deserved "to be stoned to death, like the treacherous, black-hearted dog that he is." The citizens of Arizona Territory should, the *Miner* suggested "dump the old devil into the shaft of some mine, and pile rocks upon him until he is dead."[8]

When Colyer departed for the East, New Mexico editors and others assessed his work and found it wanting. Themestocles, a correspondent to the *Borderer* announced, "This miserable fizzle has swung around the circle and arrived safely in Washington, thanks to a strong escort."[9] He accomplished nothing, and "Every cañon and mountain peak in New Mexico and Arizona echoes a groan of contempt for this old civilized deformity."[10] In another issue, Bennett exclaimed, "Great Scott! Is there no one to take this villain by the neck and choke him in the interest of Christian civilization."[11]

In general, the New Mexico press concluded that Colyer's visit had been a total failure. Editors of, and correspondents to, territorial newspapers expressed the hope that there would be peace, but they did not expect the new reservation at Tularosa to succeed because the Indians had not been consulted when the reservation was selected. The *Borderer* was convinced that the Warm Springs Apaches did not like that region and would refuse to go there.[12] In fact, hostilities did continue, leading to the expectation that Gen. George Crook, commander of the Department of Arizona, would be released to punish raiding parties and drive them to their reservations. The San Francisco *Bulletin* offered the opinion from afar that Colyer's "sugarplum policy" had failed. "Having waved his shepherd's crook in vain over these wild lambs, a crook of another sort will be employed to control them...."[13] It was with a certain degree of satisfaction that the *Republican Review* of Albuquerque announced under the headline "One More Barnacle Rubbed Off" that the "Undiluted humbug Vincent Colyer" had resigned from the Board of Indian Commissioners.[14]

Many Southwesterners were dismayed when they learned that President Grant did not loose General Crook and that instead had determined upon another peace commissioner to negotiate a peace with the Apaches. Grant selected Gen. Oliver O. Howard, Civil War veteran and director of the Freedman's Bureau. Howard's courage was beyond question, for he had lost an arm in the Civil War, and his humanitarian and religious activity had won him the label of "the Christian soldier." As a result, New Mexico editors showed him more courtesy and respect than they offered Colyer, but they expressed little hope that he would be successful. *The Borderer,* for example, exclaimed, "We regard his mission as a pusillanimous and foolish attempt to conciliate savages who have deserved severe punishment."[15] However, the combination of Howard's courageous and determined efforts and General Crook's military campaign did bring temporary peace to the Southwest.

It would be unwise for the historian to assume that newspapers are a fully reliable indicator of public opinion, but it would be equally foolish to ignore these important and colorful sources. The press provides one barometer of public attitudes, and in the case of the Colyer visit to the Southwest in 1871 appears to reflect a widespread skepticism and hostility. New Mexico newspapers were unanimous in their criticism of the peace commissioner and his program. Moreover, there are many indications that a large portion of the population of the territory approved of this position. Letters to the various newspapers berated Colyer, and territorial officials in both New Mexico and Arizona indicated their disagreement with his proposals. Citizens of Grant County went further by holding a mass meeting in July that produced a series of resolutions that threatened action against the Indians if raids continued. Richard Hudson, a probate judge in Grant County, also warned that if the Cañada Alamosa agency became a refuge for Indian raiders, the citizens would act and "the Camp Grant massacre will be thrown entirely in the shade, and Alamosa will rank next to Sand Creek."[16]

Nineteenth century editors were usually openly partisan and attempted to mold public opinion, but in the case of the Colyer visit it appears that little molding was neeessary. New Mexicans did not like Colyer's proposals and predicted he would fail.

NOTES

1. See *Peace with the Apaches of New Mexico and Arizona. Report of Vincent Colyer, 1871* (Government Printing Office, Washington, D.C., 1872) for Colyer's report and related correspondence.

2. *Borderer* (Las Cruces), March 30, 1871.

3. *Ibid.*

4. *Ibid.,* April 6, 1871.

5. *Ibid.,* July 19, 1871.

6. *Daily New Mexican* (Santa Fe), July 27, 1871.

7. *Ibid.,* Sept.

8. *Peace with the Apaches,* p. 29. On other occasions, J.H. Marion, editor of the *Weekly Arizona Miner,* called Colyer a "profligate scoundrel and masked robber" (Sept. 23, 1871), a "knave," "fool," "old sinner," and an "old foo-foo" (Sept. 2, 1871). On Oct. 7, 1871, Marion wrote, "an ill wind, from the Plutonic regions, has wafted to our Territory a demon of ill omen, a mock priest and pseudo-philanthropist, if not a sugar-coated thief and scoundrel in the person of one Vincent Colyer." And on Nov. 11, 1871, he announced, "let him keep a still tongue in his head, or he may have but an imperfect head to keep it in."

9. *Borderer,* Oct. 18, 1871.

10. *Ibid.,* Nov. 15, 1871.

11. *Ibid.,* Nov. 1, 1871.

12. *Ibid.;* see also *Daily New Mexican,* Dec. 20, 1871.

13. Quoted in the *Weekly Post* (Santa Fe), May 11, 1872.

14. *Republican Review* (Albuquerque), March 9, 1872.

15. *Borderer,* April 24, 1872.

16. *Peace with the Apaches,* p. 40.

Richard N. Ellis obtained his doctoral degree at the University of Colorado in 1967, taught at Murray State University (Ky.) in 1967-68, and presently is Associate Professor of History at the University of New Mexico, where he directed the Doris Duke Indian Oral History Project. He is a member of the council of the Western History Association and the Advisory Council for the National Archives and Records Service, Region 8. Publications include *General Pope and U.S. Indian Policy; New Mexico, Past and Present; The Western American Indians; Case Studies in Tribal Histories;* and a dozen or so articles.

THE MARMON BATTALION AND THE APACHE CAMPAIGN OF 1885

Austin Nelson Leiby

On a mild but sunny afternoon in late August of 1917, at the Indian Pueblo of Laguna in New Mexico, a U.S. Department of Interior official solemnly handed certificates of service and pension to "The Last of The Marmon Battalion."

Certainly no stranger nor more wistful ceremony has ever been held within the boundaries of this nation, for the simple honors of that day officially terminated the services not only of The Marmon Battalion but also of one of America's oldest and most faithful auxiliary military forces - quietly, without fanfare, almost without notice.

The 12 assembled warriors comprised the last remaining members of what had been Troop F, Company I, 3rd Battalion, 1st Regiment, New Mexico Volunteer Militia (Cavalry). They were: Fred Seracino, Topatata, Kowteya, Burns, Sinai, Tsitai, Goyetia, Levantonio, Angus Perry, George Pino, John M. Gunn, and Robert G. Marmon.[1] They were better known as "The Laguna Scouts."

These men were but the last of a long line of Laguna warriors, who had bravely fought, and just as bravely died, for their Pueblo culture and for the white man's civilization in company with Spanish, Mexican, and United States military forces.[2] The quiet ceremony on the bluff overlooking Rio San José de la Laguna took place in the absence of the "Old Man," Col. Walter G. Marmon, who was gone - gone to that place where no pension can follow and no trumpet can sound. He had died at Ramah on November 11, 1899 while serving as Deputy-Surveyor of the Territory of New Mexico.

When the Spaniards returned to New Mexico in the last decade of the 17th century, the fundamental problem confronting them was the reconquest and control of the Pueblo Indian population. By the end of the century, this task had been essentially accomplished and the problem had changed. The Spaniards now became embroiled in a bitter defensive struggle with the nomadic Indians of the Southwest, a struggle which was to outlast them and the sovereignty of their Mexican descendents in the region.

211

Remaining Members, Troop F, Company I, 1917

An official Laguna auxiliary military force was first formed in March of 1702, used to augment a Spanish military force enroute from Santa Fe to Zuni in order to suppress a minor rebellion. By 1704, the governors of New Mexico began to organize, arm, and use Pueblo Indians in formal militia forces against the *Indios Barbaros*. Such use became standard practice and was dropped only during the Anglo "peace campaign" of the period 1848-1868, a campaign that failed ultimately to solve the ancient problem of Apacheria.[3]

Employment of Laguna military forces during the four decades of 1704 to 1748 was sporadic, but during the Spanish period of sovereignty Laguna military forces took part in no less than 14 campaigns in the Apacheria region. During the Mexican Period they participated in 7 major expeditions against Apaches.

The role played by Laguna military forces in New Mexican history cannot be measured by victories in battle; there were few major battles fought and even fewer clear-cut victories won. The significance of their role must rather be measured in the strategic importance of having a constant defensive bastion located in a central position astride both the Western Apache and the Northern (Navajo) Apache foray routes.

When the United States assumed sovereignty over New Mexico Territory in 1848, the government in Washington instituted a strict policy prohibiting the formation or use of all-Indian units of militia and forbade inter-tribal warfare, even in self-defense. New Mexico Territorial Militia units were formed during the Civil War but were exclusively composed of Anglo and Mexican-American personnel. During Apache campaigns of the 1870s, Pueblo and other Indian personnel were utilized by regular and militia units as scouts, but the Washington policy of not utilizing Indians in battle against Indians was strictly obeyed.

In 1880, the Washington policy was changed, and Indians were permitted to enlist as regular members of territorial militia units. Pueblo Indians served in militia units during the Apache campaigns of 1880-1882, particularly in those against Victorio, Juh, Nana, and Chihuahua. In addition, Laguna and Zuni pueblos mounted paramilitary forces in efforts to protect their cattle and sheep, particularly in areas which now lie between the routes of U.S. highways 60 and 66.

The New Mexico Territorial Militia was reorganized several times after the Apache campaigns of the 1870s. Placement of units and

213

their war-plan use was coordinated with the general Southwest war plans of the Military District of New Mexico under the command of Brig. Gen. Ranald S. MacKenzie. In 1883, as a result of experience in the Indian campaigns of 1882-1883, the militia was reorganized again. Basic organization of the Territorial Militia now consisted of a command echelon and three regiments, one of cavalry and two of infantry, each with a different geographical distribution of companies and mission. The cavalry regiment was organized into three battalions, one in the south, one in the north, and one in west-central New Mexico.

As the Apache problem increased in the 1880s, the distribution of companies within battalions became unbalanced and companies were assigned to battalions in accordance with the danger in each region, and in line with the Regular Army plan. During 1883-1884, the greatest concentration of companies, infantry as well as cavalry, was in the south where experiences of 1882-1883 indicated a greater need for a "picket-line" in depth, 13 cavalry companies being assigned there.

In 1882, Walter Marmon petitioned Governor Lionel A. Sheldon in behalf of Laguna Pueblo for aid in battles with marauding Apache bands that threatened the Pueblo and their surrounding farmlands. The governor's reply was in effect a call-to-arms for the old soldier. He answered by forming Company I and devising strategy in accordance with the basic Territorial Militia Plan. Laguna would again become a western bastion.

There were four Troops in Company I, each with 15 assigned troopers. Walter Marmon was commissioned "Captain Commanding" of the Company and "Mustering Officer" for the first ceremonies. Also assigned were an adjutant, a 2nd lieutenant, a sergeant major, and two musicians (a trumpeter and a drummer). A sergeant had charge of each troop. In December 1882, Marmon organized the first Troop F as the first unit of Company I. Troop F was always the Old Man's favorite. It contained his closest Indian friends from the Pueblo, was trained by his brother, Robert G. Marmon,[4] and was commanded by his second cousin John M. Gunn.

During 1883, Walter Marmon traveled back and forth between Laguna and Santa Fe, procured weapons and equipment, planned the Company's role in the new and evolving militia system, and coordinated training and tactics. He personally supervised the qualification-firing of the raw recruits with new Army rifles, and he devised a fast and efficient system for weapons issue during emergencies. He trained the troopers until they were razor-sharp, and they became the pride of the local countryside.[5]

The Old Man also encouraged and assisted in the organization of other militia companies in the region, but to him his "Laguna Boys" were always first and always the best. He had been piqued and chagrined with the first Table of Organization and Equipment from Santa Fe. He cajoled and argued with Army and militia "brass" until they transferred his boys into a cavalry unit - back in the saddles where they belonged!

Walter Marmon was well-suited for his commission and position of military leadership. Born on March 12, 1843 in Bellefontaine, Logan County, Ohio, he studied engineering at Northwestern Ohio Normal School in Lebanon. His diary reveals that he enlisted as a Private in the 87th Ohio Volunteers "at the breaking out of the Civil War." He was promoted to First Sergeant during 1861 and to 2nd Lt. in early 1862. Captured by Confederate forces at the second battle of Harpers Ferry during September 1862, he was later paroled and exchanged. He immediately reenlisted in the 2nd Ohio Heavy Artillery, where he served until mustered out of service in October 1865. The muster roll for his first commission in the New Mexico militia reflects that he "Served in A.A.A.G. for about one year Dept Cumberland. Served in 87th O.V.S. & 2nd OV HA from 62/65 2nd Lt & Dept Missouri." His diary states that he was promoted to 1st Lt. prior to being mustered out of the Army.

In 1868, Walter Marmon entered New Mexico with the Darling Survey Party,[6] and in 1870 he settled in Laguna Pueblo. He was appointed Government School Teacher for Laguna in 1871, and he remained in that position until the spring of 1878. In 1877, Walter married Mary Seracino, daughter of Pueblo official Luis Seracino, and in the same year he was selected to serve on the Laguna Council. He helped draft the written Laguna Constitution. As noted before, he died while still serving his Pueblo and the Territory of New Mexico.

The Laguna region soon mustered and trained four full companies of territorial militia. With the formation of a battalion organization, Walter Marmon was promoted to major and assumed command.

The Marmon Battalion[7] seems to have been the only militia battalion to have ever operated as a unit in the field; all other companies of New Mexico Volunteers operated as separate units under the direct command of a regimental headquarters. The Marmon

215

Troop F and Capt. Walter G. Marmon, 1882

216

ROSTER OF COMPANY I

Third Battalion, New Mexico Volunteer Militia

December, 1882*

Walter G. Marmon	Captain	Garra ci neh	
George H. Pradt	1st Lt	Gau yea, Ramon	
Robert G. Marmon	2ns Lt	Skate way, Henry	
John M. Gunn	1st Sgt	Show i ty	Act Corp
Jose V. Pasano	Sgt	Sinai	
William Watemah	Sgt	Se o se weh	
Joseph Kewery	Sgt	Se o gu a	
Neovy	Sgt	Francis se wa kery	
George Watery	1st Corp	Si we a	
Angus Kytshe	2nd Corp	Scho te kuh	
Iateyeh	3rd Corp	John Get te	
Frank Kao wa	4th Corp	Li neh	
Chawa Kum	Pvt	Lo ya	
Chaveh		Luh wi cea	
Elvin		Phillip Luk bin is Ky	
Eah ny		Lo rey	
Guero		Le a ria, George	
He co		U ni, Harmon	Act Corp
John Wa ah a		Yastea	
Hi ow		Kow i ty	
Kow y misuch	Act Corp	Ghe y such	Died
Bob Ki ate yeh	Act Corp	Palle Batiste	
Ko wi cu ry		Francisco Ghli	
Walter Koity		Ha pi	
Kow u ni		He oh yi	
Ka eh		Kow u ni	
Kow t yea		Kow y u ni	
Ki tu meh		Murushe	
Joseph Lion	Act Corp	Antonio Pasano	
Ka such		Pedro Gurricino	
Po ni		Si ki eh	
Ow astie		Se on yea	
Peter		Sa to eh	

*Muster Roll of "Company I of the Second Regiment of New Mexico Volunteers, Captain Walter G. Marmon At Laguna Valencia County Number of men, including non comm officers 63 Rec'd and filed in A.G.O. December 2nd 1882. Certificate of Mustering Officer Territory of New Mexico County of Valencia, I . . . , 1st day of December 1882. Captain Commanding I of the 2nd Regiment N.M.V.M."

1st Lt. Walter G. Marmon, 1865

Battalion, while not then officially formed, was in effect a field expedient first tried in 1882 only to control the routine supply and deployment of other companies of the region as they became active in the campaigns of '82-83. Later, after full deployment of Companies I, K, L, and M during 1883 had proven inefficient without a formal battalion staff, Headquarters Company was officially organized and added to the Table of Organization and Equipment.

George H. Pradt normally served as adjutant of Headquarters Company.[8] The battalion was unique in having an assigned command echelon, but it was also unique in another aspect: each of the companies of the battalion comprised an ethnic group. Company I, located in Laguna under command of Robert Marmon, was composed almost entirely of Pueblo Indians (exceptions were the Marmons and Pradt in command positions; and the Marmons and Pradts were actively Indians - they had married into the tribe and taken clan vows).

The three other companies of the battalion were composed of Spanish-Americans, with some few Anglo-Americans who had married into local families. Company K at San Rafael was under command of Capt. Dumas Provencher. Company L from Cubero was commanded by Capt. Gregorio N. Otero, and Company M at San Mateo on the steep side of Mount Taylor was led by Capt. Manuel Chaves. Many of the personnel of Company M were from Cebolleta where a great battle had taken place in the Spanish period.[9]

Pay and allowances for members of the Marmon Battalion were the same as that for other units of the Territorial Militia. Troops were paid only for active service approved by the governor. Privates received 45¢ per day and a $2.00 per day allowance for forage of their privately owned horses. The divergence of pay between private and private's-horse drew an especially strong blast from the adjutant general in his 1884 report to the governor! Officers and NCO's (non-commissioned officers) were paid according to a monthly pay scale, which in 1885 was captain - $155.35 per month, lieutenant - $129.00 per month, first sergeant - $83.65 per month, sergeant - $79.55 per month, and corporal - $77.50 per month. The pay scales were roughly the same as Regular Army pay of the same period.

Uniforms were not furnished, either to enlisted or to officer personnel, nor was any defrayment made for wear and tear of the uniform while in service in the field. Uniforms were, however, highly prized by all volunteer troopers, and The Adjutant General Re ort for 1884 made special note of the cavalry uniforms of Laguna Company at the annual militia competitions held in Santa Fe. These had been purchased by the Laguna Scouts at great expense when they were transferred to cavalry in 1833, and they were completely worn out in the campaigns of 1884 and 1885.

While the uniform was not a required item for enlisted personnel, General Order No. 10 of The Adjutant General Office, dated March 16, 1882, required officers of the Territorial Militia to wear the same uniform as that prescribed for Regular Army officers (with exceptions for types of buttons, fatigue hats, and trouser stripes), while for the NCO the word "may" was used which, in the time-honored jargon of military service, meant that they'd better!

Another General Order set forth militia policies on training, and the requirements matched those of the regular army. Weekly drill schedules were strictly adhered to, annual marksmanship training and competitions were held, within the battalion and at Territorial level, and the Laguna Scouts were always among the best. The Adjutant General Office Report for 1884 stated that "the troop of cavalry at Laguna is composed entirely of Laguna Indians, and though they do not speak English, all commands are given in that language, and their proficiency in the drill and manual is remarkable." The report further stated that "the Zuni Indians, who were present at the drill in Santa Fe, became emulous of the Lagunas, and... authorized Mr. Frank Cushing to take the necessary steps to form a company from among them."[10]

In accordance with the Table of Organization and Allowance outlined in Adj. Gen. Edward L. Bartlett's militia reorganization of 1883-1884, each company of the Marmon Battalion was required to attain and maintain a strength of 60 officers and enlisted personnel. Only Company I at Laguna ever attained that strength. According to muster rolls at the beginning of the 1885 campaign, Company I was at full strength, Companies K and M at 45 each, and Company L at Cubero had 40.

The companies of the battalion were armed with caliber .50 Springfield rifles until late 1883. These were withdrawn at the time of their transfer from infantry to cavalry, and the caliber .50 Sharps carbine was issued. As in the Regular Army, officers furnished their own sidearms and sabers.

The mission of the Marmon Battalion was to serve as the moving anvil of a new defense plan. The battalion was located in four key positions on the line of the Atlantic & Pacific Railroad, near the southern border of the Navajo Reservation and within striking distance of an imagined picket line across the north of the Mogollon, Fox, Escondido, Datil, and Gallinas Mountains. Thus the battalion could swiftly repulse any unlikely thrusts from the Navajos on the north and, hopefully, contain any Apache forays from the south. The "hammers" of this defense arrangement were the 13 companies of volunteer cavalry on the line of the Atchison Topeka & Santa Fe Railroad and on the Mexican border (eight east of the center-line of the mountain chain and five west of it), and the five companies of cavalry situated along the west northwest and the north northwest borders with Arizona and Utah. The movements of the Marmon Battalion during the campaign of 1885 were part of the general plan to meet the threat of Apache uprisings in the Southwest. Units in the field were kept abreast of the developing situation by the Adjutant General Office through use of the telegraph. It is apparent that many messages were coordinated and dispatched from Santa Fe so as to arrive at small telegraph stations just prior to the calculated arrival there of a field unit.

The campaign of 1885 was touched off by Geronimo's foray which began on May 17, 1885. Pursued by regular and militia forces under the overall command of Gen. George C. Crook, he led raids into westcentral New Mexico and then fled into Mexico. But Chihuahua and his band remained in western New Mexico and eastern Arizona until late June, and both he and Geronimo raided into New Mexico in September, October, and in December.

On the morning of May 30, 1885, pursuant to telegraphic orders from the governor of New Mexico, Col. Walter Marmon directed that the four companies of 3rd Battalion be mustered-in and assembled.[11] Meeting with the battalion staff, all of whom resided in the Pueblo of Laguna, he decided that they would be formed into two combat groups, one to be composed of Companies I and L under the command of Capt. Robert Marmon and the other to be composed of Companies K and M under the command of Battalion Adjutant Major Pradt. Colonel Marmon attached the now reduced battalion staff to the group under Capt. Robert Marmon. The morning was occupied with planning and directing the procurement of supplies and equipment.

In the afternoon, the battalion staff met and discussed a plan for the situation. A report had been received that a raiding party had entered the region to the north of the Datil Mountains and was moving rapidly towards the North Plains area. The battalion, in

221

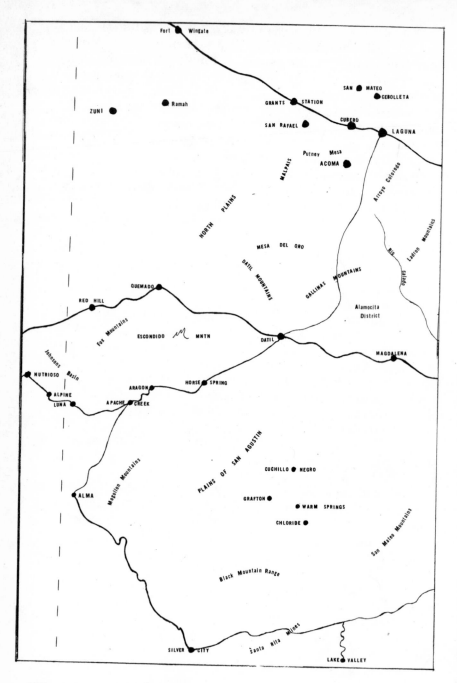

The Apacheria Region, 1885

moving south to meet the main threat, would have to reconnoiter that area. For that reason, Major Pradt was ordered to assemble his combat group at San Rafael and to proceed southeast and to the east of the Malpais (an area of an ancient volcanic flow) which lies south of Grants, and to cross the North Plains on the east side while proceeding in the general direction of Quemado. The other combat group would proceed south through Arroyo Colorado and toward the gap between the Datil and Gallinas Mountains, and then would swing west toward Quemado. Both groups would maintain contact with home base at Laguna by courier. Normal cavalry tactics would be followed, and troops of each Company would be assigned patrol sectors as the situation required. Upon arrival and regrouping at Quemado, the campaign would proceed in accordance with the situation and orders from Santa Fe.

The second group was the first to take up the line of march. Company I departed Laguna in the early afternoon of May 31. The battalion staff, now accompanied by an "Infantry Surgeon", made a detour to Cubero in order to speed up the movement of Company L and to direct the line of march so that it would intersect that of Company I south of Laguna. Company I marched south through Arroyo Colorado and passed the mouth of Dripping Spring Canyon. The 60 troopers, accompanied by a pack-train of 21 horses and mules, made camp about sundown near the present site of the Marmon Ranch, north of Mesa del Oro.

They broke camp early on the morning of June 1, preceded by the usual scouts and skirmishers, and marched for about five hours, stopping about noon near the Gunn Ranch north of Blue Water Creek and about 30 miles south of Laguna. There the group was joined by battalion staff and Company L, they having departed San Rafael the previous day and having marched a distance of some 55 miles around the malpais country and across the Acoma reservation. The march was taken up by the consolidated group after the noon break and reached the Alamocito district that day, having traveled a distance of about 30 miles. A base camp was set up, and the group remained in the district for four days. Patrols were sent out to the east and south, and they reconnoitered the entire area. Robert Marmon's report states that these patrols scouted "the adjacent country for a distance of 25 miles," which would indicate that the scouting parties operated as semi-autonomous units, perhaps remaining overnight in sub-camps. It would also mean that the patrols reconnoitered the Rio Salado and Ladron Mountains, areas

223

which had long provided sanctuary for renegade Navajo bands. In the meantime, the first group under the command of Major Pradt assembled at Grants Station. On June 1, provisions and ammunition were procured and a pack-train made ready. The group marched to San Rafael on June 2 and was quartered in houses for the night by townspeople. On June 3, it completed a march of 25 miles, proceeding southeast across the malpais, then east along the edge of the malpais, finally camping near Cebolleta Ranch west of Putney Mesa. Very early in the morning of June 4, because of reports of raids farther east and south, Major Pradt split his command and changed direction, personally leading a small squad east directly over Putney Mesa while the main body proceeded around the mesa under the command of Captain Provencher of Company K. The squad reached Cebolla Ranch (a sheep corral and station) near Acoma Creek at about 8 a.m., and the main body arrived at about 4 p.m. Major Pradt detached a squad to guard the ranch and patrol the area and marched that same evening with the main body to the Blue Water Creek area some ten miles farther south. On June 5, he continued about 22 miles, south and east through Estacado Spring area and over Cachow Mesa, camping somewhere near the present Martin Ranch in the gap between the Datil and Gallinas Mountains. According to reports of Major Pradt and Capt. Robert Marmon, both groups must now have been camped within six or seven miles of each other, or at least were in close proximity. Major Pradt reported that he "arrived at the Belleview Ranch [i.e. the Martin Ranch] at 4 p.m. and reported [to Colonel Marmon] for further orders." There is no record in any of the archives or in Colonel Marmon's diary of his order to Major Pradt, but ensuing actions indicate that he must have decided to change his original plan, for Major Pradt's group remained in the Datil-Gallinas Mountains gap area on patrol duty while Captain Marmon's group slipped through the gap and proceeded west. A review of the situation reveals that the change was warranted.

On May 31, General Crook reviewed the situation and reported to his superiors that the outlook "indicates troubles similar to the Victorio outbreak, which will be very difficult to suppress." On June 2, he reported an even dimmer view.

> The Indians shortly after crossing the New Mexican line evidently divided into small parties which raided in widely separated localities, while the women and children were hidden away in the mountains. Troops

have been following around different raiding parties without other than to break down their stock. It is impossible with troops to catch the raiding parties or afford citizens so scattered among the mountains protection from such parties.

Crook was worried about the area to the east of the upper Gila River and reported troop dispositions. "Maj Van Vliet with five troops...and thirty Apache scouts, is moving north...towards Datil Range. Capt. Chaffee with one troop...is in vicinity of Cuchillo Negro. Capt. Lee with three troops...is moving across Black Range between Smith and Van Vliet." He indicated that the pressure was beginning to provide results, that the raiding parties were beginning to turn south. But the danger was still high, for Crook figured that by this time they had killed at least 17 civilians, 7 near Alma, 5 near Silver City, 2 near old Camp Vincent, and 3 near Grafton. "If the Indians get among these mountains again...!"

That some of the Apaches had never left "the mountains" was borne out by a later event. In July, "a band of ten or twelve who had been hiding in the New Mexican mountains swooped down on the border from the north driving forty or more head of horses before them," giving southern New Mexico a good scare!

Major Pradt's troops remained in a blocking position between the Datil-Gallinas Mountains and the Plains of San Agustin until June 21, when the Laguna courier delivered a message from the governor addressed to Colonel Marmon and directing termination of the campaign. Until that time, patrols were maintained daily, in the North Plains, through the *trincheria* (trench) separating the northern from the southern Datils, and in the gap between the Gallinas and Magdalena Mountains. On June 10, one of Pradt's scouting parties took up the trail of a raiding party of four fleeing north. The trail was lost in the northern Datils, but non-militia Indians picked up the trail. Three of the raiding party turned south and disappeared. The remaining raider, a renegade Laguna named Huisia, was tracked down and killed. On June 21, Major Pradt directed recall of all patrols and the assembly of all his troops for return to Laguna. He also sent a courier to notify Colonel Marmon of the withdrawal in accordance with the governor's message.

On June 6, Captain Marmon's group broke base camp, passed through the Gallinas-Datil gap, and turned west on the "Rito Quemado" road. Marmon's report details his group's movements until June 20, when he was dispatched with a squad to "take the sick and disabled back to Laguna."

225

It proceeded through Datil and, turning south along the route over which State Highway 12 now is constructed, made camp in the vicinity of Horse Springs. Maintaining constant patrols and utilizing standard Army cavalry procedures, the 100-man unit passed down the valley, through old Fort Tularosa at Aragon, around the now deserted Apache Creek, and on the evening of June 8 made camp in the area of Cienega Canyon on the San Francisco River. Progress through the tortuous valley of the San Francisco was slow, and on June 9 it made camp in the vicinity of Luna, New Mexico, just 25 miles north of Alma which had suffered heavy casualities in a savage raid by Apaches on June 2. On June 10, patrols were dispatched to reconnoiter the entire Luna Valley, and a guide, James Taylor of Springerville, Arizona, was hired for five dollars a day to advise the Colonel and lead the battalion in the unknown region.

Early on the morning of June 11, the group moved out in formation, with scouting parties posted toward Blue River on the south, Lake Luna on the west, and Hell-Roaring Mesa on the north. About noon, the Marmon Battalion crossed the boundary and entered the Territory of Arizona near Alpine. Turning north, the battalion continued the march until it arrived at the foot of Escudillo Mountain some five miles east of Nutrioso, Arizona. There a base camp was set up, outguards were posted, and the Marmon Battalion settled down to reconnoiter the area. As Robert Marmon reports in his Record of Actions on the back of the July Muster Roll,

> The time up to the 20th was spent in scouting the Escudillo Range Luna Valley Blue Creek Johnsons Basin on which date I was ordered to take a detail of 10 men and proceed to Laguna as bearing dispatches also as guard to a wagon containing two ladies and a little child fleeing from the Apaches..Which detail I performed and on the evening of 29 June arrived in Laguna.

With the departure of Captain Marmon, John M. Gunn was promoted to captain and placed in command of Company I. José Pasano, a Laguna Indian, was promoted to 2nd Lt., a rare occurence in the militia and in the history of the West, and he was designated as Adjutant of Company I.

On June 25, the couriers sent by Major Pradt arrived to deliver the withdrawal notice. Base camp was taken up and preparations made for the long trip home. The line of march to Springerville was completed that day, and there James Taylor was issued a Territorial Voucher for his services as guide and released from service. On June

226

26, the group arrived in Red Hill, New Mexico, on June 27, at Quemado, on June 28, at Datil, and on June 30, at Laguna. The role of the Marmon Battalion in the Apache Campaign of 1885 was ended.

Records available in New Mexico archives and in the U.S. Army Adjutant General files do not indicate with certainty when the battalion disbanded. After 1893, the companies of the battalion gradually waned in strength from lack of volunteer personnel, and they no longer appear on State or Territorial militia muster rolls after 1894.

At the ceremony on the bluff in 1917, certificates were handed to each of the surviving warriors. A trumpet sounded taps from the opposite bank of the river. The assembled Indians and their families moved to the feast tables set under the broad limbs of the elms and oaks. The official of the Interior Department hurried off on his way back to Washington. The silence of eternity descended on the Marmon Battalion.

NOTES

The author became aware of the history of The Marmon Battalion while engaged in historical investigations as a Research Assistant for The American Indian Historical Research Program (AIHRP) of the Doris Duke Foundation. Much of the personal history of this work is derived from archives in the possession of Mrs. W.K. Marmon, daughter-in-law of Robert G. Marmon, of Mrs. Alice (Marmon) Day, daughter of Col. Walter G. Marmon, and of Mrs. Edith (Marmon) Lorenzo. Much of the "flavor" of this account derives from long discussions with Mr. Charlie Atsie of Magdalena and Laguna, cowboy, railroadman, former lt. governor and member of Laguna Pueblo Council, and almost certainly descendent of "Ow astie" listed on the 1882 Muster Roll. Official documentation and authentication was accomplished in close association with Dr. Myra Ellen Jenkins, Deputy for Archives and State Historian, New Mexico State Records Center (NMSRC) in Santa Fe.

1. The members in the photograph were identified by Mrs. W.K. Marmon and by Mr. Wallace Gunn of Cubero, N.M., nephew of John Gunn. Identification was collated with names appearing in documents of the Governor's Papers, Edmund G. Ross, Militia, NMSRC.

2. A rather complete history of New Mexican Pueblo Indian military auxiliary forces may be found in Oakah L. Jones Jr., *Pueblo Warriors and Spanish Conquest* (University of Oklahoma Press, Norman, 1966) and Austin N. Leiby, *Western Bastion-Laguna Military Auxiliaries* (University of New Mexico, M.A. Thesis, Albuquerque, 1969).

3. A complete outline of the history of Apacheria can be found in Max L. Moorhead, *The Apache Frontier, Jacobo Ugarte and Spanish-Indian Relations in Northern New Spain, 1769-71* (University of Oklahoma Press, Norman, 1968) and in Dan L. Thrapp, *The Conquest of Apacheria* (University of Oklahoma Press, Norman, 1967).

4. Robert Gunn Marmon was born in Kenton, Ohio and studied engineering at Northwestern Ohio Normal School in Lebanon. All of the Marmons and Gunns were inter-related and all who entered New Mexico seemed to have been competent surveyors. There is no evidence of military experience in Robert's background prior to his entry into New Mexico Volunteer Militia service in 1882. He accompanied surveyor George H. Pradt into New Mexico and to Laguna in the fall of 1875, apparently upon notification from his brother that a great need existed for surveyors for the Atlantic & Pacific Railroad construction. Robert married a Laguna and started a cattle ranch at Dripping Springs, south of Laguna. He later organized a lumber mill in Laguna, and near the turn of the century he organized the Territory's first tourist agency in Laguna. He was commissioned a 2nd Lt. in N.M.V.M. at the time of the organization of Company I by his brother. Robert was promoted to 1st lt. in 1883, to captain in 1884, and to major in 1885. He was serving as lt. colonel when the 1st Regiment Cavalry was disbanded in 1894. During 1899-1901, he was promoted to colonel and appointed Inspector for Training of the N.M.V.M. Robert became a trader at Laguna and built a store there which still stands. He lived until 1929, and it was he who carried on the long struggle, after the Old Colonel's death, with Washington bureaucracy which culminated in recognition of and pensions for survivors of The Marmon Battalion in 1917.

228

5. They had already purchased their distinctive uniforms and were highly trained (AIHRP Records, University of New Mexico Project, Laguna Scouts, n.p., no date).

6. Capt. Ehud N. Darling was commissioned by The U.S. Cadastral Engineer to survey the Navajo Reservation and other western regions beginning in 1868. Hiring and training Indians on survey chain gangs and employing local equipment, Darling and Walter Marmon surveyed a two-section swath around the huge area in just 13 months. In 1870, Darling and Marmon surveyed the Atlantic & Pacific Railroad route from Albuquerque to the Arizona border. It was during that survey that Walter Marmon first became acquainted with Laguna Pueblo.

7. Beginning almost immediately with the organization of a headquarters company in 1883, documents in the NMSRC indicate that the term was used almost exclusively to designate the 3rd Battalion, that term appearing even in Regular Army documents of the period.

8. George H. Pradt was born on April 28, 1844 in Jersey Shore, Lycoming County, Pennsylvania. He served in the 40th Wisconsin Volunteers during 1864-65 and was discharged as corporal after the end of hostilities. Pradt secured employment as a government surveyor shortly after entering New Mexico Territory in 1875 and continued alternately in that capacity until his death in 1918. He was commissioned 1st Lt. of Company I in 1882 and remained in The Marmon Battalion until its disbandment in 1893-94. He was promoted to captain in early 1883, and to major in early 1884.

9. Apparently, the great battle took place in late fall of 1819. John M. Gunn, in his narrative of old Laguna tales, described a Navajo attack on Cebolleta, about ten miles from Laguna. "...the Navajos laid seige to the town in earnest. The village was...surrounded by a high wall, but the Navajos, numbering about 3,000 succeeded in forcing the gates and would have massacred the entire population but for the timely assistance of the Laguna Indians...When the Navajos broke through the gates the settlers were compelled to barricade themselves in their houses, and then the fight began at close quarters. It is said that a woman killed a Navajo chief by dropping a metate from a window on his head. The story says that there was an American in the village at the time. They called him sargento. He received a desperate wound from an arrow, but with the fighting instinct peculiar to those old pioneers, he climbed to a window, and there with his trusty rifle fought until he died from the effect of his wound. The Laguna Indians in the meantime had attacked the Navajos in the rear, and the latter were compelled to retreat."

10. Cushing, an ethnologist with the Bureau of American Ethnology, worked for many years at Zuni and often referred to himself as "First War Chief of the Zunis." He had taken clan vows and become an Indian. The Zuni Company was formed, and uniforms purchased, but it was not sufficiently well-organized nor trained to take part in the Apache campaign of 1885. See Adjutant General Office Report for 1884, Muster Rolls, May - December 1885, NMSRC.

11. Troop movements of Regular Army and militia or scout forces attached to Regular Army forces referred to in this article are derived from Dan L. Thrapp, *The Conquest of Apacheria* (University of Oklahoma Press, Norman, 1967). All movements of the Marmon Battalion in the Apache Campaign of 1885 are derived from archival documents in the New Mexico State Records Center in Santa Fe, in most cases from accounts written on the reverse side of muster rolls by officers in charge of companies.

Austin N. Leiby was born in Clairton, Pennsylvania on July 26, 1926. He enlisted in the U.S. Navy in October, 1943 and served through World War II. After separation in September 1947 he resided in Mexico, until March 1949 when he entered the U.S. Air Force. Upon retirement from the Air Force in August 1966, Mr. Leiby and his family settled in Albuquerque where he entered the University of New Mexico and received his M.A. in History in June 1969. The Leibys - Austin, his wife and two sons - now live in Scottsdale, Arizona, and he is serving in the position of State Archivist for the National Guard of Arizona.

THE INFLUENCE OF
J. WALTER FEWKES ON
NAMPEYO: FACT OR FANCY?

Theodore R. Frisbie

Introduction

For those interested in Pueblo ceramics, Nampeyo is associated with the revival of the prehistoric Sikyatki polychrome style at Hano, a First Mesa village in the Hopi country of northeastern Arizona. Further, the name of an anthropologist, J. Walter Fewkes, is frequently coupled with that of Nampeyo, for it was he who conducted excavations at the site of Sikyatki in 1895, the year associated with the beginning of the renaissance in Hopi ceramics. Fewkes is credited with having encouraged or aided Nampeyo in the revival. This information is readily conveyed by the majority of craft shop personnel to those who show interest or who purchase Hopi vessels of characteristic well-polished creamy yellow-to-orange background with dark brown and red paint. It is also the information found in the majority of publications available to the general public (e.g., Brody 1971:67; Dunn 1968:99; Euler and Dobyns 1971:72; Frisbie 1971; Judd 1967:27-28; Sikorski 1968:21-22; Simpson 1953:77-78; Underhill 1944:99). For the anthropologist, a wide range of popular to technical resources may be consulted, but specific data pertaining to the interaction of Nampeyo and Fewkes are sketchy and inconclusive. Nevertheless, there is information which makes me strongly suspect that the relationship between the two individuals was quite different than what published sources and "common knowledge" would have us believe.

In order to comprehend more fully the reasons for questioning the influence of Fewkes on Nampeyo, it is necessary to present some background material. This setting will allow the reader to begin formulating his own conclusions prior to those which I will offer.

Nampeyo, The Potter of Hano and the Revival of the Sikyatki Style

Unfortunatley, unlike Maria, the potter of San Ildefonso (Marriott 1948), Nampeyo has not been the subject of an extensive biography,

231

and therefore little is known about her personal life. The available data, other than those of purely ceramic interest, occur in brief obituaries (Hodge 1942; Nequatewa 1943; Colton and Colton 1943) and in various short notes (Douglas 1942; Judd 1951; 1968:104-105). The "notes" are concerned primarily with the age of Nampeyo at the time of her death, July 20, 1942. The exact date of her birth is unknown; however, an 1875 photograph of her by W.H. Jackson suggests that Nampeyo probably was born either in 1859 or 1860. It pictures her as a young woman with a hair style of squash blossom side-whorls, indicating that she was of marriageable age (approximately fifteen or sixteen), dressed in a woolen *manta* (i.e. old style dress), wearing multiple necklaces and turquoise pendants, and barefooted (Jackson and Driggs 1929:257; Jackson 1940:240; Jackson 1947:228).

Little is known about Nampeyo's early life. She was named Tcu-mana (Snake Girl) by her paternal Hopi grandmother; however, since she was a native of Hano, settled by Rio Grande Indians in 1696, her name was translated into its Tewa counterpart, Nampeyo. As a child, she frequently observed her paternal grandmother at Walpi making pottery in the "decadent" Hopi style. It was painted and since has been classified as "Crackle Ware", based on the fact that the thick, white slip crackled upon firing (Fewkes 1898a:660). In contrast, Hano potters at this time were producing only undecorated utility wares (Stephen 1936:1021, 1190; Sikorski 1968:20-21). With the encouragement of her grandmother, Nampeyo began making miniature vessels, and by the time she was a young woman, she had acquired the reputation of being a fine potter, as fine as any then producing ceramics on First Mesa. Her ability to design and decorate were exceptional, and in addition to her own work, she decorated or finished all of the vessels formed by her grandmother. During this period or slightly later, Fewkes (1919a: 275 and fig. 108) stated that one of her frequently used designs was that of Shalako Mana (Corn Maid).

The year 1875 was a significant one for the Hopis and particularly for Nampeyo because on August 31, 1875, Thomas Keam established what soon became known as Keams Canyon Trading Post some 12 miles east of First Mesa (McNitt 1962:161). Prior to this time, there were no white traders in the immediate Hopi area and non-Indian goods were rare. Acquisition of such items now became easier, and the Hopis brought in their handicrafts to exchange for them. It was reported that Keam's storeroom shelves were "loaded" with Hopi pottery, woven plaques, baskets, textiles, and some ceremonial items. Nequatewa (1943:40) noted that once white traders were operant in the area, Nampeyo found a good market for her

Nampeyo, Hopi Pottery Maker

233

pottery, and she tried to improve upon her already fine work. A member of the Hayden Survey party reported that Nampeyo was a gracious hostess, having poise and exceptional beauty. At this time (1875) she kept house for her brother, Captain Tom, chief of the village, who provided food and lodging for the visiting group (Jackson and Driggs 1929:257).

Nampeyo's beauty was reputed to have caused the termination of her first marriage to Kwi-vio-ya. From data based on interviews with family and friends, Nequatewa (1943:40) stated that the marriage took place about 1879, but the groom refused to live with his new bride for fear that some other male, drawn by her beauty, would take her away from him. Nampeyo's second marriage, in 1881, was to Lesou from the neighboring village of Walpi. The marriage seems to have been quite stable, and at least five children were born to the couple.

Lesou assisted his wife in her ceramic work, and the vessels produced by 1890 have been classed as outstanding by the Coltons (1943:43). It may be assumed that the Shalako Mana and other Hopi designs, as well as a number of designs, motifs, and elements adapted from Zuni pottery, were among those employed. Fewkes (1919a:217) suggested that there also was evidence of designs derived from the Rio Grande Tewa villages of New Mexico and that a few vessels exhibited Sikyatki surface color and designs on otherwise typical Crackle Ware (Fewkes 1898a:660 and Plate CXXVI; cf. Hough 1917:322; 1919:275). The Coltons asserted (1943:43) that in 1892 Nampeyo and Lesou began collecting potsherds for their designs from ruins; however, it is quite possible that Nampeyo and/or others had done this at an earlier date or perhaps copied designs from heirloom pieces. In any event, it would appear that some vessels bearing Sikyatki designs on Crackle Ware were produced prior to 1892.

With the present evidence that Nampeyo and Lesou were collecting and using designs from prehistoric potsherds at least by 1892, it is not surprising that when Fewkes began excavating at the Pueblo IV ruins of Sikyatki in 1895, the decorated mortuary vessels unearthed attracted their attention. The interest of Nampeyo and Lesou went far beyond the designs, however, for the complete renaissance of Hopi ceramics was to occur that year. Of particular importance to Nampeyo was the discovery of the location of the clay beds originally used to produce the ancient Sikyatki ware. She experimented with the local clays and found what she considered to be the correct one; she also was fully successful in duplicating shapes (i.e. forms), surface characteristics, and matching the paints which had been used (Hough 1917:322). According to Fewkes (1896a:577), both Nampeyo and Lesou copied designs from the vessels, of which there were about 500 (Ibid. 1896b:159). Lesou was one of 15 Hopi males employed by Fewkes to assist in the excavation. It is likely, therefore, that he copied designs before and after working hours. The designs were drawn in pencil or, lacking this media, charcoal. When the supply of paper was depleted, any handy scrap was used, including soda cracker wrappers, and as a last resort, cardboard.

Fewkes (1919a:218) was of the opinion that the vessels produced by Nampeyo were decorated with modified Sikyatki designs, but the Coltons (1943:44) suggested that there may have been some copying, although they believed the chances of this were minimal. Hough (1917:322-323) offered the interpretation that while Nampeyo's early revival pieces were close copies, she gradually developed a degree of freedom in design and finally completely mastered the style. Hough accompanied Fewkes on his 1896 expedition, which included partial excavation of "Old Cuñopavi" at Second Mesa. He stated (Ibid.) that Nampeyo was present, copying Sikyatki designs to gain further inspiration for her vessels. At this time, Hough secured examples of her early revival pieces for the United States National Musuem.

As is well known, Nampeyo's revival of the Sikyatki style was an immediate success. Lesou continued the search for different designs by collecting pottery (sherds and possibly vessels) from Awatovi, as well as Payupki, Tsukuvi, and numerous other ruins on the reservation (Nequatewa 1943:41-42). With the success of the revival, and particularly because of the resulting material benefits, First Mesa women became jealous of Nampeyo. She instructed those interested in the style, which raised the economic level of many First Mesa families. Nampeyo, however, surpassed the others in technical mastery and creative ability. Her vessels, according to Bunzel (1929:67-68) and the Coltons (1943:44), were recognizably superior to those of other potters. This was due primarily to her sense of freedom, flowing quality, and the use of space or open background. Hough (1917:323), when discussing her artistic abilities, stated: "Nampeyo is progressive and as long as she lives her taste and skill will grow." Well before 1917, she was a recognized artist and had traveled far beyond the confines of her reservation home.

The anthropologists and traders who have been cited as helping Nampeyo to attain recognition are numerous and vary according to the source consulted. However, for the moment, a consideration of only those who were involved *after* the revival in 1895 seems most appropriate. In 1898, under the auspices of the Santa Fe Railroad and with arrangements made by Dr. G.A. Dorsey and H.R. Voth, who had worked together studying Second and Third Mesa Hopi ceremonialism for the Field Museum in Chicago, Nampeyo and Lesou demonstrated pottery-making at the Santa Fe Railroad Exposition at the Coliseum in Chicago (Nequatewa 1943:42).

Six years later, Lorenzo Hubbell (Jr. seems more likely since Keams Canyon Trading Post was purchased in 1902-McNitt 1962: 199) suggested that the Fred Harvey Company employ Nampeyo at their Grand Canyon establishment to demonstrate her art. Apparently the arrangements were made through Mr. H. Schweizer of the Fred Harvey Company, and Nampeyo was thus employed for a year, and then for another, in 1907. Although this may be considered an exploitative venture, the Company provided an excellent outlet for her pottery (Colton and Colton 1943:44; Nequatewa 1943:42). Indeed, Fewkes (1919a:218) wrote:

> The extent of her work, for which there was a considerable demand, may be judged by the great number of Hopi bowls displayed at every Harvey store from New Mexico to California.

The final, recorded pottery demonstration trip by Nampeyo and some members of her family took place in 1910, when the destination was again Chicago (Nequatewa 1943:42).

The remaining years of Nampeyo's life are somewhat obscure, although her ceramic work continued. In later life, undoubtedly her greatest personal problem was blindness. The date when this occurred is unknown; however, Judd (1951) stated that when he visited her in 1920 to deliver a copy of the well known photograph taken by Jackson in 1875, she was either totally blind or very nearly so. The last contemporary publication to discuss Nampeyo's career without an indication of blindness is that of Hough (1917). There is no doubt of total blindness by 1924-1925 (Bunzel 1972) when Bunzel had several interviews with her while researching her masterful study, *The Pueblo Potter* (1929).

Blindness, of course, precluded Nampeyo's decorating her own fully formed and polished vessels. This task was assumed by Lesou as did Julian for Maria at San Ildefonso Pueblo (Burton 1936:60; Chapman 1971:33-35; Marriot 1948). Lesou's ability to decorate in the revived style is reputed to have been equal to that of his wife (Nequatewa 1943:42). This raises a question whether Lesou

236

had assisted in decorating the vessels earlier, and, if so, how much earlier? Since Nampeyo's three daughters had learned the revival style and were adept in its production, it is also possible that they assisted Lesou in the final finishing processes. The Coltons (1943: 44-45) indicated that the work of Fanny was closest to that of her mother. If Fanny decorated vessels, it might prove difficult to distinguish them from Nampeyo's, particularly if she attempted to duplicate what her mother might have done.

Lesou died in 1932. Nampeyo was cared for by her children, and she continued to mold pottery, which her daughters probably decorated, almost to the day of her death, July 20, 1942.

In retrospect, it may be said that Nampeyo's contribution to her own people has been immeasurable. Not only did she revive a ceramic style which completely overtook and replaced the decadent Crackle Ware, but she also stimulated other women to become potters. Their pottery found a ready market which in turn helped improve the general socio-economic level of First Mesa residents. This movement, inaugurated by Nampeyo, continues at the present time with its own evolutionary trends and encouragement from the Museum of Northern Arizona (Colton 1938; Stanislawski 1969; Sikorski 1968).

The Influence of J. Walter Fewkes on Nampeyo

The primary figure credited with substantially influencing Nampeyo's revival of the Sikyatki style in 1895 is J. Walter Fewkes. In the previous section, commentary has been provided on the circumstances leading to and following the revival. The critical points, namely the revival itself and Fewkes' involvement with it, remain to be discussed.

Fewkes undoubtedly had met Nampeyo during his association with the Hemenway Southwestern archeological expedition while engaged in anthropological research among the Hopis from 1890 to 1894. But Fewkes himself did not report any interaction until his 1895 expedition for the Bureau of American Ethnology. At this time he directed partial excavation of the Sikyatki ruins (Fewkes 1896a:577; 1898a:660). In the preliminary report, Fewkes (1896a: 577) stated:

The best potter of the East mesa, an intelligent woman from Hano, named Nampio, acknowledged that her productions were far inferior to those of the women of Sikyatki, and she begged permission to copy some of

237

the decorations for future inspiration. The sight of this dusky woman and her husband copying the designs of ancient ware and acknowledging their superiority was instructive in many ways.

The final report on the season's work provided the following remarks:

> The most expert modern potter at East Mesa is Nampéo, a Tanoan woman who is a thorough artist in her line of work. Finding a better market for ancient than for modern ware, she cleverly copies old decorations, and imitates the Sikyatki ware almost perfectly. She knows where the Sikyatki potters obtained their clay, and uses it in her work. Almost any Hopi who has a bowl to sell will say that it is ancient, and care must always be exercised in accepting such claims (Fewkes 1898a: 660).

At this point it is already possible to detect some of Fewkes' own personal feelings prior to and following the revival; however, before interpreting them, it is instructive to interject a statement he made considerably later:

> ...in 1895...there was a renaissance of old Sikyatki patterns, under the lead of Nampeo. In that year Nampeo visited the excavations at Sikyatki and made pencil copies of the designs on mortuary bowls. From that time all pottery manufactured by her was decorated with modified Sikyatki symbols, largely to meet the demand for this beautiful ancient ware. The extent of her work, for which there was a large demand, may be judged by the great number of Hopi bowls displayed at every Harvey store from New Mexico to California. This modified Sikyatki ware, often sold by unscrupulous traders as ancient, is the fourth, or present, epoch of Hopi ceramics. These clever imitations, however, are not as fine as the productions of the second epoch. There is a danger that in a few years some of Nampeo's imitations will be regarded as ancient Hopi ware of the second epoch, and more or less confusion introduced by the difficulty in distinguishing her work from that obtained in the ruins (Fewkes 1919a:218).

The first of these statements reveals an aloof but permissive attitude toward Nampeyo; this changes to one of distrust in the second, and finally, in the third, Fewkes formalizes a statement about the potential dangers of revival pieces. Nowhere does he comment on the merits of the renaissance, once it has occurred; rather, he views it with what might best be termed distaste.

From what Fewkes himself said, it would appear that he took no more than casual notice of Nampeyo and Lesou during the onset of the renaissance. Perhaps his assistant during 1895, Frederick W. Hodge, acted differently; however, supportive evidence for even this possibility is lacking. Further evidence of Fewkes' lack of positive interest is evident from his 1896 expedition, which included a brief period of excavation at Old Cuñopavi of Second Mesa. There is no mention in Fewkes' report (1898b) of Nampeyo's visits to copy designs, although Hough, who assisted Fewkes, not only mentions the visits (Hough 1917:322), but also purchased examples of her wares as previously noted. The positive statements made by Hough indicate his own, rather than Fewkes' keen interest in the revival and its evolution.

Swanton and Roberts (1931:611) in their obituary of Fewkes perpetuate the idea that Fewkes strongly influenced Nampeyo by crediting him with fostering "the beginnings of a renaissance in Hopi pottery making" and offering Nampeyo "encouragement and advice" to such an extent that "she was so successful in her endeavors that other women turned to the ancient wares for their inspiration." The fact that both of these anthropologists did not become acquainted with Fewkes until his later years is important in evaluating their supposition of his important influence on Nampeyo; perhaps it even excuses their assumption.

In the obituaries of Fewkes by Hough (1931; 1932), there is no mention of the Fewkes-Nampeyo relationship. Since Hough accompanied Fewkes on the 1896 expedition and knew him very well, had the latter's interest in and/or influence on Nampeyo been strong, or even noticeable, it undoubtedly would have received comment.

Of perhaps even greater significance is the fact that Fewkes himself, in what is thought to be his autobiography (Fewkes 1919b), failed to mention Nampeyo in any context whatsoever. Surely, had his influence on her been what it is so often reputed to be, he would have discussed it in this work, or at least in one of his several hundred other publications.

The Fewkes-Nampeyo relationship remains a topic worthy of further study, and, as one of the many aspects of Fewkes' career and numerous anthropological contributions, is continuing to receive consideration (Frisbie n.d.). On the basis of the available facts, however, it would seem that the major contribution of J. Walter Fewkes to the Hopi ceramic revival was simply that he, as the archaeologist in charge of the Sikyatki excavations, permitted Nampeyo and Lesou to examine recovered vessels and reproduce the designs. For this, Fewkes does, indeed, deserve credit, for his actions not only facilitated the work which Nampeyo and Lesou had already begun, but also illustrate a fact worthy of recognition and

239

consideration by contemporary archaeologists and ethnologists: that the material objects recovered during an excavation can further enhance a native craft development already in process.

BIBLIOGRAPHY

BRODY, J.J.

1971   *Indian Painters and White Patrons.* University of New Mexico Press, Albuquerque.

BUNZEL, R.L.

1929   The Pueblo Potter: A Study of Creative Imagination in Primitive Art. *Columbia University Contributions to Anthropology* 8.

1972   Personal communication, March 18.

BURTON, H.K.

1936   The Re-establishment of the Indians in Their Pueblo Life Through the Revival of Their Traditional Crafts. Teachers College, *Columbia University Contributions to Education* 673.

CHAPMAN, K.M.

1971   *The Pottery of San Ildefonso Pueblo.* University of New Mexico Press for the School of American Research, Albuquerque.

COLTON, M.R.

1938   The Arts and Crafts of the Hopi Indians: Their Historic Background, Processes and Methods of Manufacture and the Work of the Museum for the Maintenance of Hopi Art. *Plateau* 11:3-24.

COLTON, M.R. and H.S. COLTON

1943   An Appreciation of the Art of Nampeyo and Her Influence on Hopi Pottery. *Plateau* 15:43-45.

CURTIS, E.S.

1922   *The North American Indian,* Vol. 12: *The Hopi,* edited by F. W. Hodge. Published by E. S. Curtis, Seattle and Cambridge.

DOUGLAS, F.H.

1942   The Age of Nampeyo the Potter. *Masterkey* 16:223.

DUNN, D.

1968   *American Indian Painting of the Southwest and Plains Areas.* University of New Mexico Press, Albuquerque.

EULER, R.C. and H.F. DOBYNS

1971   *The Hopi People.* Indian Tribal Series, Phoenix.

241

FEWKES, J.W.

1896a   Preliminary Account of an Expedition to the Cliff Villages of the Red Rock Country and the Tusayan Ruins of Sikyatki and Awatobi, Arizona in 1895. *Smithsonian Institution Annual Report for 1895*:557-588.

1896b   The Prehistoric Culture of Tusayan. *American Anthropologist* 9:151-173.

1898a   Archeological Expedition to Arizona in 1895. *Bureau of American Ethnology Annual Report* 17:519-744.

1898b   Preliminary Account of an Expedition to the Pueblo Ruins near Winslow, Arizona in 1896. *Smithsonian Institution Annual Report for 1896*:517-541.

1919a   Designs on Prehistoric Hopi Pottery. *Bureau of American Ethnology Annual Report* 33:207-284.

1919b   *Biography and Bibliography of Jesse Walter Fewkes.* Bibliography compiled by Mrs. F.S. Nichols. Privately printed, Washington.

FRISBIE, T.R.

1971   Introduction to J. W. Fewkes, Archeological Expedition to Arizona in 1895. *Bureau of American Ethnology Annual Report* 17:519-744. Reprinted by the Rio Grande Press, Inc., Glorieta, New Mexico.

n.d.   Biography, Critical Evaluation, and Bibliography of Jesse Walter Fewkes. In *Selected Papers of Jesse Walter Fewkes*, edited by Theodore R. Frisbie. In preparation.

HODGE, F.W.

1942   The Death of Nampeyo. *Masterkey* 16:164.

HOUGH, W.

1917   A revival of the Ancient Hopi Pottery Art. *American Anthropologist* 19:322-323.

1919   The Hopi Indian Collection in the United States National Museum. *United States National Museum Proceedings* 54:235-296.

1931   Jesse Walter Fewkes. *American Anthropologist* 33:92-97.

1932   Jesse Walter Fewkes (1850-1930). *National Academy of Sciences Biographical Memoirs* 15:261-283.

HUCKEL, J.F.

1926   *First Families of the Southwest.* Fred Harvey Company, Kansas City.

JACKSON, C.S.

1947   *Picture Maker of the Old West: William H. Jackson.* Chas. Schribner's Sons, New York.

JACKSON, W.H.

1940   *Time Exposure.* G.P. Putnam's Sons, New York.

JACKSON, W.R. and H.R. DRIGGS

1929   *Pioneer Photographer.* World Book Company, New York.

JUDD, N.M.

1951　Nampeyo, an Additional Note. *Plateau* 24:92-93.

1967　*The Bureau of American Ethnology: A Partial History.* University of Oklahoma Press, Norman.

1968　*Men Met Along the Trail: Adventures in Archaeology.* University of Oklahoma Press, Norman.

MARRIOTT, A.

1948　*Maria: The Potter of San Ildefonso.* University of Oklahoma Press, Norman.

McNITT, F.

1962　*The Indian Traders.* University of Oklahoma Press, Norman.

NEQUATEWA, E.

1943　Nampeyo, Famous Hopi Potter. *Plateau* 15:40-42.

SIKORSKI, K.A.

1968　Modern Hopi Pottery. *Utah State University Mongraph Series* 15:2.

SIMPSON, R.D.

1953　The Hopi Indians. *Southwest Museum Leaflet* 25.

STANISLAWSKI, M.

1969　The Ethno-archaeology of Hopi Pottery Making. *Plateau* 42:1:27-33.

STEPHEN, A.M.

1936　Hopi Journal, edited by E. C. Parsons. *Columbia University Contributions to Anthropology* 23.

SWANTON, J.R. and F.H. ROBERTS, JR.

1931　Jesse Walter Fewkes. *Smithsonian Institution Annual Report for 1930:*609-619.

UNDERHILL, R.

1944　Pueblo Crafts. *United States Department of the Interior, Bureau of Indian Affairs,* Branch of Education, Washington.

Dedication

This paper is dedicated to the memory of Julia Solomon, my adopted Zuni Mother, who had hoped to begin working in ceramics. Whether her creative ability in turquoise and silver jewelry would have carried over into pottery is something we shall never know. Her untimely death on March 24, 1972 greatly saddened her family and many friends.

243

Theodore R. Frisbie attended the University of New Mexico where he earned his B.A. in Anthropology in 1963 and an M.A. in 1967. He obtained his Ph.D. at Southern Illinois University in 1971. Dr. Frisbie, a member of a number of societies and recipient of awards and fellowships, has published on facets of the archeology and ethnology of the greater Southwest and currently is an Assistant Professor of anthropology at Southern Illinois University, Edwardsville. He is assembling a biography and critical evaluation of Fewkes' contributions to Southwestern studies which is nearing completion and will accompany a collection of papers by Fewkes selected for reprint.

THE GILA RIVER PIMAN
WATER PROBLEM:
AN ETHNOHISTORICAL
ACCOUNT

Alfonso Ortiz

This essay represents an attempt to chronicle the development of the Gila River Pimans' water problem from the beginning of American sovereignty over what is now Arizona, from the middle of the 19th century to the present time. Because this problem arose out of the Pima people's dealings with and treatment by the American government, this essay may be understood, in the broadest context, as an attempt to present an important chapter in the history of these people as a part of the American political experience. A secondary aim of this essay is to establish precisely the time of and the reasons for the Pima-Maricopa settlement on the Salt River, which is today known as the Salt River Pima-Maricopa Reservation.

Given inherent space limitations and the nature of the problem, the following qualifying points are in order. First, the earlier Spanish and Mexican periods of recorded Pima history will only be touched upon briefly; the Gila River Pimas had no extended water shortage in their recorded history or tribal memory prior to the occupation of lands along the upper Gila River above them by American settlers. Second, no attempt can be made to assess the lasting consequences for Pima society and culture of the extended water shortage and continuing disputes beyond what is apparent from the available documents, the principal ones of which are cited here. Detailed, quantifiable data simply are not available for the period of greatest social and economic upheaval which coincided with the period of the most acute and sustained water shortage on the Gila, a 40 year time span between 1871 and 1910 which the Pimas refer to today as the "forty years of famine."

Third, the Yuman-speaking people, now known as Maricopas, who also reside on both the Gila and Salt River reservations and who comprise single political units with the Pimas on each reservation, will not be treated separately here. On the one hand their political, economic, and other fortunes have been inextricably bound up with those of their Pima hosts since well before American sovereignty over the area, and on the other they have apparently always comprised a small numerical fraction, today less than ten percent, of the combined total population of the two reservations. Moreover, historical documents and other data pertaining to their agricultural water use are not as readily available or as reliable as those for the Pimas, and what documents are available (Castetter and Bell 1942, 1951) indicate that there are no appreciable differences bearing upon our problem between the two peoples' agricultural practices.

When the Spaniards first came into the area of the middle Gila or into the northwest reaches of Pirmeria Alta, as the area was then known, they found the Pima inhabitants to be settled farmers, depending primarily on the waters of the river along which they lived for their subsistence. The first visits by a Spaniard into this area for which there are adequate documentation were by Padre Eusebio Kino in 1694 (Bolton 1919:171-172) and in 1697. Others who reported upon their observations included Padre Jacobo Sedelmayr in 1744, Padre Francisco Garces in 1770, Capt. Juan Bautista de Anza and Padre Juan Diaz in 1774, and Padre Pedro Font in 1775. All of these travelers commented at one time or another on the extensive irrigated fields of the Pimas. Anza's observation (Bolton 1930(2)127) made at one of the Pima villages in 1774 is especially noteworthy, although very likely exaggerated:

> The fields of wheat which they now possess are so large that, standing in the middle of them, one cannot see the ends, because of their great length. They are very wide too, embracing the whole width of the valley on both sides...

The addition of wheat and alfalfa to the old staples of maize, beans, and squash during the Spanish period aided in expanding the agricultural activities of the Pimas. Thus by approximately 1770, wheat had rivaled maize as a major crop (Ezell 1961:34). Early American travelers into the middle Gila continued to be impressed by the agriculture of the Pimas. James O. Pattie in 1826, Philip St. George Cooke and W. H. Emory in 1847, and John R. Bartlett in 1854 all make references to the Pimas' irrigated agriculture. Although the American period did not begin officially until 1853, with the Gadsden Purchase, the year 1849 signifies the beginning of intensive American contact with the Gila River Pimas (Ibid.:30). For nearly 20 years after the middle of the 19th century, they sold, traded, and, at times, gave away thousands of tons of wheat, maize, beans, squash, and melons to American settlers passing through on their way to California. American military establishments in this area during the same period were largely maintained by Pima agricultural surpluses.

It is obvious thus far, and will become much more clear as we proceed, that the Pimas were historically an agricultural people, depending primarily upon the waters of the Gila River for their agricultural subsistence. Castetter and Bell, in their very thorough study of Pima Indian agriculture, stated "...the cultivated crop supplied approximately from ¼th of the total food requirements among several families to nearly the entire amount among others." Later they added:

> In conclusion we are forced to draw from our own field studies as well as historical accounts as to the ancient basis of Pima subsistence, which is that before White contact radically disturbed the economic pattern, the Pima cultivated crop in average years comprised about 50 to 60 per cent of the total food supply, wild plants and animals constituting the remainder (1942:56-57).

The period of Pima prosperity and abundance, which was expanded during the period of American contact, continued nearly two decades longer. Since the early 19th century, the Pimas had been acquiring improved agricultural techniques and tools from the Spaniards and later the Mexicans, so when the American period was fully ushered in, the Pimas were up to the task of providing food for the hundreds of gold-seekers and settlers on their way to California. From these settlers and from military expeditions during the period, the Pimas received in trade primarily metal tools, livestock, cloth, garments, and items of adornment.

In American sources we find numerous references to the industry of the Pimas: Charles D. Poston, writing in 1854 (1894:91), stated: "At the time of our first exploration there was virtually no civilized population in the recently acquired territory [referring to the Gadsden Purchase]...The Pima Indians on the Gila River number from seven to ten thousand, and was the only producing population." In 1856, Emory reported:

> As we journeyed along the portion of the valley of the Gila we found

lands fenced in, and irrigated by many miles of acequias [ditches], and our eyes were gladdened with sight of rich fields of wheat ripening for the harvest...a view differing from anything we had seen since leaving the Atlantic States (1856:117).

The following year Sylvester Mowry (1857:588) wrote: "Their [Pimas'] stores of wheat and corn have supplied many a starved emigrant and restored his broken down animals." In 1859, Mowry again reported:

> They have under fence and in cultivation 15,000 acres of land this year, an increase of one-third over last. They have this year disposed of, to the trading posts, 220,000 pounds of wheat, and the corn and bean crops, planted on the same ground from which the wheat is harvested during the months of May and June, promise an amount equally large...(1859:728-729).

By 1866, the amount of agricultural produce sold had grown to an estimated million and a half pounds for that year alone (Ruggles 1867:163-164). This prosperity, however, was not to last, for by 1863 one gets a preview of things to come from Poston (1863). "If, in the eager rush for farms or embryo cities, the land above them should be occupied by Americans, and their supply of water reduced, it might produce discontent." By this time, settlers were beginning to trickle into the area of the middle Gila, and above in the Safford and Duncan valleys. Thus it is that by 1871, we are already well into our problem. There had already been, by that time, sufficient diversion of water by settlers above the Pimas' natural habitat to cause the Gila River below to run dry at planting time. The single most enlightening document for the period is a letter written by J.M. Stout (1871), U.S. Special Indian Agent, Arizona Territory, to Hon. Vincent Colyer, Secretary of the Board of the Indian Commission, in 1871. It is quoted in part:

> DEAR SIR: When you were here it was supposed from the amount of water in the bed of the river above here that there would be a sufficient quantity to reach the lower part of this reserve to enable our Indians to irrigate their fields as usual in preparing them for the reception of their crops. Though there was apparently plenty of water for that purpose, and though it continued to rise for a while after you left, it has now fallen to its normal state, and not a drop of it has reached their fields. The time for preparing their lands is now at hand, but having no water they can do nothing.

People who have lived on the Gila for years tell me there never was before such a thing as a dry riverbed on this reserve this time of the year. As a matter of course, our Indians are much dissatisfied and blame the settlers who are above us for taking away their water. On Sunday morning last, Chin-kum, a chief of one of the lower villages, and one of the best chiefs on the reserve, came to me and said that for many years he and his people had "lived from what they planted," but now they had no water; white men up the river had taken it from them. After spending a few moments in telling me of his wrongs, he made known the object of his visit, which was to obtain leave to take the warriors of his village, numbering one hundred and twenty-seven men, and by force of arms drive the whites from the river.

I was not a little astonished at this manifestation, but quietly told Chin-kum he must not go. I spent an hour in telling him of the fearful results which must surely follow such a step, and finally succeeded in inducing him not to go. But he told me this, that he would wait one month, and if the water did not come to them he would take his whole village, which number one hundred and move to the Salt River settlements, where, as he said, there is always water. As the settlers of that vicinity are and have been for years at enmity with these Indians, I assured him that trouble would certainly follow such a step as that, and urged him to remain on the reserve. He then asked me how he could stay here next year, with nothing to eat. I told him that the Great Father at Washington would not let him or his people starve. He went away silenced, but not satisfied, and I have not the slightest doubt that in a month from now he and his village will leave the reservation.

Day before yesterday Ku-vit-ke-chin-e-kum, chief of the Va Vak [present day Wet-Camp area] village, called and said he was going to Salt River with his tribe, as there is no water for his fields. I, of course told him not to go, but am afraid it did no good. There are six or seven other villages on that part of the reserve, which is about the only part of it that can ever be reached by the water, the rest of the land being too high; and if the water does not come soon I think they will all leave.

Those villages which did threaten to move to Salt River did so later that same year (Stout 1872). This is how the Salt River Pima community was founded.

By 1872, the situation had apparently grown so acute that the same agent was recommending the Pimas' removal:

> If these facilities, such as good land, plenty of water, etc. cannot be furnished them here, they should be at once removed to some locality offering all these advantages...The Indian Territory [Oklahoma] offers the best field for realizing these ends; and I would recommend that measures be taken for their removal there at the earliest possible opportunity (Ibid.).

249

Again, in 1878, Stout reports that 50,000 acres of the 70,000-acre reservation had become worthless due to the lack of water. For the same reason, he states that only one-fourth of the remaining 20,000 acres were available in 1877. The area available for farming is reported as being much less the following year but he does not say how much less (Stout 1878). With reference to the people themselves, Stout added:

> In consequence of the foregoing facts, as a matter of self-preservation, more than one-half of these Indians have been forced to leave their reserve, in order, to use their own language, "that they might not hear their women and children cry for bread," and there are now about 2,500 of them living beyond its lines (Ibid.).

By this time, in addition, the other native wild plants which the Pimas had gathered for food were adversely affected by the lack of water. Mesquite beans, which Frank Russell (1908:74) cited as probably constituting the single most important item of the Pimas' diet, was "almost an entire failure in the vicinity of the reserve" (Ibid.). Referring once again to the statement of E. F. Castetter and W. W. Bell, cited above, that "wild plants and animals constituted the remainder" (40-50%) of the Pimas' diet, we can easily see that the condition of the Gila River Pimas at this time was one of destitute poverty.

In examining the annual reports of the Commissioner of Indian Affairs for the next decade, there are indications that the completely waterless situation was alleviated a little in the 1880s by some rainfall. Furthermore, there was some interest taken by the government through the Pima Agency at Sacaton to actively help the Pimas improve their agricultural techniques. Implements were distributed and instructions given to those still engaged in agriculture. A school was also established during the period, a small agency farm started in connection with the school, and a dam and a canal were constructed in 1883 (Jackson 1883).

The Pimas themselves also hand-dug some wells on the reservation and in adjoining areas. A number of these were pointed out to the author by Pima elders, who indicated that these were primarily for domestic use and for the watering of stock. A series of extremely dry years just after the turn of the century resulted in the abandonment of these, and the cattle and wild horses brought into captivity were sold or died out.

On the negative side, these years of poverty also saw the Pimas reduced to eating wild horses and rats and begging and working for subsistence wages off the reservation. One of their major sources of income, meager as it was, during this period consisted of cutting mesquite on the reservation and shipping it to nearby white settlements for use as firewood. At least two older Pimas have told the author that this extensive cutting of the trees on and near the reservation is the reason why there are no tall and extensive growths of mesquite visible today. They have not yet had time to grow back.

As early as 1875, the prediction was made that unless some major steps were taken to remedy the water problem, Pimas would soon become dependent upon the government for support (Stout 1875). These and other warnings went unheeded, but by 1880 some rations of wheat were issued to "destitute Indians" (Ludlam 1880). This occurred several times during the later years of want, well into the turn of the century. As a not unexpected consequence, there was also sòme pilfering from white settlements reported during this period, as well as much idleness.

By 1888, one of the more perceptive of the Indian agents was willing to admit that better irrigation facilities for Indian use held the answer.

> The river runs through this reservation from end to end, a distance of forty-five miles, but if the water is all "corralled off" by the whites above, this fertile valley will remain a barren desert, peopled by paupers. There is enough tillable land on the [Gila River] Reservation to support all the Indians of the three tribes, and a system of irrigation can be constructed that will be beyond the reach of grasping settlers. It is possible to redeem an area of one-half mile from each river bank, extending nearly the whole length of the reservation, without injury to the people above it. A substantial dam, properly constructed near the head of the reservation would form a "catchment basin" for the storage of sufficient water for use during the dry seasons, when it is most needed... (Johnson 1888:6-7).

In 1895, and each year between 1900 and 1903, the same suggestion was made by three different Indian agents, but there were no results. There were, however, just as predicted, distributions of food by the government for four years between 1894 and 1901.

The first real attempt to supplement the Pimas' sporadic river water supply was made in 1904, when five wells were dug at Sacaton, the Pima Agency (Alexander 1905:147-148). By 1906, eight additional wells were dug, and a short canal and side ditches were constructed to divert flood waters. But this affected only a few hundred acres, and in concentrated areas at that. Pima elders who grew up during this period have stated to the author on several occasions that only the few families who resided near each of these wells had enough to eat even during these years. The majority of the population still had to rely on other means to support themselves. .

By approximately 1910, the Roosevelt Dam was completed, and one of the purposes behind its construction was to restore some of the Pimas' water. Yet, when the dam was finally finished, the government took a long, hard second look and decided that money could not be expended to construct a canal all the way to the reservation. Instead, most of the water went toward the development of new lands being opened up in the Chandler area just north of the reservation. The Pimas got instead, as a cheaper substitute for the canal, the eight wells referred to above. This period between 1871-1910 has been referred to by the Pimas as the "Forty Years of Famine."

Actually, any date we could give signaling the end of the "Years of Famine" would be arbitrary at best, but I select 1910 because it is the one to which the Pimas themselves most often refer. In retrospect, federal government affairs with the Pimas during this period are noteworthy for their amusing contradictions. Thus, while one agent would recommend a program of action one year, a new agent would put forth a contradictory program the next, all of which usually went unheeded in Washington anyway. Furthermore, a new agent during his first year would often paint a picture of the Pimas' condition so different from that of his predecessor that it was obviously designed to please his superiors. Only two themes emerge from the Bureau of Indian Affairs records from this period: first, that the Pimas were not doing very well with their agriculture; and, second, that the government seemed powerless to act on their behalf.

By 1910, however, conditions had improved somewhat for the Pimas. Although the wage scales were low, numerous jobs had become available off the reservation in the growing towns of Florence, Casa Grande, Chandler, Mesa, Tempe, and Phoenix. Furthermore, there was still a ready market for wood and whatever agricultural surplus the Pimas could accumulate. They were still hopeful also that they would get their dependable source of water by the construction of a dam on the Gila. For years thereafter, they and their friends kept up a steady plea to the government to restore some of their lost water. By this time the Winters Case of 1908 had become the basis for Western water law. It stated, in effect, that the law of river-water use is decided on a first come, first served basis.

Finally, on June 7, 1924, the U.S. Congress passed the Coolidge Dam Act (43 Stat. 475), authorizing construction of a dam in a box canyon of the upper Gila River. It took a dozen years from the time the first surveys and estimates were made by army engineers to the passage of the Act, but the Pimas had remained hopeful during that time.

The Coolidge Dam Act was specific to the order of priority of use for the waters to be subjugated.

> For the purpose, first of providing water for the irrigation of lands allotted to Pima Indians on the Gila River Reservation, Arizona, now without an adequate supply of water, and second, for the irrigation of such other lands in public or private ownership, as in the opinion of the Secretary [of the Interior], can be served without diminishing the supply necessary for said Indian lands...

With the completion of the Coolidge Dam in 1926, the case should have been closed, but instead a suit was filed by dissatisfied non-Indian farmers in the upper Gila to decide the question raised by a Congressional act on June 30, 1917. This act had provided that water diverted from the Gila River should be given to both Indians and non-Indians alike, respecting the "rights and priorities" of each. These rights and priorities were to be determined by the Secretary of the Interior "or by a court of competent jurisdiction."

Theoretically, the Indians' rights should not have been included in the suit since both acts had treated them as a special case, but the matter wound up in the courtroom anyway, with the solicitor for the Department of the Interior presumably representing the Indians. Yet, there is no one living on the reservation today who can give an account of the proceedings since no one was present on their behalf but the solicitor. When they requested a private attorney to attend on their behalf, this man was prevented from entering the room.

The final determination of this hearing was a curious 113 page document entitled the "Gila River Decree," entered in the District Court of the United States, for the district of Arizona, on June 20, 1935. Nearly 15 years later, Judge Alfred C. Lockwood, Former Chief Justice of the Arizona Supreme Court, had this to say about the Gila River Decree: "I have never read a decree of an English speaking court more fraudulent on its face than the Gila River Decree" (Personal Communication-1). Why this unequivocal condemnation? The Decree stipulated, incredibly, that all Indian and white users were entitled to share equally in all of the stored and pumped water of the project, ignoring the directives of the two previous acts.

There were further complicating factors. Pima canals of the early days were constructed in such a way that they were easily repaired and easily rebuilt after a flood. After the completion of Coolidge Dam, the canals were rebuilt and greatly enlarged by modern engineers; elaborate drops, siphons, and regulating gates were constructed. Now ditch cleaning required expensive heavy equipment. Moreover, the Pimas were asked to make annual cash payments in order to have water delivered to their land, something they certainly were ill-prepared to do. Even here the government was not blameless; it had broken up the Pimas' irrigable land into ten-acre allotments many years previously. These small plots kept the Indians from becoming any more than subsistence farmers, very unlike the years after the mid-19th century.

Not surprisingly, the Pimas refused to pay operation costs for the canal; lacking the funds, they simply had no other choice. The government then hit upon another "inexpensive" solution: an 11,279-acre plot of desert land just to the northwest of Sacaton was cleared and brought under the canal. The intent was that the land would be leased to non-Indian farmers and the income used to pay operation and maintenance costs on all Pima lands. Again, the Pimas had little choice but to agree to this decision. This was in 1919, and the farm was run by the Bureau of Indian Affairs until 1952.

Meanwhile, white farmers living around the periphery of the reservation drilled wells, claiming that the water they were tapping was not a part of the San Carlos Project. These wells were pumped day and night and, as a natural consequence, the underground water table dropped rapidly. During these same years, in the 1930s, the storage behind the Coolidge Dam disappeared entirely. Indian farmers failed to make a crop year after year. The only successful farms during these years were those served by deep wells.

In 1949, the Pimas retained a private attorney, and through him they renewed their pressure upon the government to finance the drilling of wells to serve the Pima farms. For four years the Bureau

254

of Indian Affairs seemed unable to make the necessary expenditures. In 1950, the returning war hero, Ira Hayes, was sent to Washington to make this and other pleas, but to no avail. Finally, in 1953, the Pimas took matters into their own hands by drilling four irrigation wells without official sanction from Washington. The cost of each well can be estimated at around $15,000, and the necessary funds came from revenues for cropping operations on tribal land.

After the wells were complete, the electric power to drive the pumps was refused them. A telegram from the Secretary of the Interior was received ordering the Pimas not to use water from their own wells until the chief legal officer of the department could render an opinion as to whether they were entitled to it. By these red-tape measures the Pimas lost another full growing season. The order was finally rescinded in February 1955 (Fey and McNickle 1959:44).

Even after 1952, when the 11,000-acre Pima Farm was finally turned completely over to the tribe, the Pimas received continuous pressure from the local agency of the Bureau of Indian Affairs encouraging them not to grow crops which were in direct competition with nearby white farmers. When the storage behind Coolidge Dam was low, these pressures came in the form of encouraging the the Pimas to plant crops which required little water so that they would not use the 210 acre-feet of water allotted to them (Personal Communication-2). This was distributed to other farmers within the project. Only during the last decade and a half, through the steadfastness from increasingly more capable leaders and by efforts of the tribal attorney, has the Bureau relaxed its own form of high pressure salesmanship. Today they will run surplus water into the desert to the west to prove that the Indians are getting their fair share.

This has been the recent record. What has been the net result of the Pimas' long-standing fight for water, which is as yet far from won, and which may indeed be subverted again in the last third of this century? It can be summed up in one statement: Today the Pimas are farming about one-half the acreage of their peak years a century ago, despite a doubling of their population since that time.

BIBLIOGRAPHY

ALEXANDER, J.B.

1905   Annual Report to U.S. Commissioner of Indian Affairs. *Secretary of Interior's Annual Report.* In House Executive Documents, 58th Congress, 3rd Session, 19:146-148, Washington.

BOLTON, HERBERT E.

1919   *Kino's Historical Memoir of Pimeria Alta,* 2 vols. University of California Press, Berkeley.

1930   *Anza's California Expeditions.* 4 vols. University of California Press, Berkeley.

CASTETTER, EDWARD F. and WILLIS H. BELL

1942   *Pima and Papago Indian Agriculture.* Inter-American Studies I. University of New Mexico Press, Albuquerque.

1951   *Yuman Indian Agriculture:* Primitive Subsistence on the Lower Colorado and Gila Rivers. University of New Mexico Press, Albuquerque.

EMORY, W.H.

1856   *Report to Secretary of the Interior.* Senate Doc. 108, vol. 1, Washington.

EZELL, PAUL H.

1961   *The Hispanic Acculturation of the Gila River Pimas.* American Anthropological Association Memoirs 90. Menasha, Wisc.

FEY, HAROLD E. and D'ARCY McNICKLE

1959   *Indians and Other Americans.* Harper and Brothers, New York.

JACKSON, A.H.

1883   Annual Report to U.S. Commissioner of Indian Affairs. *Secretary of the Interior's Annual Report.* In House Executive Documents, 48th Congress, 1st Session, 11:63-65, Washington.

JOHNSON, CLAUDE M.

1888   Annual Report to U.S. Commissioner of Indian Affairs. *Secretary of the Interior's Annual Report.* In House Executive Documents, 50th Congress, 2nd Session, 2:1-7, Washington.

LUDLAM, A.E.

1880   Annual Report to U.S. Commissioner of Indian Affairs. *Secretary of the Interior's Annual Report.* In House Executive Documents, 46th Congress, 2nd Session, 9:112, Washington.

MOWRY, SYLVESTER

1857   Annual Report to U.S. Commissioner of Indian Affairs. *Secretary of the Interior's Annual Report.* In House Executive Documents, 35th Congress, 1st Session, 2:584-593, Washington.

1859   *Annual Report to the Commissioner of Indian Affairs.* Secretary of the Interior's Report. In Senate Executive Documents, 36th Congress, 1st Session, 1(2) pt. 1:728-730, Washington.

PERSONAL COMMUNICATION

1.   From Z. Simpson Cox, tribal attorney for the Pimas and son-in-law of the late Judge Alfred C. Lockwood, May 1962.

2.   As told to the author during interviews conducted in the spring of 1962. Both of these points were corraborated independently by two Pimas who each served as tribal chairman, for an aggregate of several years between them, during the period under discussion.

POSTON, CHARLES D.

1863   Annual Report to U.S. Commissioner of Indian Affairs. *Secretary of the Interior's Annual Report.* In House Executive Documents, 38th Congress, 1st Session, 3:503-510, Washington.

1894   Building a State in Apache Land. *Overland Monthly.* XXIV: 87-93, 203-213, 291-297, 403-408.

RUGGLES, LEVI

1867   Annual Report to G. W. Dent, Superintendent of Indian Affairs, Arizona Territory. *Secretary of the Interior's Annual Report.* In House Executive Documents, 40th Congress, 2nd Session, 3(1):161-165, Washington.

RUSSELL, FRANK

1908   *The Pima Indians.* Bureau of American Ethnology Annual Report 25. Washington.

STOUT, J.H..

1871   Annual Report to U.S. Commissioner of Indian Affairs. *Secretary of the Interior's Annual Report.* In House Executive Documents, 42nd Congress, 2nd Session, 1:769-774, Washington.

1872   Annual Report to U.S. Commissioner of Indian Affairs. *Secretary of the Interior's Annual Report.* In House Executive Documents, 42nd Congress, 3rd Session, 3:700-704, Washington.

257

Alfonso Ortiz, a social anthropologist from Santa Clara Pueblo, received his Ph.D. from the University of Chicago and is currently associate professor of anthropology at Princeton University. He has many publications to his credit, a recent one being, *The Tewa World,* a penetrating study of the cosmological and ritual systems of the Tewa Pueblos. He also serves as President of the Association of American Indian Affairs, Inc.

ANGLOS AMONG THE NAVAJOS: THE DAY FAMILY

Clifford E. Trafzer

Many white pioneers overlooked the Indians' colorful history because the natives were considered mere obstacles to be overcome before "civilization" could be established.[1] Nonetheless, some pioneers attempted to understand the Indians and worked to preserve their past. These enlightened individuals sought to bridge the gap of misunderstanding that existed between Indians and Anglos by studying Indian language, culture, and prehistory. They felt an obligation to learn about their neighbors and to help others learn more about Indians.[2] Such was the case of Samuel Edward Day and his family.[3]

Sam Day was born in Canton, Ohio in February 1845. He received a fine elementary education at a local public school, and he began work on a college degree in Newark, New Jersey at the age of 13. In 1861, his studies of civil engineering came to an abrupt halt when he quit school and joined Mr. Lincoln's Army.[4] After the Civil War, Day journeyed to South Dakota to seek the gold hidden in the deep canyons of the Black Hills. He encountered great hardships on the Dakota mining frontier and made little profit; therefore, he moved to Iowa and accepted a position as a surveyor of public lands. In Plymouth County, Iowa, Day met Anna P. Burbridge whom he courted for two years and married in 1878. A year later, the Day family traveled by prairie schooner to Colorado where Sam surveyed the first rail line to ascend Pikes Peak.[5]

Day first came to New Mexico in 1883 to survey the eastern and southern extension lines of the Navajo Indian Reservation.[6] He took great interest in the Navajo way of life and informed his son in 1884 that the cultural life of the Indians was indeed interesting and far different than that of Anglos.[7] Not long after Day wrote to his son, he sent for his entire family to come to Arizona where he had staked a claim in a region known as the Cienega Amarilla. His family included three young boys named Charles, Samuel, and William, all of whom grew to manhood on their father's ranch at the Cienega Amarilla.[8] The boys had an intriguing childhood because they lived among the Navajo children of the area;

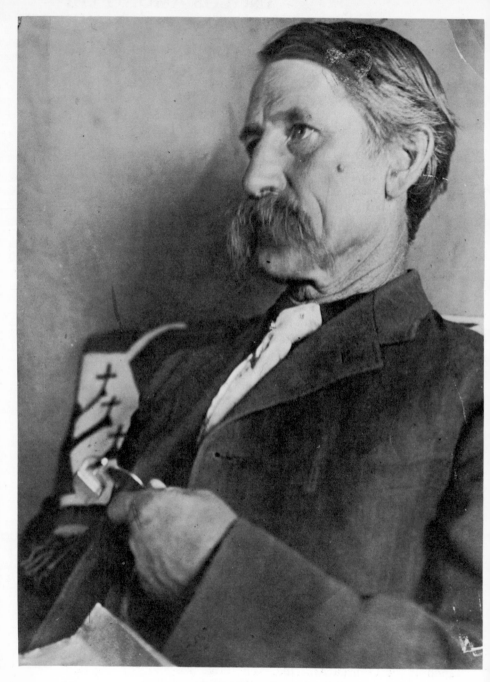

Samuel Edward Day

the Indians taught the Days to speak the Navajo tongue as well as their cultural ways.[9]

There were no schools near the Cienega Amarilla, but Anna Day, a former school teacher from Iowa, gave her children a fundamental knowledge of the "three R's". As her sons grew older, she realized that they needed a formal education, but she was unable to send them east.[10] Good fortune intervened, for in the mid-1890s a group of Franciscan Fathers, under the leadership of Reverend Mother Kathren Drexel, established a Catholic mission for the Navajos in St. Michaels, Arizona. Realizing that the Franciscans were highly educated men, Mr. and Mrs. Day approached them with a unique idea. One of the priests later recalled that on December 18, 1898, Sam Day "paid us a visit and gave us an idea of shocking irregularity." The Days persuaded the priests to enter into an educational barter whereby the boys would instruct the priests in the Navajo language and the friars in turn would teach the boys math, literature, and history.[12]

Three days before Christmas, the final arrangements were made; however, the mutual instruction did not begin until January 23, 1899. The language instruction commenced in a haphazard manner until late February when a more orderly system of study was devised. The Franciscans found an old copy of *Webster's Dictionary* and put the boys to work translating it into Navajo.[13] Reverend Mother Drexel and Charles began with the letter A, while Father Anselm Weber and Sam, Jr., began with the letter Z. Each group translated the words into Navajo and worked toward the middle of the dictionary "until the 26th of April when we had a peaceful encounter at the letter L."[14]

Mr. and Mrs. Day were delighted to have their children educated by such competent men as the Franciscans and wanted the mutual instruction to continue. However, circumstances intervened. In 1900, Charles left the ranch to begin Indian trading south of Chinle, Arizona. In 1901, Sam Day, Sr., sold his homestead and moved his family north of St. Michaels to live with Charles. The Day family lived at the old Bill Meadows Trading Post for approximately one year before moving to Chinle.[15]

When Day arrived at Chinle, he was struck by the great beauty of the Canyon de Chelly, with its sandstone walls and reddened buttes that rose thousands of feet above the canyon floor. Day was impressed with the area so much that he wrote two descriptive articles about the colorful canyon. He called Canyon de Chelly

Anna and Sam Day

Day's Trading Post, Canyon de Chelly

"one of the little known regions, which promises to become a veritable mecca for...scientist, palaeontologist, archaeologist, anthropologist, [and] ethnologist."[16] Day was enthusiastic about the rich cultural remains that could be drawn from this region and expressed his beliefs in his articles. He observed that prehistoric ruins, tools, weapons, and clothing could be unearthed in the canyon and that these archeological treasures could be of great value to serious students of prehistoric life, challenging them to dig in the region. Day stated that the cliff dwellings would attract the most interest because they were easy to reach, although most were "built in caves that are from one hundred to four hundred feet from the bottom of the canyon."[17]

Sam suggested that scholars throughout the United States could benefit from examining the ruins, such as White House, Sentinel, Antelope House, Standing Cow, Mummy Cave, and Massacre Cave. This last site is located in a branch of the canyon known as Canyon del Muerto, or the Canyon of the Dead One. The cave is said to have received its name from an incident which occurred in the winter of 1805 when a party of Spaniards, led by a Leather Jacket Soldier named Lt. Antonio Narbona, pursued some Navajos into Canyon de Chelly. The Navajo men hid their women and children in a large cave high on the canyon wall. The soldiers located the cave and commenced firing. Bullets ricochetting off the back of the cave took their toll of the women and children in the cave.

Because of the Navajos' fear of their dead, few would venture inside Massacre Cave, and no white man did so until 1902 when Sam Day, Jr., entered the rock shelter. He had heard Navajo legends regarding the cave and had enlisted the services of a Navajo to show him the cave's location. When he entered, he found over 50 well-preserved desiccated bodies, clay pots, loom sticks, spindles, bags of quills, woven baskets, bows, arrows, iron arrow points, woolen fabric, and cotton clothing.[19] Sam, Jr., realized that finding such a rare collection carried with it the responsibility of making it available to others. Thus he made the artifacts available to Steward Culin, the curator of ethnology, at the Brooklyn Museum.[20] Samuel was interested in the prehistory of the Southwest because he believed a better understanding could result if Anglos could understand the cultural heritage of the Indians.[21]

The Day family was interested in preserving and protecting ruins and artifacts in the Chinle area for scholarly study.[22] They worked closely with the United States Department of Interior in its effort

264   Charlie Day

to end all unauthorized excavations in the area. In 1903, the Indian Office argued that "considerable injury has already been done by unskilled excavators who have visited these canyons and recovered... the antiquitees buried in the ruins." Furthermore, governmental officials maintained that as "these canyons [Canyons de Chelly and del Muerto] are the most important prehistoric remains in the Southwest, no greater misfortune could befall the work of historical research than to permit further excavation except...for the purpose of enlarging either the National Museum of other musuems in the United States." After conferring with officials of the Department of Interior, Charles L. Day stated that he "would be glad to do what he could to prevent further excavations" of the canyons in question.[23] A few days later, he was appointed custodian of the Canyons de Chelly and del Muerto and was instructed to prevent all unauthorized excavations.[24] Nonetheless, illicit diggings continued.

Sam Day, Jr., had excavated in the canyons prior to the decision of the government to halt such diggings, but he had sold most of his first collection to Brooklyn Museum. Moreover, he realized that it would be selfish to retain the remainder of it without making it available to researchers.[25] Sam felt that his "collection should be in some institution...in Arizona, as the relics were all gathered in this state."[26] He contacted Bryon Cummings, the founder of the Department of Anthropology at the University of Arizona, and offered his collection to the Arizona State Museum. Day spoke to Cummings about the collection, and the professor decided that Day should receive a small compensation for the artifacts. Between 1924 and 1926, Cummings tried to purchase Day's collection and once explained to Samuel that "I find on returning to Tucson that the University situation is no more straightened out than when I went away." Cummings commented that the "regents and everybody else seem 'up in the air' and no budget has been arranged for the present college year, consequently I can see no hope in securing your collection from the present University funds."[27] Nevertheless, the collection eventually did rest at the Arizona State Museum; whether it was purchased or donated we do not know. However, most evidence indicates that Day's collection was donated.[28]

Cummings knew that Sam Day, Jr., was interested in archeological work, and in 1926 he asked him to consider "going out for a couple of months...to make investigations and collect material for the State Museum."[29] And indeed Sam was eager to assist in en-

265

Sam Day, Jr.

A Gathering of Navajos

larging the archeological holdings of the museum. He and Cummings particularly hoped that the expedition would uncover "some early cave peoples' (Basketmakers') homes and graves."[30]

The expedition was delayed until the spring of 1927, when on April 8, Day and a colleague of Cummings' named Mr. Hauds began to explore the ruins of the Canyon de Chelly. Between April 10 and April 30, Day and Hauds excavated in many ruins near Mummy Cave. Their work was delayed by snow, ice, and mud, and the expedition proved a disappointment. No major findings were made, and the trip was largely a failure. This was due to the fact that many of the ruins in the canyons had been visited previously by other excavators. Nonetheless, Sam learned a great deal regarding archeological field techniques from Mr. Hauds.[31]

Sam Day, Jr., was not the only member of the Day family who was interested in the Indians and who gave his time to help scholars. Charles Day was of great service to Edward S. Curtis, an educator, lecturer, and author from Seattle, Washington. Curtis came to the Southwest to study the Indians by making photographs and motion pictures, and Day acted as Curtis' guide, interpreter, and educator. Together they gathered information from all the remote regions of the Navajo Reservation.[32] By 1907, Curtis informed Day that he had completed five volumes of his study and was "more than impatient for the day when they will be ready for delivery."[33] At five volumes Curtis just had begun his work because he ultimately produced 20 volumes in a famous series, *The North American Indian*. Charles helped Curtis collect most of the information regarding the Navajos, including studies on their Creation Myth, Happiness Chant, Nightway Chant, and Puberty Ceremony. He helped describe and picture "all features of the Indian life and environment--types of the young and the old, with their habitations, industries, ceremonies, games and everyday customs."[34] Day and Curtis produced a study which presented a basic insight into Navajo life, a study yet available to students of the American Indian.

Sam Day, Sr., like his sons, also helped scholars in their educational endeavors. In the early spring of 1909, Day was contacted by his friend, Frank G. Bames, a university professor from Detroit, Michigan. Bames had made many previous trips to the Southwest and felt that the region held a wealth of educational attractions. He proposed to lead a group of university students on a Southwest study tour. Bames wanted the tour to spend some time at Day's ranch so his students could question Day about Navajo culture, and

267

he also wanted Sam to guide the group through the Canyons de Chelly and del Muerto.[35] On June 19,1909, the touring party arrived at St. Michaels, and Day began a series of provocative lectures and guided tours.

The Days themselves were concerned with learning more about their neighbors. For example, Charles translated the Navajo Creation Myth into English as it was told to him by Hosteen Diel, an old Navajo medicine man. In 1900, Diel was believed to have been one of the few men then alive who knew the entire myth in detail; and since the Navajos nad no written language, Charles provided a valuable service to the Navajos by preserving the myth.[36]

Charles translated other important accounts into English, including children's tales of the coyote, the elk, and the deer. One of the more detailed translations which he made available in English was the Navajo Moccasin Game. Day learned from a Navajo informant that the Moccasin Game originated long ago when "all the living birds, animals and reptiles held intercourse and conversed with each other." The story explains that all the animals were in a great dispute as to whether there should be perpetual day or perpetual night. The animals decided to play a game to decide the matter, with the "day animals" on one side and the "night animals" on the other. The game commenced "with varying success until the night animals had all...but six [of the points]...and the day animals were alarmed and afraid they would lose." The day animals "stopped to council with themselves on what they should do." They decided to "send for the Magpie who had only recently been married and was off on his honeymoon."[37]

The day animals sent three consecutive messengers to ask the Magpie to return and to help win the game. The fourth messenger (the fourth or the number four being the lucky number of the Navajos) persuaded the bird to return with him. When the Magpie arrived he took a hammer and struck each moccasin saying each time that the ball was not there. The Magpie then "went to owl who was on the side of night, and struck him on one foot saying the ball was not there." Then the Magpie struck the owl "so hard on the other foot that he dropped the ball." The owl had taken the ball when it seemed that the game was going to end in a draw. At dawn the game ended with neither team winning--this is why there is day and night in the world today.[38]

Many Navajo ceremonials now are extinct (i.e. the Pretty Chant or the Eagle Dance) because the Navajos had an oral tradition and no written language. Therefore, the precious past that could have been preserved in those ceremonies vanished with the death of the old medicine men. Few Anglos in the Southwest were sufficiently interested in the Indians to preserve this information--the Days were the exception, not the rule.[39]

Navajo ceremonials are not performed for the express purpose of pleasure alone. Each chant is part of a sacred ritual and each sand painting has a legend behind it.[40] Sand paintings are important particularly in Navajo healing rituals, and Charles Day was extremely interested in these legends. On one occasion he described the legend behind a painting used to cure Navajos ill because of contact with snakes. A Navajo medicine man named Hosteen Bezaad told Charles that the legend originated many years before when a young warrior was out hunting.[41] One evening as he lay by his campfire, he saw flames rising from a nearby mountain. When morning came the warrior climbed the mountain but failed to find a trace of the fire. For three consecutive nights he saw the fire but never found evidence that a fire had occurred. On the fourth morning, he again climbed the mountain which suddenly turned into a large snake right before his eyes. The snake was extremely large because it had four other snakes attached to its body. The wind told the Navajo to be brave and to enter the great snake's mouth. He did this and serpent's mouth closed behind him. Bravely the warrior walked on until he saw another snake named Clish Tso sitting at the west end of the chamber.[42] When he saw Clish Tso, the Navajo fainted and remained unconscious for many hours. Clish Tso used a "Naatoebaca" buckskin painting to awaken the warrior as the painting had great healing power. When the Navajo regained consciousness, he talked with Clish Tso who taught the warrior sacred songs, saintly ceremonies, and healing procedures. The youth pleaded with Clish Tso to allow him to take the buckskin painting with him, but Clish Tso refused saying that Navajos throughout the ages would quarrel over the ownership of the painting. He argued that Navajos could possess the painting's power merely by reproducing it in the sand. Clish Tso showed the warrior how to grind rocks and plants to be used as colorful designs in reproducing the "Naatoebaca" sand painting.

Sand paintings still are used in healing ceremonials and are a significant part of Navajo culture. Charles Day and his brother Sam knew that the Navajos needed their legends preserved before the old medicine men passed away. They spent much of their leisure time collecting accounts of a vanishing culture.

At the turn of the 20th century, few if any sand paintings were constructed anywhere except on the ground. Sam Day, Jr., was one of the first Anglos to reproduce Navajo sand paintings in a permanent form, on paper and wood with the use of adhesives.[43] Other individuals foresaw their value and hired Sam to collect paintings and legends. One such person was John Frederick Huckel, who worked for the Fred Harvey Company and who wanted the sand paintings for his personal collection of Indian arts and crafts.[44]

In addition to sand paintings, Huckel wanted descriptions of the legends and ceremonies related to each painting. Sam began his work eagerly but soon was confronted with an obstacle which had plagued anthropology students for years--the older Indians who knew the ceremonies were dying. Day informed Huckel that he "would like very much to...take each and every ceremony by itself and write them down from beginning complete [to the end] so as to preserve them as the old men who know the ceremonies are dieing [sic] out fast." Sam was alarmed because "within the last month three of the eldest medicine men have died and one of them I had expected to get the Pretty ceremony from and he was the last old man who knew it."[45]

Day told Huckel that "the Old Laughing Doctor of the Night Chant died three weeks ago," and the Night Chant thus was recorded incomplete. Furthermore, Day stated that he had seen Old Captain Sam (a Navajo) who had told him that "he wanted me to come to his home and write down all that he knew about Eagle and Buffalo Chants...of which he is the only surviving performer [sic] or singer." Old Captain Sam was a very old man who "says himself that he expects to die anytime now." Day promised the Indian that he would visit him as soon as he could but evidently Sam was not in time. The Eagle and Pretty ceremonies are extinct today because the only Navajos who knew the chants, medicine men like Old Captain Sam, died without passing on the ceremonies. Nonetheless, Sam Day preserved the sand paintings that were related to these ceremonies.[46]

Consistent with promoting knowledge of the Navajos' culture, the Day family did not condone people who misrepresented the Indians. In May of 1932, Sam Day, Jr., was troubled when he read an article in *Scribner's Magazine* entitled "Death of a Medicine Man." The author, Mrs. Richard Wetherill, gave a detailed description of "barbaric" customs of the Navajos. Sam was disgusted with

270

Mrs. Wetherill and could not "understand how any person could draw on their immagination [sic] to the extent which...[she] did." Day felt that the Indians had been dealt a "rank injustice" and that he had a personal obligation to inform K.S. Crichton, the editor of *Scribner's Magazine,* of this misrepresentation of facts.[47]

Sam wrote Crichton to "point out a few of the most impossible things in the article" as well as the "utter absurdity of some of Mrs. Wetherill's assertions." Day declared that the author's description of a sacrificial ceremony in the "Canyon of Human Sacrifice" was ludicrous. He stated that "as for the putting to death of a medicine man because of three failures in curing his patients, it is a thing unheard of even by the oldest Indian." Moreover, Sam maintained that Mrs. Wetherill's "detailed description of such an execution to which she claims to have been an eye witness, never occured [sic] outside of [her] elastic mind." Sam had lived on the reservation for nearly 50 years, and he argued that neither he nor any of the Navajos had ever heard of a Canyon of Human Sacrifice. The controversy ended when Crichton refused to permit the *Readers Digest* to reprint the "Death of a Medicine Man."[48]

Because they wanted to acquaint Anglos with Indians, Samuel Edward Day and his sons engaged in a search for new knowledge about the Navajos. They believed this knowledge could help close the void of misunderstanding that existed between the Anglo and the Indian cultures. They were conscientious individuals who served as middle men for scholars and labored to preserve the cultural heritage of the Navajo Indians. Their importance in the history of the Southwest, too long unappreciated, was indeed great.

271

NOTES

1. Douglas Edward Leach, *The Northern Colonial Frontier* (Holt, Rinehart and Winston, New York, 1966):6-14.

2. One of the first men to take an intellectual or cultural look at the Navajo Indians was Washington Matthews, an United States Army officer who was stationed in New Mexico Territory during the post-Civil War era. He wrote a number of accounts for the Bureau of Ethnology about the legends, arts, and crafts of the Navajo Indians. Others who pioneered the study of Southwestern anthropology were John G. Bourke, Byron Cummings, and Berard Haile.

3. Frank McNitt, *The Indian Traders* (University of Oklahoma Press, Norman, 1962): 247; Robert L. Wilken, *Anselm Weber, O.F.M.* (Bruce Publishing Company, Milwaukee, 1955):43-44; Elizabeth C. Hegeman, *Navaho Trading Days* (University of New Mexico Press, Albuquerque, 1963):198-199.

4. Discharge paper of Samuel Edward Day, Sr., from the United States Army, September 25, 1862. Samuel Edward Day, Sr., Collection, Northern Arizona University Library, Flagstaff, Arizona (hereafter cited as Day Collection, N.A.U.).

5. Biographical Sketch of Samuel Edward Day, Sr., Day Collection, N.A.U.

6. McNitt 1962:247.

7. Samuel Edward Day, Sr., to Charles L. Day, December 3, 1884, Day Collection, N.A.U.

8. Biographical Sketch of Samuel Edward Day, Sr., Day Collection, N.A.U.

9. Wilken 1955:43-44.

10. McNitt 1962:247; Wilken 1955:43-44.

11. Wilken 1955:23-24.

12. The Indian Mission Among the Navajos, December 28, 1898, Day Collection, N.A.U. This work was written by one of the Franciscan Fathers at the Catholic Mission at St. Michales, Arizona. Also see Wilken 1955:43-44.

13. Charles and Samuel Day, Jr., translated many of the words in the Franciscan Fathers' *An Ethnologic Dictionary of the Navaho Language* (Max Breslauer Company, Germany, 1910).

14. The Indian Mission Among the Navajos, Day Collection, N.A.U., Wilken 1955:44.

15. McNitt 1962:250. Chinle, Arizona is located 50 miles northwest of St. Michaels at the mouth of the Canyon de Chelly.

16. Samuel Edward Day, Sr., Canyon de Chelly, Gallup Independent, (1916):1-2. Other Anglo Indian traders felt the same way about the archeological wealth in northeastern Arizona. One such trader was Richard Wetherill who helped scholars unearth many ruins of the Anasazi. For an excellent account of Wetherill's work see Frank McNitt, *Richard Wetherill: Anasazi* (University of New Mexico Press, Albuquerque, 1957).

17. Samuel Edward Day, Sr., Canyon de Chelly, Day Collection, N.A.U.

18. John Upton Terrell, *The Navajo* (Weybright and Talley, New York, 1970):70-71; Ruth Underhill, *The Navajos* (University of Oklahoma Press, Norman, 1956):72-73.

19. Stewart Culin, Report of a Collecting Expedition Among the Indians of New Mexico and Arizona, April-September, 1903. This note was extracted from the files of the Brooklyn Museum by Albert H. Schroeder, May 4-5, 1961. Also see Hegemann 1963:198-199.

20. Wilken, 1955, 128.

21. Samuel Edward Day, Jr., to Byron Cummings, March 24, 1924, Day Collection, N.A.U. Byron Cummings was born on September 20, 1860. He received his Master of Arts at Rutgers University in 1892 and taught at the University of Utah from 1893 to 1915. He began teaching at the University of Arizona in 1915 where he remained until retirement. Cummings was the founder of the Department of Anthropology at the University of Arizona and served twice as president of the university. A.C. Tonner to Secretary of Interior, June 1, 1903, Day Collection, N.A.U.

22. Wilken 1955:128.

23. A.C. Tonner to Secretary of Interior, June 1, 1903, Day Collection, N.A.U.

24. Secretary of Interior to Superintendent Reuben Perry, June 1, 1903, Letter book in the Window Rock Tribal Museum, Window Rock, Arizona.

25. Byron Cummings to Samuel Edward Day, Jr. September 14, 1926, Day Collection, N.A.U.

26. Samuel Edward Day, Jr., to Byron Cummings, March 24, 1924. Day Collection, N.A.U.

27. Byron Cummings to Samuel Edward Day, Jr., September 14, 1926, Day Collection, N.A.U.

28. A very detailed list of all artifacts which Samuel Day, Jr., sent is in the Day Collection, N.A.U., this list is dated 1936. However, there is no mention in this account or anywhere else of who purchased the artifacts. The only correspondence regarding such a purchase is with Byron Cummings. The Arizona State Museum reported that they had "no specimans in [their] collection credited to Mr. Day, although records prior to 1938 are rather meagre [sic]."

29. Byron Cummings to Samuel Edward Day, Jr., September 14, 1926, Day Collection, N.A.U.

30. Byron Cummings to Samuel Edward Day, Jr., November 3, 1926, Day Collection, N.A.U.

31. Samuel Edward Day, Jr., Archaeological Exploration Account, Arpil 8, 1927, Day Collection, N.A.U.

32. Edward S. Curtis, *The North American Indian,* I (Johnson Reprint Corporation, New York, 1970):i-xiii. This is a multi-volume pictorial and descriptive history of the North American Indians, edited by Frederick Webb Hodge. There are four supplements to the work which features photographs of American Indians.

33. Edward S. Curtis to Charles L. Day, November 19,1908, Day Collection, N.A.U.

34. Curtis 1970:xiii.

35. Frank G. Bames to Samuel Edward Day, Sr., March 21, 1909, Day Collection, N.A.U. Bames was the General Secretary of the University Research Extension, University of Chicago, and former professor at the University of Indiana.

273

36. The 40 page account and numerous works on Navajo ceremonies, superstitions, myths, chants, games, clan names, paintings, and drawings can be found in the Day Collection, N.A.U.

37. Charles L. Day, "Moccasin Game Description," No Date, Day Collection, N.A.U. The Moccasin Game is played with eight moccasins, a stone ball, and a heavy stick called a hammer. Soap Weed or Yucca, used as counters are actually a physical means of keeping score. There are four moccasins for each side that are filled with sand and buried leaving only the open tops showing. The ball is hidden in a moccasin by one side and the other side guesses where the ball was hidden by pointing to the moccasin with the hammer.

38. Ibid.

39. For general discussions on the preservation of Navajo myths, legends, and games, see Leland C. Wyman, *Blessingway* (University of Arizona Press, Tucson, 1970); Mary C. Wheelwright, *Emergence Myth* (Museum of Navaho Ceremonial Art, Santa Fe, 1949); Franc J. Newcomb, *Navaho Folk Tales* (Museum of Navaho Ceremonial Art, Santa Fe, 1967); Berard Haile, *Origin Legend of Navaho Flintway* (University of Chicago Press, Chicago, 1943).

40. Haile 1943:1-10; J. W. Lesueur, *Indian Legends* (Zion's Printing and Publishing Company, Independence, 1928):143-174.

41. This legend was taken from the "Naatoebaca" sand painting as told to Charles L. Day by Hosteen Bezaad, a Navajo medicine man. Day Collection, N.A.U.

42. Clish Tso was a Navajo god who is also known as Big Snake or Old Man Big Snake. In Navajo lore, the "Naatoebaca" painting was once only placed on buckskin, but after this incident above described, the painting was drawn in the sand.

43. Samuel Edward Day, Jr., to John Frederick Huckel, August 20, 1923, Day Collection, N.A.U.

44. John Frederick Huckel to Samuel Edward Day, Jr., July 26, 1923, Day Collection, N.A.U.; Leland C. Wynn, *Sandpaintings of the Navaho Shootingway and the Walcott Collection,* (Smithsonian Institution Press, Washington, D.C., 1970):19. The Huckel Indian arts and crafts collection can be seen today at the Taylor Museum in Colorado Spring, Colorado.

45. Samuel Edward Day, Jr., to John Frederick Huckel, August 20, 1923, Day Collection, N.A.U.

46. Ibid.

47. Samuel Edward Day, Jr., to K.S. Crichton, March 18, 1933, Day Collection, N.A.U.

48. Ibid.; Michael Harrison to K.S. Crichton, February 25, 1933, Day Collection, N.A.U.

Clifford E. Trafzer received his Bachelor's degree in 1970 and his Master's degree a year later from Northern Arizona University, Flagstaff. In 1970, he was hired by the Special Collections Division of the Northern Arizona University Library to organize and to calendar the papers of Samuel Edward Day. His association with the Day Papers led him to write about the role played by the Days in the northern part of the Southwest. Mr. Trafzer is the author of other scholarly articles on the American West, and he is presently a Ph.D. candidate in history at Oklahoma State University, Stillwater.

Index